AF335332

Bayesian Econometrics

Bayesian Econometrics

Editors

Mauro Bernardi
Stefano Grassi
Francesco Ravazzolo

MDPI • Basel • Beijing • Wuhan • Barcelona • Belgrade • Manchester • Tokyo • Cluj • Tianjin

Editors
Mauro Bernardi
Department of Statistical
Sciences, University of Padova
Italy

Stefano Grassi
Dipartimento di Economia e
Finanza, University of
Rome 'Tor Vergata'
Italy

Francesco Ravazzolo
Associate Professor at Faculty of
Economics and Management at
Free University of Bozen
Italy

Editorial Office
MDPI
St. Alban-Anlage 66
4052 Basel, Switzerland

This is a reprint of articles from the Special Issue published online in the open access journal *Journal of Risk and Financial Management* (ISSN 1911-8074) (available at: https://www.mdpi.com/journal/jrfm/special_issues/bayesian).

For citation purposes, cite each article independently as indicated on the article page online and as indicated below:

LastName, A.A.; LastName, B.B.; LastName, C.C. Article Title. *Journal Name* **Year**, *Volume Number*, Page Range.

ISBN 978-3-03943-785-6 (Hbk)
ISBN 978-3-03943-786-3 (PDF)

Contents

About the Editors

Mauro Bernardi is a senior Assistant Professor at the Department of Statistical Sciences at University of Padova. His research focuses on Bayesian statistics, risk measures and time series analysis. He has published in several leading academic journals.

Stefano Grassi is an Associate Professor of Economic Statistics at the Faculty of Economics at University of Rome 'Tor Vergata'. His research focuses on Bayesian econometrics, financial econometrics and macroeconometrics. He has published in several leading academic journals.

Francesco Ravazzolo is a Full Professor of Econometrics at the Faculty of Economics and Management, Free University of Bozen-Bolzano, and a Visiting Professor at Center for Applied Macro and Commodity Prices, BI Norwegian Business School. His research focuses on Bayesian econometrics, energy economics, financial econometrics and macroeconometrics. He has published in several leading academic journals. Francesco has several academic roles: he is on the Editorial Boards of the following journals: *Annals of Applied Statistics*; *International Journal of Forecasting*; *Journal of Applied Econometrics*; *Studies in Nonlinear Dynamics and Econometrics*. He is also a member of the executive committee of the Society of Nonlinear Dynamics and Econometrics and of the steering committee of the Italian Econometric Association.

Journal of
*Risk and Financial
Management*

Editorial

Bayesian Econometrics

Mauro Bernardi [1], Stefano Grassi [2] and Francesco Ravazzolo [3,4,5,*]

[1]   Department of Statistics, University of Padova, 39100 Padova, Italy; mauro.bernardi@unipd.it
[2]   Department of Economics and Finance, University of Rome 'Tor Vergata', 00133 Rome, Italy;
     stefano.grassi@uniroma2.it
[3]   Faculty of Economics and Management, Free University of Bozen-Bolzano, 39100 Bolzano, Italy
[4]   Centre for Applied Macroeconomics and Commodity Prices, BI Norwegian Business School,
     0442 Oslo, Norway
[5]   Rimini Centre for Economic Analysis (RCEA), Waterloo, ON N2L3C5, Canada
*   Correspondence: francesco.ravazzolo@unibz.it; Tel.: +39-0471-013133

Received: 26 October 2020; Accepted: 26 October 2020; Published: 29 October 2020

Abstract: The computational revolution in simulation techniques has shown to become a key ingredient in the field of Bayesian econometrics and opened new possibilities to study complex economic and financial phenomena. Applications include risk measurement, forecasting, assessment of policy effectiveness in macro, finance, marketing and monetary economics.

Keywords: Bayesian econometrics; forecasting; MCMC methods; macroeconomic and financial applications

---

This special issue aims to contribute to this literature by collecting a set of carefully evaluated papers that are grouped amongst two topics in financial economics: the first three papers refer to macro-finance issues for the real economy; the last three papers focus on cryptocurrency and stock market predictability.

The first paper, written by Nguyen Ngoc Thach, studies the elasticity of factor substitution (ES) in the Cobb–Douglas production function (see Thach 2020). It proposes a new Bayesian nonlinear mixed-effects regression via Random-walk Metropolis Hastings (MH) algorithm to estimate the average ES through the specification of an aggregate constant elasticity of substitution (CES) function and applies it to the Vietnamese nonfinancial enterprises. Results indicate that the CES function estimated for the researched enterprises has an ES lower than one, i.e., capital and labor are complimentary. This finding shows that Vietnamese nonfinancial enterprises can confront a downward trend of output growth.

The second paper, written by Marco Lorusso and Luca Pieroni, investigates government public spending components in order to analyze their effects on the economy (see Lorusso and Pieroni 2019). It develops a Dynamic Stochastic General Equilibrium Model (DSGE) model with civilian and military expenditures and is applied to U.S. data. It estimates it on U.S. data taking account of financial liberations with Bayesian methods. Results show that total government spending has a positive effect on output, but it induces a fall in private consumption. Moreover, sizeable differences between the effects of civilian and military spending exist: civilian spending has a more positive impact on output than military expenditure.

The third paper, written by Martin Feldkircher and Florian Huber, focuses on quantitative easing, monetary policy and economics (see Feldkircher and Huber 2018). Employing a time-varying vector autoregression with stochastic volatility studies the transmission of a conventional monetary policy shock with that of an unexpected decrease in the term spread, unconventional monetary policy shocks. Results indicate that the spread shock works mainly through a boost to consumer wealth growth, while a conventional monetary policy shock affects real output growth via a broad credit/bank lending channel. Moreover, the conventional monetary policy shock has a small effect during the period of the global financial crisis and stronger effects in its aftermath, whereas the spread shock has affected output growth most strongly during the crisis and less so thereafter.

The fourth paper, written by Rick Bohte and Luca Rossini, studies the forecasting ability of cryptocurrency time series (see Bohte and Rossini 2019). Working on the four most capitalised cryptocurrencies, Bitcoin, Ethereum, Litecoin and Ripple, different Bayesian models are compared, including models with constant and time-varying volatility, such as stochastic volatility and GARCH. Results show that stochastic volatility improves both point and density forecasting accuracy. Using a different type of distribution, for the errors of the stochastic volatility, the student-t distribution is shown to outperform the standard normal approach.

The fifth paper, written by Camilla Muglia, Luca Santabarbara and Stefano Grassi, investigates whether Bitcoin is a good predictor of the Standard and Poor's 500 Index (see Muglia et al. 2019). Using Bayesian dynamic model averaging (DMA) and Bayesian dynamic model selection (DMS) methodologies, the analysis shows that Bitcoin does not show any direct impact on the predictability of Standard and Poor's 500.

The sixth paper, written by Chiari Limongi Concetto and Francesco Ravazzolo, investigates how investor sentiment affects stock market returns and evaluates the predictability power of sentiment indices on U.S. and EU stock market returns (see Limongi Concetto and Ravazzolo 2019). Investor sentiment indices have an economic and statistical predictability power on stock market returns. Moreover, comparing the two markets, the analysis indicates a spillover effect from the U.S. to Europe.

The guest editors want to thank all referees for a speedy and high quality evaluation procedure.

References

Bohte, Rick, and Luca Rossini. 2019. Comparing the Forecasting of Cryptocurrencies by Bayesian Time-Varying Volatility Models. *Journal of Risk and Financial Management* 12: 150. [CrossRef]

Feldkircher, Martin, and Florian Huber. 2018. Unconventional U.S. Monetary Policy: New Tools, Same Channels? *Journal of Risk and Financial Management* 11: 71. [CrossRef]

Limongi Concetto, Chiara, and Francesco Ravazzolo. 2019. Optimism in Financial Markets: Stock Market Returns and Investor Sentiments. *Journal of Risk and Financial Management* 12: 85. [CrossRef]

Lorusso, Marco, and Luca Pieroni. 2019. Disentangling Civilian and Military Spending Shocks: A Bayesian DSGE Approach for the US Economy. *Journal of Risk and Financial Management* 12: 141.

Muglia, Camilla, Luca Santabarbara, and Stefano Grassi. 2019. Is Bitcoin a Relevant Predictor of Standard & Poor's 500? *Journal of Risk and Financial Management* 12: 93.

Thach, Nguyen Ngoc. 2020. How to Explain When the ES Is Lower Than One? A Bayesian Nonlinear Mixed-Effects Approach. *Journal of Risk and Financial Management* 13: 21. [CrossRef]

Publisher's Note: MDPI stays neutral with regard to jurisdictional claims in published maps and institutional affiliations.

Journal of
Risk and Financial Management

Article

How to Explain When the ES Is Lower Than One? A Bayesian Nonlinear Mixed-Effects Approach

Nguyen Ngoc Thach

Institute for Research Science and Banking Technology, Banking University HCMC, Ho Chi Minh City 70000, Vietnam; thachnn@buh.edu.vn

Received: 16 December 2019; Accepted: 21 January 2020; Published: 1 February 2020

Abstract: Most studies in Vietnam use the Cobb-Douglas production function and its modifications for economic analysis. Extremely rigid presumptions are a main weak point of this functional form, particularly if the elasticity of factor substitution (ES) is equal to one, which hides the role of the ES for economic growth. The CES (constant elasticity of substitution) production function with more flexible presumptions, concretely its ES, is not unitary, and has been used more and more widely in economic investigations. So, this study is conducted to estimate the average ES through the specification of an aggregate CES function for the Vietnamese nonfinancial enterprises. By performing Bayesian nonlinear mixed-effects regression via Random-walk Metropolis Hastings (MH) algorithm, based on the data set of the listed nonfinancial enterprises of Vietnam, the author found that the CES function estimated for the researched enterprises has an ES lower than one, i.e., capital and labor are complimentary. This finding shows that Vietnamese nonfinancial enterprises can confront a downward trend of output growth.

Keywords: ES; CES function; Bayesian nonlinear mixed-effects regression

---

1. Introduction

Since appearing in 1928, the Cobb-Douglas function has been a highly crucial tool in economic research. This functional form has become very popular due to its ease of use and empirical adaptation to different data sets. Solow (1957) and his followers used the Cobb-Douglas in their growth theories. However, this type of function is criticized because of its rigid premises. One of them is the unit ES, which, according to many empirical results, does not coincide with facts. Moreover, the unit ES masks the role of the ES for economic growth processes. Several theoretical and empirical studies published have explored this limitation. For example, among others, Antrás (2004) stated that the ES is not appropriate for the US economy, and Werf (2007) argued that the Cobb-Douglas function is not suitable for modeling policies for climate change, while Young (2013) revealed that the ES of the aggregate production function and the production function of most U.S. industries could not be equal to one and had estimates less than 0.62. Therefore, the CES function with an ES other than one was announced in 1961 (Arrow et al. 1961). Since then, an increasing amount of studies around the world have used the CES function for economic analysis, while the number of works evaluating elasticities using the Cobb-Douglas function decreased substantially. Specifically, Heubes (1972) theoretically argued that either the time path or the level of the output growth rate depends on the ES value. Among empirical studies, Ferguson (1965), La Grandville (1989), Klump and Grandville (2000), Pitchford (1960), Azariadis (1993), and Galor (1995) focussed on the effects of the ES on economic growth. In Vietnam, to the knowledge of the author, the Cobb-Douglas function and its different modifications are commonly used, and at present, no empirical research on the CES function has been carried out. Besides, most previous research on production functions applied mainly traditional quantitative methods, such as the accounting method or the frequentist approach, being a subject of much criticism from modern statisticians as it gave unreliable results in many cases (Briggs and Nguyen 2019; Anh et al. 2018; Kreinovich et al. 2019).

Because of the above reasons, the author conducted this study to estimate the ES via specifying an aggregate CES function using a non-frequentist method, namely the Bayesian nonlinear mixed-effects regression.

The remainder of the paper is structured as follows. Section 2 introduces the theoretical framework of the ES and its relationship with economic growth. Section 3 provides the theoretical analysis of the ES in the CES. Empirical studies on the ES in the CES and its association with economic growth are reviewed in Section 4. Section 5 discusses the data and estimation method. Bayesian simulation results are provided in Section 6. Section 7 includes the conclusion.

2. Theoretical Background of the ES

2.1. The ES

Production functions are an important instrument of economic analysis in the neoclassical tradition. They are often utilized to analyze the economic performance of an economy, as well as those of enterprises, industries and industrial complexes. Homogeneity and returns to scale particularize a neoclassical production function under the conditions of uniform changes in all inputs. Nonetheless, when the inputs change at different rates, how does the function change? In this case, the nature of the production function varies depending on the ES. In general, the ES plays a significant role in economic growth process.

The marginal rate of technical substitution between two inputs (MRS_{ij}) illustrates the rate at which one input must decrease to hold a production level unchanged when another input increases:

$$MRS_{ij} = -\left(\frac{dx_j}{dx_i}\right) = \frac{f_i}{f_j}$$

where x_i, x_j are the first and second inputs, respectively.

The limitation of this coefficient is that it is dependent on the measurement unit of resources. Therefore, the usage of the ES instead is more appropriate:

$$\sigma_{ij} = \frac{\partial(x_j/x_i)}{\partial MRS_{ij}} \times \frac{MRS_{ij}}{x_j/x_i},$$

where σ_{ij}—the ES of input x_i for input x_j.

The ES denotes how the ratio of inputs changes if the marginal rate of technical substitution between them varies by one percent. Hicks (1932) first proposed this definition for the case of two inputs. In the case of n inputs, the method of calculating the ES is inconsistent. In a later work of Hicks and Allen (1934), a generalized ES was suggested. Accordingly, the formula for the two-input case is applied to any two inputs in a multivariate function with the assumption that other inputs remain unchanged. This is the Hicks Elasticity of Substitution (HES). However, the restriction of the HES is that because the optimal quantity of all inputs is simultaneously decided by enterprises, the ratio between any two inputs is affected not only by relative prices but also by the prices of other inputs. The optimization behavior of enterprises requires:

$$MRS_{ij} = \frac{f_i}{f_j} = \frac{p_j}{p_i}.$$

then

$$\sigma_{ij} = \frac{\partial(x_j/x_i)}{\partial(p_j/p_i)} \times \frac{p_j/p_i}{x_j/x_i}.$$

where p_j, p_i are the price of x_j, x_i, respectively.

Under the optimization condition, the ES indicates how the input ratio varies if their price ratio changes by one percent. Let us consider a function with three inputs $f(x_1, x_2, x_3)$. With this preposition, $MRS_{12} = \frac{p_2}{p_1}$. The HES between x_1 and x_2 shows how the ratio between them changes if $MRS_{12} = \frac{p_2}{p_1}$ changes by one percent with the assumption of a fixed amount of x_3. However, it is noted that a change of $\frac{p_2}{p_1}$ may make the amount of x_3 vary due to variations in the ratios of $\frac{p_2}{p_3}$ and $\frac{p_1}{p_3}$. Thus, the assumption of a fixed quantity of the third input is not always correct. The use of the HES is correct only for the Cobb-Douglas and the CES because the change in the third input does not impact on the ratio between the first two inputs. In the meanwhile, for generalized functions, the HES may yield biased results.

Hicks and Allen proposed a Partial Elasticity of Substitution to measure the ES. Later, this coefficient was studied in detail by Allen and Uzawa, so it was called the Allen-Uzawa Elasticity of Substitution (AUES). AUES is calculated by the following formula:

$$\sigma_{ij} = \frac{x_1 \times f_1 + \cdots + x_n \times f_n}{x_i \times x_j} \times \frac{F_{ij}}{F},$$

where $F = det[0 \; f_1 \ldots f_n \; f_1 \; f_{11} \ldots f_{1n} \; f_n \; f_{n1} \cdots f_{nn}]$,

$$f_{ij}(y, p) = \frac{\partial^2 f}{\partial x_i \times \partial x_j},$$

where F_{ij} denotes algebraic addition to element f_{ij} in F.

In the two-input case, AUES is reduced to the HES. Nevertheless, Blackorby and Russell (1981) claim that deduction from the ES between two inputs to the ES between multiple inputs is not correct. They proved the non-informativeness of AUES in several cases. So, the Morishima Elasticity of Substitution (MES) was proposed instead:

$$M_{ij}(y, p) = \frac{p_i \times C_{ij}(y, p)}{C_j(y, p)} - \frac{p_i \times C_{ij}(y, p)}{C_i(y, p)}.$$

where $C(y, p)$ is a cost optimization function derived from:

$$C_i(y, p) = \frac{\partial C(y, p)}{\partial p_i}, \; C_{ij}(y, p) = \frac{\partial^2 C(y, p)}{\partial p_i \times \partial p_j}.$$

McFadden (1963) created a new development in the elasticity theory showing the possibility of the ES to have different values for various input pairs. According to this author, it is not possible to construct a neoclassical production function with an arbitrary set of the ES when the number of inputs is more than two. That is, if we propose different ES for various input groups, it is necessary to use a different type of production function that may not be fixed at different input quantities and at various prices.

In this study, the author uses the ES between the two inputs, capital and labor. In this case, the ES is a measure of the ease of substitution between capital and labor, or a measure of their similarity from a technological view. When the ES is large, the inputs are similar to each other. So when an input increases, the technology enables this factor to be easily substituted for the element remaining constant. In the case of a small ES, the technology views the inputs as unsimilar, so it is difficult to substitute one input for the other. In other words, as expressed by Nelson (1965), the ES can be referred to as an index of the rate at which diminishing marginal return sets in as one input increases in relation to the other. If the ES is great, then it is easy to substitute one input for the other or to increase output by increasing one input. Hence, a diminishing marginal return will set in slowly or not set at all. From here, we could confirm that the ES has an effect on the economic growth as long as inputs grow at different rates so their proportions change.

2.2. Impact of the ES on Economic Growth

In order to show the positive effect of the ES on economic growth, let us use a 2-factor linear homogenous production function with Hicks-neutral technical change (A):

$$y = A(t) \times F(K, L) \tag{1}$$

Differentiating (1), we get:

$$\frac{dy}{dt} = \frac{\partial A}{\partial t} \times F(K, L) + A \times \frac{\partial F}{\partial K} \times \frac{\partial K}{\partial t} + A \times \frac{\partial F}{\partial L} \times \frac{\partial L}{\partial t} \tag{2}$$

As known, $1 - \alpha = \frac{\partial y}{\partial K}\frac{K}{y}$, $\alpha = \frac{\partial y}{\partial L}\frac{L}{y}$. Hence, the output growth rate is the following:

$$\frac{\Delta y}{y} = \frac{\Delta A}{A} + (1 - \alpha)\frac{\Delta K}{K} + \alpha \times \frac{\Delta L}{L} \tag{3}$$

We have:

$$g_y = g_A + g_k + \alpha(g_l - g_k) \tag{4}$$

The elasticity of production with respect to labor is written as a function of the ES:

$$\alpha = (1 - \alpha)\frac{w/r}{K/L}, \quad w = \frac{\partial y}{\partial L}, \quad r = \frac{\partial y}{\partial K}, \tag{5}$$

or in logs and differentiating with respect to time:

$$\frac{dln\alpha}{dt} = \frac{dln(1 - \alpha)}{dt} + \frac{dln(w/r)}{dln(K/L)} \times \frac{dln(K/L)}{dt} - \frac{dln(K/L)}{dt} \tag{6}$$

It is known:

$$\frac{dln(w/r)}{dln(K/L)} = \frac{1}{\sigma} \tag{7}$$

Therefore

$$\frac{dln\alpha}{dt} = \frac{dln(1 - \alpha)}{dt} + \frac{dln(K/L)}{dt}\left(\frac{1 - \sigma}{\sigma}\right) \tag{8}$$

and

$$\frac{\Delta \alpha}{\alpha} = -\frac{1}{1 - \alpha} \times \Delta \alpha + \frac{1 - \sigma}{\sigma}\left(\frac{\Delta K}{K} - \frac{\Delta L}{L}\right) \tag{9}$$

So, we get:

$$\Delta \alpha = \alpha(1 - \alpha)\frac{\sigma - 1}{\sigma}(g_l - g_k) \tag{10}$$

Assuming the constant growth rates of technical progress and the inputs, the output growth rate (g_y) may vary only because of changes in α. Combining (4) with (10), we obtain:

$$\frac{dg_y}{dt} = \alpha(1 - \alpha)\frac{\sigma - 1}{\sigma}(g_l - g_k)^2 \tag{11}$$

In case $g_l \neq g_k$, the sign of (11) will be positive if $\sigma > 1$ and negative if $\sigma < 1$. Thus, the magnitude of the ES effects is dependent of the difference between the growth rates of capital and labor. In case $g_l \approx g_k$, the variation of g_y over time is small or the impact of the ES on economic growth rate is weak.

In addition, Heubes (1972) stated that not only the time path but also the level of the output growth rate are functions of the ES. Let us differentiate (4) with respect to time and σ to get for small dt and $d\sigma$;

$$dg_y = \left(\frac{\partial \alpha}{\partial t}dt + \frac{\partial \alpha}{\partial \sigma}d\sigma\right)(g_l - g_k) = \left\{ \alpha(1-\alpha)(g_l - g_k)dt - \frac{c\alpha}{\sigma^2}\frac{ln(K/L)}{c + (K/L)^{\frac{1-\sigma}{\sigma}}}d\sigma\right\}(g_l - g_k) \qquad (12)$$

In case $g_l > g_k$ $(g_l < g_k)$ and $K/L < 1$ $(K/L > 1)$, the higher growth rate of output is correlated to a greater ES. Hence, $\frac{\delta g_y}{\delta \sigma} > 0$. If the ES is low, a strong impact of the relatively scarce input on output emerges as its elasticity of production is great. With a growing σ, the elasticity of production diminishes for the scarce input, but it increases for the relatively abundant factor. The impact of the ES change on the output growth rate becomes small for high levels of the ES. The growth rate is independent of the ES when $K/L = 1$.

3. ES in the CES Function

Before analyzing the ES in the CES, we consider the Cobb-Douglas function. The work of Cobb and Douglas (1928) is a turning point in the field of production functions. It can be said, although there have been some previous studies on production functions (Schumpeter 1954; Stigler 1952; Barkai 1959; Lloyd 1969; Velupillai 1973; Samuelson 1979; Humphrey 1997), for the first time the relationship between inputs and outputs is mathematically formulated and empirically assessed in (Cobb and Douglas 1928). During a vacation at Amherst, Paul Douglas asked math professor Charles Cobb to suggest an equation describing the relationship between capital and labor and output based on time series data on the U.S. manufacturing sector for the period 1889–1922. As a result, a joint paper showed up, where the authors concluded that their model fits the data well. The initial Cobb-Douglas function has the following form:

$$y = A \times x_1^\alpha \times x_2^{1-\alpha} \qquad (13)$$

where x_1 is capital (K), x_2 is labor (L); A, α are parameters.

However, in the later works, Douglas removed the assumption that sum of elasticities of output by capital and labor equals one, and used the functional form (14):

$$y = A \times K^{a_1} \times L^{a_2} \qquad (14)$$

where A denotes technical change; a_1, a_2 are exponentials and elasticities of output by capital and labor, respectively.

The Cobb-Douglas has some properties. First, it belongs to the neoclassical class with $0 < a_1 < 1$, $0 < a_2 < 1$ and therefore, reflects the law of positive and diminishing marginal productivity. Second, its homogeneity is $a_1 + a_2$. In case $a_1 + a_2 = 1$, we get a linear homogenous function. If $a_1 + a_2 > 1$, then the multiplicative function points to a growing economic system as the output grows faster than the inputs. Then, returns to scale (ε) increase. Meanwhile, if $a_1 + a_2 < 1$, returns to scale decrease. $a_1 + a_2 = 1$ denotes constant returns to scale. Returns to scale are also the homogeneity of the production function and equal to $a_1 + a_2$:

$$\varepsilon = \frac{dy/y}{ydx/x} = a_1 + a_2 \qquad (15)$$

where $\frac{dy}{y} = a_1 \times \frac{dx_1}{x_1} + a_2 \times \frac{dx_2}{x_2}$; $\frac{dx_1}{x_1} = \frac{dx_2}{x_2} = \frac{dx}{x}$.

As we know, in the Cobb-Douglas function, the ES equals one.

Although the Cobb-Douglas is a powerful mathematical tool to describe production processes, as mentioned above, this functional form has extremely rigid premises. Hence, the CES function came into sight. The CES was established by Arrow et al. (1961) or ACMS for short. The authors dedicated the analysis to the ES. The production functions at that time assumed that the ES receives a fixed value, such as zero for Leontieff and one for Cobb-Douglas, which, in their view, is too rigid. Moreover, in order to assess the impact of economic policies on factor income, the CES is more appropriate (Miller 2008) or the Cobb-Douglas hides the role of the ES on economic growth and technical progress (Pereira 2003).

To examine the goodness of fit of the Leontieff and Cobb-Douglas functions, ACMS performed econometric analysis of the behavior of the ratio of labor income to nominal output. As long as output and input prices remain unchanged, the proportion is fixed and determined only by the parameters of the function. Rejection of the Cobb-Douglas (and Leontieff) functions are based on the arguments below.

The invariance of labor share in the Cobb-Douglas is expressed as follows:

$$\frac{p_2 \times L}{y} = a_2 \tag{16}$$

Equation (16) is rewritten in logs:

$$ln\frac{y}{L} = a + ln(p_2) \tag{17}$$

where $ln\frac{1}{a_2} = a$.

For the Leontieff function, the ratio between inputs arises from the production process, but is not influenced by price, i.e.,:

$$\frac{L}{y} = \gamma \tag{18}$$

Equation (18) takes the form of logs:

$$ln\left(\frac{y}{L}\right) = a \tag{19}$$

where $ln\left(\frac{1}{\gamma}\right) = a$.

Hence, we need to analyze the following function:

$$ln\left(\frac{y}{L}\right) = c + b \times ln(p_2) + \varepsilon \tag{20}$$

where ε is a random error.

It is necessary to test the hypotheses $b = 0$, $b = 1$. Investigating a data sample of 24 industries of 19 countries, ACMS came to the conclusion that, in most cases, the hypotheses $b = 0$, $b = 1$ are rejected.

The above finding encouraged the researchers to construct a new type of production function with a more flexible labor share, which is expressed in the following:

$$ln\left(\frac{y}{L}\right) = c + b \times ln(p_2) \tag{21}$$

where parameter b can have any value, but not zero or one.

From (21), under a condition of nonexistence of restraints on b, we can get a CES function. Through some transformations, the last version of the CES is the following:

$$F(K, L) = \gamma(\delta \times K^{-\theta} + (1-\delta)L^{-\theta})^{\frac{-1}{\theta}} \tag{22}$$

where $\theta = \frac{1-b}{b}$ is substitution parameter, $\delta = a_1 \times \gamma^\theta$ is distribution parameter; γ is efficiency parameter and $a_1 + a_2 = \gamma^{-\theta}$, the ES, $\sigma = \frac{1}{1+\theta}$.

So that the CES function (22) is a neoclassical one, assumptions $0 < \delta < 1$; $\gamma > 0$; $\theta > -1$ must be made. The premise of Hicks-neutral technical progress in the CES implies that the output produced by combining capital with labor is assumed to grow exponentially in a way that does not alter the marginal rate of technical substitution between the inputs. Therefore, the parameters of the production function will be stable over time.

In case $\sigma > 1$, i.e., $-1 < \theta < 0$, capital and labor are substitutable, so rising K/L leads to an increase in capital share.

If $\sigma < 1$, i.e., $0 < \theta < \infty$, capital and labor are complementary, and thus, when K/L increases, labor share rises.

In case $\sigma = 1$ ($\theta = 0$), then the Cobb-Douglas is obtained.

4. Empirical Research on the Elasticity of Factor Substitution and Its Association with Economic Growth

4.1. Estimation of the ES

Solow (1957) was a pioneer, and his followers used the Cobb-Douglas function, where technical change is referred to as neutral, and therefore changes in the ES were completely ignored (the ES is always equal to one). In their models, technical change is called total factor productivity (TFP). Nevertheless, in many empirical studies, the ES varies. For example, among others, Nerlove (1967) on a survey found that changes in period or concept may generate the different values of the ES. Comparing ES estimates from six alternative functional forms, five different measures of the rental price of capital, and two estimation techniques, Berndt (1976) went to a similar conclusion. McFadden (1978) tested the constancy of the ES for the steam-electric generating industry and revealed that the ES obtains a value of approximately 0.75. Hamermesh (1993) showed that the ES varies from 0.32 to 1.16 in the US and from 0.49 to 6.86 in the UK.

The consideration of the U.S. processing industry over a 200-year period indicates that ES values tend to change. The evidence shows that the ES was close to zero in the 19th century (Asher 1972; Uselding 1972; Schmitz 1981), close to one in the mid-20th century (Zarembka 1970), and greater than one in the late 20th century (Blair and Kraft 1974; Hsing 1996). Duffy and Papageorgiou (2000) estimated the ES based on a CES function on a cross-section of 82 countries and found the ES greater than one for developed economies and lower than one for developing economies. These authors concluded that the ES level is related to a country's stages of development. Using a Variable Elasticity of Substutution (VES) for 12 OECD countries (1965–1986), Genç and Bairam (1998) revealed that the average ES is greater than one. It is noteworthy that the diversity of results is because of the difference in data sets and estimation techniques. The above analyses also revealed that the ES is stable for a sample period, but rises with economic development.

4.2. Impact of the ES on Economic Growth

Theoretically, in early growth theory, some authors attempted to prove the significance of the ES. Solow (1957), Pitchford (1960), and Sato (1963) stated that allowing the ES to get any value will generate multiple growth paths, and some of them will be unbalanced. Recently, Azariadis (1993), using the overlapping generations model of growth, showed the possibilities of poverty traps depending on the values of the ES.

Ferguson (1965) ensured that in the case of a non-unitary ES, the output growth rate is dependent on the ES, as well as the growth rate of the savings ratio. La Grandville (1989), making use of the Slutsky equation, provided another evidence on the positive relationship between the ES and the output. The larger the ES, the higher production level that can be obtained. Barro and Sala-i-Martin (1995) found that under certain conditions, a large ES generates endogenous, steady-state growth. Later, Klump and Grandville (2000) proved that a greater ES leads to more probable endogenous growth and higher long-term growth rates. Also, the greater the ES, the higher steady-state income per capita. If the ES is more than one, we can achieve a unique steady-state and possibility of endogenous growth (Barro and Sala-i-Martin 1995). In the meantime, Pitchford (1960), Azariadis (1993), and Galor (1995), among others, considered that an ES lower than one in a CES function indicates multiple steady-states and poverty traps for per capita output. Two studies relying on La Grandville conducted by Yuhn (1991) and Cronin et al. (1997) attempted to test the relationship between the ES and economic growth. Comparing the US with South Korea, Yuhn (1991) found that the ES was higher for South Korea, which helps explain the higher growth rates acquired in this country after the 1960s. Utilizing data set for the 1961–1991 period, Cronin et al. (1997) estimated an ES of 13.01 between telecommunication and capital. Changes in the ES affect growth rate since production is an increasing function of the ES. In the CES case, the ES influences growth in almost every case, except when both inputs are increasing at the same rate (Kamien and Schwartz 1968).

Most studies on production functions in Vietnam made use of the frequentist methods or accounting method to estimate the Cobb-Douglas function. As known, this production function has an ES of one. Tu and Nguyen (2012) used the Cobb-Douglas function to analyze the impact of inputs on coffee productivity in DakLak province. Q.H. Nguyen (2013) applied the accounting method to build a Cobb-Douglas function for Hung Yen province to identify the resources of economic growth of this province. Khuc and Bao (2016) built an extended Cobb-Douglas function to identify factors contributing to the Vietnamese industry growth. Using the accounting method, Le estimated Vietnam's Cobb-Douglas function based on enterprise data of mining, processing industry, electricity and water production and distribution. The results show that the proportion of labor and fixed assets in the total output of the studied sectors ranges from 0.11 to 0.39 and 0.89 to 0.61, respectively.

For other types of the Cobb-Douglas function, Pham and Ly (2016) constructed a translog Cobb-Douglas function for the manufacturing enterprises of Vietnam, having net revenue as the output and capital, labor, and other costs as the inputs, based on data extracted from the 2010 Vietnam Enterprise Survey by the General Statistics Office. Huynh (2019) used the MLE method on a dataset extracted from the Enterprise Survey of the General Statistics Office for the period 2013-2016 to build a Battese-Coelli production function and analyze the factors affecting technical efficiency of small and medium enterprises in Vietnam.

It is noted that in the production function theory, many studies have tried to «soften» the premises of the Cobb-Douglas and the CES. But so far no other functions could surpass them in terms of popularity. Moreover, because of the very rigid premises of the Cobb-Douglas, the CES is increasingly explored. Hence, in the present work, the CES is selected to estimate the ES based on the data set of the Vietnamese nonfinancial enterprises.

5. Methodology and Data

5.1. Method and Model

There are several methods applied to estimate the ES, but different techniques can be divided into two main groups: Direct and indirect. A direct method allows for estimating the ES through the specification of a production function. The indirect method explores the link between the ES and factor shares to obtain the estimates. We can estimate the ES via the first-order profit maximization condition for labor employment. McFadden (1978) considered that choosing estimation methods depends on data availability, while Mizon (1977) preferred the direct method to the indirect way as the former provides estimates for a large number of functional forms using a common estimation technique and data set. In this study, following Mizon (1977), the author chooses the direct method.

Note that most of the previous studies estimated the ES within the frequentist framework using the CES or the VES. However, in the last three decades, the Bayesian approach has been popularized in social sciences thanks to some of its important strengths (Nguyen et al. 2019; Briggs and Nguyen 2019; Thach et al. 2019; Thach 2019). So, the question of when to use Bayesian analysis and when to use frequentist analysis depends on our specific research problem. For instance, firstly, if we would like to estimate the probability that a parameter belongs to a given interval, the Bayesian framework is appropriate. But if we want to perform a repeated-sampling inference about some parameter, the frequentist approach is needed. Secondly, from what was just mentioned, frequentist confidence intervals do not have straightforward probabilistic interpretation compared to Bayesian credible intervals. A 95% confidence interval can be explained as follows: If the same experiment is repeated many times and confidence intervals are computed for each experiment, then 95% of those intervals will contain the true value of the parameter. The probability that the true value falls in any given confidence interval is either one or zero, and we do not know which. Meanwhile, a 95% Bayesian credible interval provides a straightforward interpretation that the probability that a parameter lies in an interval is 95%. Thirdly, frequentist analysis is performed to approximate the true values of unknown parameters, while Bayesian analysis provides the entire posterior distribution of model parameters.

In the current study, making use of the direct method, the author estimates the ES through specifying an aggregate CES function. To estimate the CES function, the Bayesian nonlinear mixed-effects regression is performed. The Bayesian mixed-effects models with the grouping structure of the data consisting of multiple levels of nested groups contain both fixed effects and random effects. Our two-level mixed-effects model accounts for the variability between enterprises, which are identified by the id variable. According to Nezlek (2008), the results of analyses of multilevel data that do not take into account the multilevel nature of the data may (or perhaps will) be inaccurate. Based on Equation (22), our nonlinear model has the following expression:

$$lny_i = \beta_0 - \frac{1}{\theta}ln\left(\delta \times K_i^{-\theta} + (1 - \delta)L_i^{-\theta}\right) + \varepsilon_i \tag{23}$$

where lny_i is natural logarithm of output, K_i and L_i are natural logarithm of capital and labor used, respectively, β_0 is an intercept, θ is used to calculate $\sigma = \frac{1}{1+\theta}$, ε_i is a random error. The conditions $0 < \delta < 1$, $\theta > -1$ must be satisfied so Equation (23) is a neoclassical function.

In Bayesian analysis, we use conditional probability:

$$p(B) = \frac{p(A, B)}{p(B)} \tag{24}$$

to derive Bayes's theorem:

$$p(A) = \frac{p(A|B) \times p(B)}{p(A)} \tag{25}$$

where A, B are random vectors.

Assuming that a data vector y is a sample from a probability model with the unknown parameter vector θ, this model is written using a likelihood function:

$$L(\theta; y) = f(y; \theta) = \prod_{i=1}^{n} f(y_i|\theta) \tag{26}$$

where $f(y_i|\theta)$ is a probability density function of y given θ.

Relying on given data y, we infer some properties of θ. In Bayesian analysis, model parameters θ is a random vector.

We begin Bayesian analysis by specifying a posterior model. The posterior model combines given data and prior information to present the probability distribution of all parameters. Therefore, the posterior distribution has two components: A likelihood function containing information about the model parameters based on observed data, and prior distribution, including known information about the model parameters. By Bayes' law, the likelihood function and priors are combined to form the posterior model:

$$\text{Posterior} \propto \text{Likelihood} \times \text{Prior} \tag{27}$$

Because both y and θ are random variables, we apply Bayes's theorem to obtain the posterior distribution of θ given y:

$$p(y) = \frac{p(y|\theta) \times p(\theta)}{p(y)} = \frac{f(y;\theta) \times \pi(\theta)}{m(y)} \tag{28}$$

where $m(y) \equiv p(y)$ known as the marginal distribution of y which is formulated as follows:

$$m(y) = \int f(y;\theta) \times \pi(\theta) \times d(\theta) \tag{29}$$

where $f(y;\theta)$ is a likelihood function of y given θ, $\pi(\theta)$ is a prior distribution for θ, $m(y)$ is also known as the prior predictive distribution.

In cases when the posterior distribution is derived in closed form, we can proceed immediately to the inference step. However, except for some special models, the posterior distribution is scarcely available and needs to be estimated through simulation. Bayesian methods can be used to simulate many models. To simulate Bayes models, MCMC algorithms often require effective sampling and verify convergence of MCMC chains to the stationary distribution.

Experience of fitting Bayesian models shows that the specification of priors can rest on previous studies and expert knowledge. In our research, the propositions of a neoclassical production functions and previous research can suggest us to specify priors. To specify the CES, referring to Arrow et al. (1961), Afees (2015) or Lagomarsino (2017), we proposed to assign the normal N(1,100) prior to parameter β_0, the uniform(0,1) prior to parameter δ, the gamma(1,1) prior to parameter θ, and the Igamma(0.001, 0.001) prior to the variance component for u_{1j} (σ_{id}^2) and the overall variance parameter (σ_0^2) in this research.

Our Bayesian nonlinear mixed-effects regression model is as follows:
The likelihood function:

$$lny_{ij} = \beta_0 - \frac{1}{\theta} ln\big(\delta \times lnk2010_{ij}^{-\theta} + (1-\delta)lnl_{ij}^{-\theta}\big) + u_{1j} + \varepsilon_{ij} \tag{30}$$

The priors:

$$\beta_0 \sim N(1,\ 100)$$

$$\delta \sim uniform(0,\ 1)$$

$$\theta \sim gamma(1,\ 1)$$

$$u_{1j} \sim N\big(0, \sigma_{id}^2\big)$$

$$\sigma_{id}^2 \sim Igamma(0.001,\ 0.001)$$

$$\sigma_0^2 \sim Igamma(0.001,\ 0.001) \tag{31}$$

where lny_{ij}, $lnk2010_{ij}$, lnl_{ij} are natural logarithm of output, capital, labor employed, respectively in constant 2010 prices, β_0 is efficiency parameter, θ is substitution parameter, δ is distribution parameter, ε_{ij} is the random error, year $i = 2008, \ldots, 2018$, and enterprise $j = 1, 2, 3, \ldots, 227$.

5.2. Data Description

The study utilizes panel data collected from the financial statements and annual reports of 227 non-financial enterprises listed at Ho Chi Minh Stock Exchange and Ha Noi Stock Exchange in Vietnam for the period 2008–2018. All these enterprises belong to different manufacturing industries and thus, to capture their varying effects on the outcome, we perform the mix-effects regression. Time frequency indicates the year. The dataset has 1,974 observations. In Bayesian statistics, due to combining prior information with observed data, inferential results are valid to sparse data, and thus a small sample does not affect MCMC simulation results. It is noted that the 2008–2018 sample period includes years

2008–2009, when many countries around the world faced a sharp economic decline, but the Vietnamese enterprises were much less impacted by this global crisis. Statistical figures show that the economic growth of Vietnam achieved good performance, 5.7%, in 2008, and 5.4% in 2009 (World Bank 2019). Net revenue and fixed assets represent the enterprises' output and capital variables. The figures of net revenue and fixed assets are calculated based on the 2010 production price index of the General Statistics Office. The units of net revenue, fixed assets and labor are million VND, million VND and number of employees, respectively. The nonfinancial enterprises are chosen for our analysis since this sector is a powerful engine of Vietnamese economic growth, so to a great extent it stands for the national production. Moreover, according to Karabarbounis and Neiman (2014), the use of data on the enterprises listed on the stock market allows labor and capital shares not to be skewed owing to statistical errors that often occur when we take into account the mixed incomes from households' labor and capital contributions as well as those in the state-owned sector which are difficult to be measured accurately. The measurements of the variables are presented in Table 1.

Table 1. The measurements of the variables.

	Variable	Notation	Measurement	Data Source
Input	Labor	Lnl	Natural logarithm (Number of personal)	Enterprises' annual report
	Capital	Lnk2010	Natural logarithm (net fixed assets/Production price index)	Enterprises' financial statement
Output	Product	Lny2010	Natural logarithm (net revenue/Production price index)	Enterprises' financial statement
PPI	Production price index	PPI	2010 as base year	General Statistics Office

6. Empirical Results

6.1. Descriptive Statistics

Table 2 shows that variables $y2010$, l, and $k2010$ obtain maximum value of 4.00×10^7, 19,828 and 2.27×10^7, minimum value of 5320, 17 and 270, mean of 1,519,804, 1186 and 497,570, respectively. Standard deviation (Std. Dev) measures the variation or dispersion of a set of values. It equals 3,516,699, 1793 and 1,614,555 for $y2010$, l and $k2010$, respectively.

Table 2. Descriptive statistics.

Variables	Observations	Mean	Std.Dev	Min	Max
$y2010$	1974	1,519,804	3,516,699	5,320.232	4.00×10^7
l	1974	1,185.77	1,793.31	17	19,828
$k2010$	1974	497,569.7	1,614,555	270.336	2.27×10^7

6.2. Bayesian Simulation Results

Acceptance rate and efficiency are two criteria for evaluating the efficiency of MCMC sampling in Bayesian models. The acceptance rate is the number of proposals accepted in the total number of proposals, while efficiency means the mixing properties of MCMC sampling. Both of these rates influence MCMC convergence. The simulation results demonstrate that our model has a high acceptance rate of 0.6. According to Roberts and Rosenthal (2001), acceptance rates between 0.15–0.5 are optimal. Therefore, the MCMC sampling of our regression model has reached an acceptable acceptance rate. The smallest, average and largest efficiency of the MCMC sampling is 0.044, 0.21 and 0.97, which are greater than the warning level of 0.01 (Table 3). The MC errors (MCSE) of the posterior mean estimates are close to one decimal. The smaller these values are, the more accurate the estimates.

In Bayesian analysis, posterior confidence intervals, as stated above, have a straightforward probability interpretation. For example, for our model, the probability of the posterior mean of the parameter β_0 in the range (10.7; 11.2) is 95% (Table 3).

Table 3. Estimation results of the model.

Parameters	Mean	Std.Dev	MCSE	Median	Equal-Tailed [95% Cred. Interval]	
β_0	10.93202	0.1151538	0.009685	10.92836	10.71778	11.16215
δ	0.7393157	0.1598364	0.013872	0.7644217	0.3930561	0.9687505
θ	1.932563	1.48309	0.11108	1.613252	0.0643177	5.390139
σ^2_0	0.1457225	0.0049185	0.000091	0.1455947	0.136648	0.1558061
σ^2_{id}	1.410874	0.1324938	0.002484	1.401432	1.173098	1.700959

Random intercepts for u_{1j} (id) denote the varying effects of 227 enterprises studied on the outcome of the model. Means of all the random effects get MCSE close to one decimal, which is reasonable for MCMC algorithms. For illustration, we demonstrate the random intercepts of the first 10 enterprises in Table 4.

Table 4. Estimated random effects of the first 10 enterprises.

Identifier of Enterprises	Mean	Std. Dev.	MCSE	Median	Equal-Tailed [95% Cred. Interval]	
ln$y$2010 id						
1	0.8898169	0.1584065	0.005874	0.8922153	0.57769821	0.196495
2	−0.436001	0.1433862	0.006788	−0.4331991	−0.7247438	−0.1631326
3	−0.2109199	0.1437552	0.006945	−0.2091555	−0.4940332	0.0669913
4	−0.5319857	0.1439332	0.006037	−0.5303992	−0.8170173	−0.2592058
5	0.401608	0.1442947	0.006929	0.3997867	0.1252465	0.6856987
6	0.632537	0.2053234	0.006576	0.6323702	0.23859711	0.022473
7	1.133266	0.1508498	0.006596	1.129083	0.84428331	0.429053
8	1.204492	0.144532	0.005785	1.206624	0.90718511	0.489364
9	−1.363611	0.1438093	0.005982	−1.362593	−1.648538	−1.089397
10	1.146486	0.1522397	0.006884	1.147387	0.83553091	0.442738

6.3. Convergence Test for MCMC Chains

The convergence of MCMC chains should be tested before Bayes inference is performed, because Bayesian inference is robust only when the MCMC chains converge to a stationary distribution. According to the results recorded in Figure 1, with respect to our model, the diagnostic graphs are reasonable. Trace plots exhibiting no trends, run relatively quickly through the distribution towards the constant values of mean and variance; the autocorrelation plots are acceptable; histograms resemble the shape of probability distributions (Figure 1). In general, MCMC chains of our model have good mixing. Therefore, it can be concluded that there is no serious convergence problem and the MCMC chains have converged to the target distribution.

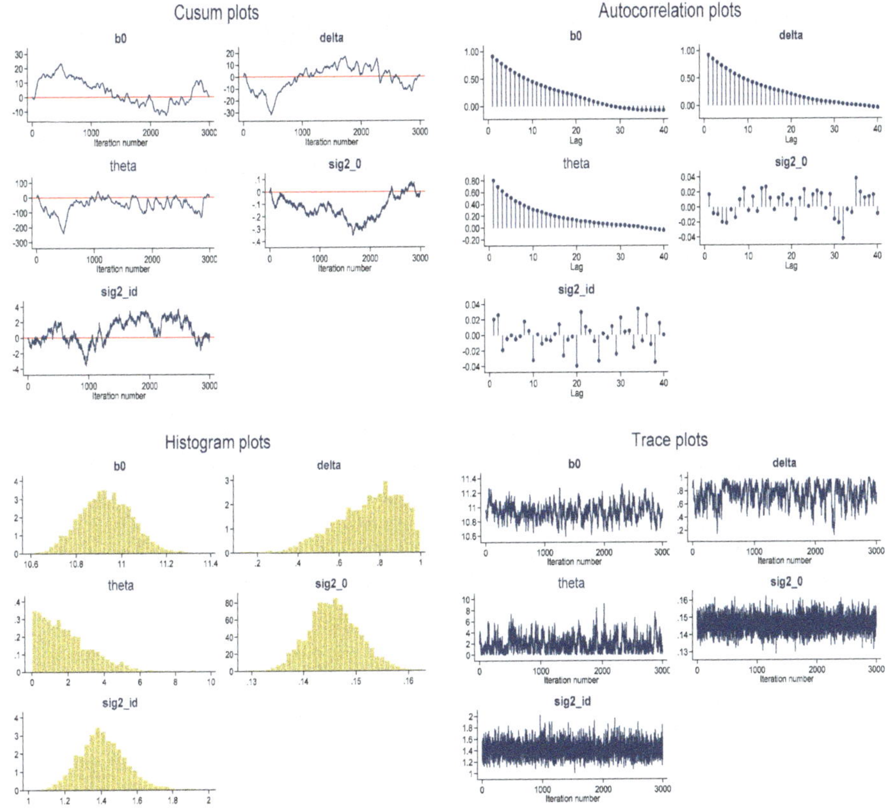

Figure 1. Graphical convergence diagnostics.

In addition, cusum plots are also a visual method for inspecting MCMC convergence. In our case, the cusum lines are not smooth but jagged, which surely points to MCMC convergence (Figure 1).

Besides visual inspection, formal test in which effective sample size can be used is a common method (Table 5). Efficiency greater than one is suggested satisfactory. Results presented in Table 5 demonstrate no sign of a non-convergence problem since the efficiency of all the model parameters is more than 4, whereas the highest correlation time is 22 lags.

Table 5. Effective sample size.

Parameters	ESS	Corr. Time	Efficiency
β_0	141.36	21.22	0.0471
δ	132.77	22.60	0.0443
θ	178.27	16.83	0.0594
σ_0^2	2903.02	1.03	0.9677
σ_{id}^2	2844.00	1.05	0.9480

6.4. Estimation Result of the ES

According to the results shown in Table 3, our estimated CES function has the value of efficiency parameter $\beta_0 = 10.9$, a distribution parameter of $\delta = 0.7$, and a substitution parameter of $\theta = 1.9$. The Bayesian simulations do not provide point estimates in a frequentist sense. Tests for MCMC convergence allow to confirm whether or not estimation results are robust. In our work, we already performed the convergence diagnostics, which produced acceptable results, as shown in the above. Once Bayesian inference is valid, MCMC iterations do yield similar estimates of the model parameters. These estimates point to the properties of a neoclassical production function. Because $\theta > 0$, the ES is smaller than one $(0 < \sigma < 1)$. These empirical results coincide with most of previous studies (for example, Berndt 1976; Hamermesh 1993; Pereira 2003; Chirinko 2008; Young 2013). In case $\sigma < 1$, we can provide two main explanations for the Vietnamese nonfinancial enterprises' output growth.

First, our data set used in this study indicates that there is a marked difference between the growth rates of capital and labor. Hence, with the ES lower than one, the sign of (12) is negative. Based on this finding, it can be concluded that the output growth rate of the Vietnamese nonfinancial enterprises has a falling trend in the long run. We should note that compared to enterprises in advanced economies, the Vietnamese ones have a very low contribution of technical change to production, and hence they are not capable of generating the unbounded endogenous growth. Therefore, stimulating R&D activities in enterprises is extremely important.

Second, as $g_l < g_K$ and $\frac{K}{L} > 1$, the higher growth rate of output is associated with a larger ES, i.e., $\frac{\delta g_y}{\delta \sigma} > 0$. According to our result, the ES is less than one, so capital as a relatively scarce factor strongly influences the output since its elasticity of production is great (≈ 0.73). While the ES is rising, the elasticity of production will be diminishing for the capital, but it will increase for the labor. Under the current conditions of the Vietnamese economy, capital is a scarce factor of the economy, so substantially increasing investment should be one of the most significant growth policies. Specifically, it is necessary to attract more foreign direct investment and expand positive spillover effects from foreign corporations to the national enterprises.

7. Conclusions

The present research uses the Bayesian non-linear mixed-effects regression method via the Random-walk MH algorithm to estimate the ES of the CES production function for nonfinancial businesses listed at Hanoi Stock Exchange and Ho Chi Minh City Stock Exchange in Vietnam. The CES was chosen over the Cobb-Douglas because its premises are more flexible, and in particular, its ES shall have useful implications for economic growth. The results of the convergence tests show that the MCMC chains converge to the target distribution so that the Bayesian inference is robust. Besides, the results of the statistical tests point out that our estimated model is consistent with the observed data. Mixed-effects estimates denote the varying impact of the studied enterprises on the model outcome. The CES function specified is a neoclassical one with a constant ES of less than one, i.e., capital and labor are complementary. So, it is concluded that the output growth rate of the Vietnamese nonfinancial enterprises is going down in the long-term. Thus, Vietnamese enterprises need to expand investment and intensify R&D activities in order to increase the capital-labor ratio as well as the contribution of technical progress to production, thanks to which the possibility of the unceasing endogenous growth can be created in the earliest prospect.

Funding: This research is supported by the Banking University HCMC, Vietnam.

Acknowledgments: The author is thankful to the anonymous referees for very useful comments.

Conflicts of Interest: The author declares no conflict of interest.

References

Afees, Salisu. 2015. Nonlinear Regression. Center for Econometric and Allied Research. Available online: http://cear.org.ng/index.php?option=com_docman&task=doc_details&gid=33&Itemid=92 (accessed on 10 January 2020).

Anh, Ly H., Si D. Le, Vladik Kreinovich, and Nguyen Ngoc Thach, eds. 2018. *Econometrics for Financial Applications.* Cham: Springer.

Antrás, Pol. 2004. Is the US Aggregate Production Function Cobb-Douglas? New Estimates of the Elasticity of Substitution. *Contributions to Macroeconomics* 4: 1–34. [CrossRef]

Arrow, Kenneth J., Hollis B. Chenery, Bagicha Singh Minhas, and Robert M. Solow. 1961. Capital Labour Substitution and Economic Efficiency. *Review of Econ. and Statistics* 63: 225–50. [CrossRef]

Asher, Ephraim. 1972. Industrial efficiency and biased technological change in American and British manufacturing: The case of textiles in the nineteenth century. *Journal of Economic History* 32: 431–42. [CrossRef]

Azariadis, Costas. 1993. *Intertemporal Macroeconomics*. Hoboken: Blackwell Publishers.

Barkai, Haim. 1959. Ricardo on Factor Prices and Income Distribution in a Growing Economy. *Economica* 26: 240–50. [CrossRef]

Barro, Robert J., and Xavier Sala-i-Martin. 1995. *Economic Growth*. New York: McGraw-Hill.

Berndt, Ernst. 1976. Reconciling Alternative Estimates of the Elasticity of Substitution. *Review of Economics and Statistics* 58: 59–68. [CrossRef]

Blackorby, Charles, and R. Robert Russell. 1981. The Morishima Elasticity of Substitution; Symmetry, Constancy, Separability, and its Relationship to the Hicks and Allen Elasticities. *Review of Economic Studies* 48: 147–58. [CrossRef]

Blair, Roger, and John Kraft. 1974. Estimation of elasticity of substitution in American manufacturing industry from pooled cross-section and time series observations. *Review of Economics and Statistics* 56: 343–47. [CrossRef]

Briggs, William, and Hung T. Nguyen. 2019. Clarifying ASA's View on P-Values in Hypothesis Testing. *Asian Journal of Economics and Banking* 3: 1–16.

Chirinko, Robert. 2008. The Long and Short of It. *Journal of Macroeconomics* 30: 671–86. [CrossRef]

Cobb, Charles W., and Paul H Douglas. 1928. A Theory of Production. *American Economic Review* 18: 139–65.

Cronin, Francis J., Elisabeth Colleran, and Mark Gold. 1997. Telecommunications, factor substitution and economic growth. *Contemporary Economic Policy* 15: 21–31. [CrossRef]

Duffy, John, and Chris Papageorgiou. 2000. A cross-crountry empirical investigation of the aggregate production function specification. *Journal of Economic Growth* 5: 87–120. [CrossRef]

Ferguson, Charles Elmo. 1965. The elasticity of substitution and the savings ratio in the neoclassical theory of growth. *Quarterly Journal of Economics* 79: 465–71. [CrossRef]

Galor, Oded. 1995. Convergence? Inference from theoretical models. *Economic Journal* 106: 1056–69. [CrossRef]

Genç, Murat, and Erkin Bairam. 1998. The Box-Cox Transformation as a VES Production Function. *Production and Cost Functions: Specification, Measurement, and Applications* 4: 54–61.

Hamermesh, Daniel. 1993. *Labor Demand*. Princeton: Princeton University Press.

Heubes, Jurgen. 1972. Elasticity of substitution and growth rate of output. *The German Economic Review* 10: 170–75.

Hicks, John R. 1932. *The Theory of Wages*. London: Macmillan.

Hicks, John R., and Roy G. D. Allen. 1934. A Reconsideration of the Theory of Value. *Economica* 1: 52–76. [CrossRef]

Hsing, Yu. 1996. An empirical estimation of regional production function for the U.S. manufacturing. *Annals of Regional Science* 30: 351–58. [CrossRef]

Humphrey, Thomas M. 1997. Algebraic Production Functions and their Uses before Cobb-Douglas. Federal Reserve Bank of Richmond. *Economic Quarterly* 83: 51–83.

Huynh, The Nguyen. 2019. Factors affecting technical efficiency in Vietnamese small and medium enterprises. *Journal of Asian Business and Economics Studies*. Available online: http://jabes.ueh.edu.vn/Home/SearchArticle?article_Id=8fbfecc6-ffc8-4ab8-84b7-5ca9b1ab8c50 (accessed on 11 January 2020).

Kamien, Morton I., and Nancy L. Schwartz. 1968. Optimal "induced" technical change. *Econometrica* 36: 1–17. [CrossRef]

Karabarbounis, Loukas, and Brent Neiman. 2014. The Global Decline of the Labor Share. *The Quarterly Journal of Economics* 129: 61–103. [CrossRef]

Khuc, Van Quy, and Tran Quang Bao. 2016. Identifying the determinants of forestry growth during the 2001–2014 period. *Journal of Agriculture and Rural Development* 12: 2–9.

Klump, Rainer, and Oliver La Grandville. 2000. Economic growth and the elasticity of substitution: Two theorems and some suggestions. *The American Economic Review* 90: 282–91. [CrossRef]

Kreinovich, Vladik, Nguyen Ngoc Thach, Nguyen Duc Trung, and Dang Van Thanh, eds. 2019. *Beyond Traditional Probabilistic Methods in Economics*. Cham: Springer.

La Grandville, Oliver. 1989. In quest of the slutsky diamond. *American Economic Review* 79: 468–81.

Lagomarsino, Elena. 2017. A Study of the Approximation and Estimation of CES Production Functions. Ph.D. thesis, Heriot-Watt University, Edinburgh, UK.

Lloyd, Peter J. 1969. Elementary Geometric/Arithmetic Series and Early Production Theory. *Journal of Political Economy* 77: 21–34. [CrossRef]

McFadden, Daniel. 1963. Constant Elasticity of Substitution Production Functions. *Review of Economic Studies* 30: 73–83. [CrossRef]

McFadden, Daniel. 1978. Estimation Techniques for the Elasticity of Substitution and Other Production Parameters. North Holland. *Contributions to Economic Analysis* 2: 73–123.

Miller, Eric. 2008. An Assessment of CES and Cobb-Douglas Production Functions. Congressional Budget Office. Available online: https://www.cbo.gov/sites/default/files/cbofiles/ftpdocs/94xx/doc9497/2008-05.pdf (accessed on 15 December 2019).

Mizon, Grayham E. 1977. Inferential procedures in nonlinear models: An application in a UK industrial cross section study of factor substitution and returns to scale. *Econometrica* 45: 1221–42. [CrossRef]

Nelson, Richard R. 1965. The CES production function and economic growth projections. *The Review of Economics and Statistics* 47: 326–28. [CrossRef]

Nerlove, Marc. 1967. Recent Empirical Studies of the CES and Related Production Functions. *The Theory and Empirical Analysis of Production* 31: 55–136.

Nezlek, John B. 2008. An Introduction to Multilevel Modeling for Social and Personality Psychology. *Social and Personality Psychology Compass* 2: 842–60. [CrossRef]

Nguyen, Quang Hiep. 2013. Sources of province Hung Yen 's economic growth. *Journal of Economic Development* 275: 28–39.

Nguyen, Hung T., Nguyen Duc Trung, and Nguyen Ngoc Thach, eds. 2019. *Beyond Traditional Probabilistic Methods in Econometrics*. Cham: Springer.

Pereira, Claudiney M. 2003. Empirical Essays on the Elasticity of Substitution, Technical Change, and Economic Growth. Ph.D. dissertation, North Carolina State University, Raleigh, NC, USA.

Pham, Le Thong, and Phuong Thuy Ly. 2016. Technical efficiency of Vietnamese manufacturing enterprises. *Journal of Economics and Development* 229: 43–51.

Pitchford, John D. 1960. Growth and the elasticity of substitution. *Economic Record* 36: 491–503. [CrossRef]

Roberts, Gareth O., and Jeffery S. Rosenthal. 2001. Optimal scaling for various Metropolis-Hastings algorithms. *Statistical Science* 16: 351–67. [CrossRef]

Samuelson, Paul A. 1979. Paul Douglas's Measurement of Production Functions and Marginal Productivities. *Journal of Political Economy* 87: 923–39. [CrossRef]

Sato, Kazuo. 1963. Growth and the elasticity of factor substitution: A comment—How plausible is imbalanced growth. *Economic Record* 39: 355–61.

Schmitz, Mark. 1981. The elasticity of substitution in 19th-century manufacturing. *Explorations in Economic History* 18: 290–303. [CrossRef]

Schumpeter, Joseph A. 1954. *History of Economic Analysis*. London: Allen & Unwin.

Solow, Robert M. 1957. Technical Change and the Aggregate Production Function. *The Review of Economics and Statistics* 39: 312–20. [CrossRef]

Stigler, George J. 1952. The Ricardian Theory of Value and Distribution. *Journal of Political Economy* 60: 187. [CrossRef]

Thach, Nguyen Ngoc. 2019. A Bayesian approach in the prediction of U.S.'s gross domestic products. *Asian Journal of Economics and Banking* 163: 5–19.

Thach, Nguyen Ngoc, Le Hoang Anh, and Pham Thi Ha An. 2019. The Effects of Public Expenditure on Economic Growth in Asia Countries: A Bayesian Model Averaging Approach. *Asian Journal of Economics and Banking* 3: 126–49.

Tu, Thai Giang, and Phuc Tho Nguyen. 2012. Using the Cobb-Douglas to analyze the impact of inputs on coffee productivity in province DakLak. *Journal of Economics and Development* 8: 90–93.

Uselding, Paul. 1972. Factor substitution and labor productivity growth in American manufacturing, 1839–1899. *Journal of Economic History* 33: 670–81. [CrossRef]

Velupillai, Kumaraswamy. 1973. The Cobb-Douglas or the Wicksell Function?—A Comment. *Economy and History* 16: 111–13. [CrossRef]

Werf, Edwin. 2007. Production Functions for Climate Policy Modeling: An Empirical Analysis. *Energy Economics* 30: 2964–79. [CrossRef]

World Bank. 2019. World Bank National Accounts Data, and OECD National Accounts Data Files. Available online: https://data.worldbank.org/indicator/NY.GDP.MKTP.KD.ZG?locations=VN (accessed on 10 January 2020).

Young, Andrew T. 2013. US Elasticities of Substitution and Factor Augmentation at the Industry Level. *Macroeconomic Dynamics* 17: 861–97. [CrossRef]

Yuhn, Ky-hyang. 1991. Economic growth, technical change biases, and the elasticity of substitution: A test of the la grandville hypothesis. *The Review of Economics and Statistics* 73: 340–46. [CrossRef]

Zarembka, Paul. 1970. On the empirical relevance of the ces production function. *Review of Economics and Statistics* 52: 47–53. [CrossRef]

Journal of
Risk and Financial Management

Article

Disentangling Civilian and Military Spending Shocks: A Bayesian DSGE Approach for the US Economy

Marco Lorusso [1,*] **and Luca Pieroni** [2]

[1]   Newcastle Business School, Northumbria University, Newcastle upon Tyne NE18ST, UK
[2]   Department of Political Science, University of Perugia, 06123 Perugia PG, Italy
*   Correspondence: marco.lorusso@northumbria.ac.uk; Tel.: +44-(0)191-349-5803

Received: 8 August 2019; Accepted: 22 August 2019; Published: 1 September 2019

Abstract: In this paper, we disentangle public spending components in order analyse their effects on the U.S. economy. Our Dynamic Stochastic General Equilibrium Model (DSGE) model includes both civilian and military expenditures. We take into account the changes in the effects of these public spending components before and after the structural break that occurred in the U.S. economy around 1980, namely financial liberalisation. Therefore, we estimate our model with Bayesian methods for two sample periods: 1954:3–1979:2 and 1983:1–2008:2. Our results suggest that total government spending has a positive effect on output, but it induces a fall in private consumption. Moreover, we find important differences between the effects of civilian and military spending. In the pre-1980 period, higher civilian spending induced a rise in private consumption, whereas military spending shocks systematically decreased it. Our findings indicate that civilian spending has a more positive impact on output than military expenditure. Our robustness analysis assesses the impact of public spending shocks under alternative monetary policy assumptions.

Keywords: military and civilian spending; DSGE model; fiscal policy; monetary policy; Bayesian estimation

JEL Classification: C11; E21; E62; E63

---

1. Introduction

The effect of an increase in government spending is a central issue in macroeconomics. In this regard, different macroeconomic models have achieved contrasting conclusions about the response of private consumption to government spending shocks (see, among others: Baxter and King 1993; Ambler and Paquet 1996; Linnemann and Schabert 2006; Forni et al. 2009; Leeper et al. 2010; Enders et al. 2011; Coenen et al. 2012; Corsetti et al. 2012; Kormilitsina and Zubairy 2018; Beidas Strom and Lorusso 2019).

It is also well known that around the early 1980s, the transmission of fiscal policy shocks actually changed (see, for example: Fatás and Mihov 2001; Blanchard and Perotti 2002; Perotti 2005; Galí et al. 2007). Such a change is related to the increased asset market participation by households (Bilbiie et al. 2008). During the 1960s and the 1970s, a large fraction of households was prevented access to financial markets due to significant restrictions. Starting from the early 1980s, financial liberalisation widened private access to financial markets. In turn, such a change had an important influence on the private consumption response to government spending shocks.

In this paper, we develop and estimate a Dynamic Stochastic General Equilibrium (DSGE) model, which includes two different components of government spending, namely civilian and military expenditures. In line with the so-called "military Keynesianism" (see Pieroni et al. 2008), we assume that spending decisions for these two different government components are independent. According to the proponents of this view, defence expenditure satisfies two particular conditions: Firstly, it is financed independently of the other public spending categories (such as education and health). Secondly, decisions about the defence sector are taken from institutions that are independent of the other government sectors (the Department of Defence in the U.S.).

Our DSGE model tries to explain the possible sources of crowding in/out effects in consumption observed in the data. To do so, we take into consideration heterogeneous households as in Galí et al. (2007) and Lorusso and Pieroni (2017). A share of households does not have access to the bond market and consumes their current disposable income at each date. On the other hand, a share of households has access to financial markets, smoothing their consumption in the desired way. Firms that produce differentiated goods decide on labour input and set prices according to the model of Calvo (1983). The fiscal policy authority purchases consumption goods, which are divided into spending for the military and non-military sectors, and raises lump-sum taxes and income taxes and issues nominal debt. Finally, our model encompasses a central bank, which sets its policy instrument, the nominal interest rate, by the rule of Taylor (1993).

We estimate our model with Bayesian techniques using U.S. data for two sub-samples: 1954:3–1979:2 (S1) and 1983:1–2008:2 (S2). This sample split allows us to analyse the changes in fiscal shocks before and after the potentially important changes to the financial markets mentioned above.

The main contribution of this paper with respect to previous literature is twofold. Firstly, we include the disaggregated components of civilian and military spending in a DSGE theoretical framework. This allows us to assess the effects of these two public spending components on several macroeconomic aggregates and, in particular, on private consumption. Secondly, we use the Bayesian approach to estimate the effects of fiscal policy shocks on the economy. This allows us to avoid the well-known shortcomings in the identification of military shocks that are associated with the neoclassical literature (Ramey and Shapiro 1999; Ramey 2011) based on the so-called "narrative approach".[1]

Our estimated results show that, in the U.S., the share of asset holders increased after the financial liberalisation that occurred in the early 1980s. Such an increase has important consequences on the effects of public spending shocks on the economy. In particular, we find that total government, non-military and military spending shocks affect the U.S. economy differently. An increase in total government expenditure has a positive effect on output, but it induces a fall in private consumption (the so-called crowding-out effect). This occurs because the negative wealth effect generated by the increase in taxation leads both non-asset and asset-holders to increase their labour supply. Accordingly, the fall in the aggregate wage lowers households' disposable income, and in turn, private consumption decreases.

On the other hand, an increase in non-military spending induced a crowding-in effect on consumption in the pre-1980s period. Such an outcome occurred because the lower persistence of the non-military spending shock implies a lower wealth effect on asset holders, and subsequently, the shift in labour demand dominates the shift in labour supply. Accordingly, the real wage increases enough to raise aggregate consumption. Our results also indicate that military spending shocks have a less positive effect on output than civilian spending shocks in both sub-samples.

Finally, we analyse the role of monetary policy in the presence of several public spending shocks. We find that a higher nominal interest rate associated with a more aggressive monetary policy tends to strengthen household incentives to postpone consumption, inducing a negative effect on output.

The rest of the paper is structured as follows. The model is presented in Section 2. In Section 3, we describe the data used for our analysis, discuss the parameters of the model, and report the estimated

---

[1] For a detailed discussion about the criticism of the narrative approach, refer to Perotti (2005).

results. Section 4 presents the impulse response analysis of our estimated models, and Section 5 provides the robustness analysis. Finally, Section 6 concludes.

2. The Model

In this section, we present our DSGE model, which is in line with the theoretical framework developed by Bilbiie et al. (2008).[2]

2.1. Households

We assume a continuum of infinitely-lived households $[0,1]$ that are divided in two fractions: asset holders and non-asset holders. Asset holders are denoted with the fraction $1 - \lambda$. They trade a risk-less one period bond and hold shares in firms. The non-asset holders are denoted by λ. They do not participate in asset markets and simply consume their disposable income.

2.1.1. Asset Holders

These households face the following intertemporal problem:

$$\max_{\{C_{A,t}, L_{A,t}, B_{A,t+1}\}} E_t \sum_{t=0}^{\infty} \beta^t \frac{\left(C_{A,t} L_{A,t}^{\varphi}\right)^{1-\sigma}}{1-\sigma} \tag{1}$$

where $\beta \in (0,1)$ denotes the discount factor, φ indicates the inverse of the Frish elasticity and σ is the inverse of the intertemporal elasticity of substitution. Moreover, $C_{A,t}$, $L_{A,t}$ and $B_{A,t+1}$ denote, respectively, consumption, leisure and nominal bond holdings for each asset holder.

The asset holder intertemporal budget constraint is expressed by:

$$R_t^{-1} B_{A,t+1} + P_t C_{A,t} + P_t T_t = B_{A,t} + (1-\tau)\left(W_t N_{A,t} + P_t D_{A,t}\right) \tag{2}$$

where τ is the income tax rate that is assumed to be constant and (T_t) denotes the real lump-sum taxes that are adjusted to a rule specified below. Moreover, we indicate by R_t the gross nominal return on bonds purchased in period t, whereas P_t is the price level, W_t the nominal wage and $D_{A,t}$ the real dividend payments to households who own shares in the monopolistically-competitive firms. Finally, $N_{A,t}$ indicates the hours worked by the asset holder. If we assume that time endowment is normalized to one, then we have: $N_{A,t} = 1 - L_{A,t}$.

2.1.2. Non-Asset Holders

In each period t, these households solve the following intratemporal problem:

$$\max_{\{C_{N,t}, L_{N,t}\}} \frac{\left(C_{N,t} L_{N,t}^{\varphi}\right)^{1-\sigma}}{1-\sigma} \tag{3}$$

subject to the following budget constraint:

$$P_t C_{N,t} = (1-\tau) W_t N_{N,t} - P_t T_t \tag{4}$$

where $C_{N,t}$ and $N_{N,t}$ denote consumption and hours worked by non-asset holders, respectively. Equation (4) implies that non-asset holder consumption equals their net income.

---

[2] Appendices A–C report the full derivation of the model.

2.2. Firms

Firms in the final goods market are competitive. They use the following aggregation technology:

$$Y_t = \left(\int_0^1 Y_t(i)^{\frac{\varepsilon-1}{\varepsilon}} \, di \right)^{\frac{\varepsilon}{\varepsilon-1}} \tag{5}$$

where $Y_t(i)$ denotes the quantity of intermediate goods $i \in [0,1]$, at time t, used as input. Moreover, ε is the constant elasticity of substitution.

Firms in the final goods market have the following profit maximization problem:

$$\max_{\{Y_t(i)\}} P_t Y_t - \int_0^1 P_t(i) \, Y_t(i) \, di \tag{6}$$

where P_t is the price index for the final goods and $P_t(i)$ denotes the price of the intermediate goods i. From the first order condition for $Y_t(i)$, we obtain the downward sloping demand for each intermediate input:

$$Y_t(i) = \left(\frac{P_t(i)}{P_t} \right)^{-\varepsilon} Y_t \tag{7}$$

This implies a price index equal to:

$$P_t = \left[\int_0^1 (P_t(i))^{1-\varepsilon} \, di \right]^{\frac{1}{1-\varepsilon}} \tag{8}$$

The intermediate goods, $Y_t(i)$, are produced by monopolistically-competitive producers that face a production function that is linear in labour and subject to a fixed cost F:

$$Y_t(i) = N_t(i) - F, \text{ if } N_t(i) > F, \text{ otherwise, } Y_t(i) = 0 \tag{9}$$

Thus, real profits for these firms correspond to:

$$O_t(i) \equiv \left[\frac{P_t(i)}{P_t} \right] Y_t(i) - \left[\frac{W_t}{P_t} \right] N_t(i)$$

We assume that intermediate goods firms face Calvo-style price-setting frictions (Calvo 1983). This implies that intermediate firms can reoptimize their prices with probability $(1 - \alpha)$, whereas with probability α, they keep their prices constant as in a given period. A firm i, resetting its price in period t, solves the following maximization problem:

$$\max_{\{P_t^*(i)\}} E_t \sum_{s=0}^{\infty} \alpha^s \Lambda_{t,t+s} \left[P_t^*(i) \, Y_{t,t+s}(i) - W_{t+s} Y_{t,t+s}(i) \right] \tag{10}$$

subject to the demand function:

$$Y_{t+s}(i) = \left(\frac{P_t^*(i)}{P_{t+s}} \right)^{-\varepsilon} Y_{t+s} \tag{11}$$

where $P_t^*(i)$ is the optimal price chosen by firms resetting prices at time t. Finally, the expression for the price law of motion is equal to:

$$P_t = \left[\alpha (P_{t-1})^{1-\epsilon} + (1 - \alpha)(P_t^*)^{1-\epsilon} \right]^{\frac{1}{1-\epsilon}} \tag{12}$$

2.3. Fiscal Policy

The government budget constraint is given by:

$$R_t^{-1} B_{t+1} = B_t + P_t \left[G_t - \tau Y_t - T_t \right] \tag{13}$$

where (τ) and (T_t) denote distortionary and lump-sum taxes, respectively. Moreover, (B_t) indicates the one-period nominal discount bonds.

We analyse two different cases: firstly, we focus on the model with total government spending; secondly, we disentangle public expenditure into civilian and military components.

2.3.1. Total Government Spending

In the model with aggregated public expenditure, total government spending is treated as an exogenous $AR(1)$ process:

$$\log\left(G_t\right) = \rho^G \log\left(G_{t-1}\right) + \epsilon_t^G \tag{14}$$

$$\text{where: } \epsilon_t^G \sim N\left(0, \sigma_G^2\right)$$

where ρ^G indicates the persistence of total government spending and ϵ_t^G is an i.i.d. distributed error term that captures the shock volatility.

2.3.2. Non-Military and Military Expenditures

In the model with disaggregated components of public expenditure, we adopt the additive principle where total government spending can be seen as the sum of its different components. Thus, government spending is divided into civilian sector spending (NM_t) and military sector spending (M_t):

$$G_t = NM_t + M_t \tag{15}$$

We assume that civilian and military expenditure levels are independent and exogenous $AR(1)$ processes:

$$\log\left(NM_t\right) = \rho^{NM} \log\left(NM_{t-1}\right) + \epsilon_t^{NM}, \tag{16}$$

$$\text{where: } \epsilon_t^{NM} \sim N\left(0, \sigma_{NM}^2\right)$$

$$\log\left(M_t\right) = \rho^M \log\left(M_{t-1}\right) + \epsilon_t^M, \tag{17}$$

$$\text{where: } \epsilon_t^M \sim N\left(0, \sigma_M^2\right)$$

where ρ^{NM} and ρ^M are, respectively, the persistence parameters of the civilian and military shocks, while ϵ_t^{NM} and ϵ_t^M are, respectively, the stochastic civilian and military terms that are i.i.d. distributed.

2.3.3. Financing Mechanism of Public Expenditure

The government primary deficit is defined as:

$$D_t = G_t - \tau Y_t - T_t \tag{18}$$

Equation (18) simply means that government primary deficit is the total non-interest spending less revenues. Moreover, we assume that the government incurs a structural deficit $(D_{s,t})$, which is given by the changes in the primary deficit adjusted by automatic responses of tax revenues resulting from deviations on output from its steady state value (Y):

$$D_{s,t} = D_t + \tau\left(Y_t - Y\right) = G_t - T_t - \tau Y \tag{19}$$

We assume that the structural deficit is adjusted according to the following log-linearized rule:

$$d_{s,t} = \eta d_{s,t-1} + \phi_g G_Y g_t \tag{20}$$

This type of rule is in line with those used by Bohn (1998) and Galí and Perotti (2003). The parameter η captures the possibility that budget decisions are autocorrelated. The parameters ϕ_g measure the response of structural deficit to changes in government spending.

2.4. Monetary Policy

We assume that the monetary authority sets the nominal interest according to the following log-linearized monetary policy reaction function:

$$r_t = \rho^R r_{t-1} + \left(1 - \rho^R\right) \left\{ \bar{\pi}_t + r_\pi \left(\pi_{t-1} - \bar{\pi}_t\right) + r_y \left(y_t - y\right) \right\} + \epsilon_t^R \tag{21}$$

where ρ_R is an interest rate smoothing parameter, whereas π_t denotes the inflation rate. Equation (21) implies that the central bank responds to deviations of lagged inflation from an inflation objective and to an output gap defined as the difference between actual and steady state output (Rabanal and Rubio-Ramírez 2001).

Our monetary policy rule assumes two exogenous shocks: The first is a shock to the inflation objective ($\bar{\pi}_t$), which is assumed to follow a first order autoregressive process:

$$\log\left(\bar{\pi}_t\right) = \rho^{\bar{\pi}} \log\left(\bar{\pi}_{t-1}\right) + \epsilon_t^{\bar{\pi}} \tag{22}$$

$$\text{where: } \epsilon_t^{\bar{\pi}} \sim N\left(0, \sigma_{\bar{\pi}}^2\right) \tag{23}$$

The second shock is a temporary i.i.d. monetary policy shock $\epsilon_t^R \sim N\left(0, \sigma_R^2\right)$.

2.5. General Equilibrium and Aggregation

The final goods market clearing condition is given by:

$$Y_t = C_t + G_t \tag{24}$$

that is production equals demand by total household consumption and total government spending. The aggregate consumption is given by:

$$C_t = \lambda C_{N,t} + (1 - \lambda) C_{A,t} \tag{25}$$

The equilibrium in the labour market is given by:

$$N_t = \lambda N_{N,t} + (1 - \lambda) N_{A,t} \tag{26}$$

that is the wage level is such that demand by firms for labour equals total labour supply. Finally, the equilibrium in the share market is given by:

$$B_{t+1} = (1 - \lambda) B_{A,t+1} \tag{27}$$

that is households hold all outstanding equity shares and all government debt is held by asset holders.

3. Estimating the Model

In this section, we focus on the estimated results of our model. We start by describing the data, then we discuss the assumptions on the prior distributions of the parameters estimated with Bayesian techniques. Finally, we present the posterior estimates of such parameters.

3.1. Data Description

Our model is estimated on U.S. data for two samples, 1954:3–1979:2 (S1) and 1983:1–2008:2 (S2). As we explained above, in the early 1980s, financial liberalisation occurred. Therefore, our choice of splitting the overall sample reflects the hypothesis of a structural break in such a period.

Our choice of ending S2 in 2008:2 is because this period coincides with the beginning of the U.S. financial crisis. As a consequence, the Fed adopted an unconventional monetary policy, which resulted in the short-term nominal interest rate approaching the zero-lower bound. As Christiano et al. (2011) and Ramey and Zubairy (2018) argued, in such a situation, the effects of fiscal spending shocks on several macroeconomic aggregates substantially changed with respect to "normal" times.

As we mentioned above, we have two separate models. In the first model, we assumed that the whole economy was driven by three exogenous shocks: total government spending (ϵ_t^G), inflation objective ($\epsilon_t^{\bar{\pi}}$) and monetary policy (ϵ_t^R). Since there were three exogenous shocks, we used three observed variables to estimate this model: total government spending, inflation rate and short-term nominal interest rate. The series of the total government spending was taken from the U.S. Bureau of Economic Analysis (BEA). The inflation rate corresponded to the quarterly growth rate of the GDP price index. For the short-term nominal interest rate, we considered the effective federal funds rate expressed in quarterly terms. The source of these two data series was the website of the Federal Reserve Bank of St. Louis.

In the second model, we disaggregated total public spending into non-military and military components. Thus, the exogenous processes governing the economy were four: non-military expenditure (ϵ_t^{NM}), military spending (ϵ_t^M), inflation objective ($\epsilon_t^{\bar{\pi}}$) and monetary policy (ϵ_t^R). Thus, we used four observed variables to estimate this model: non-military expenditure, military expenditure, inflation rate and short-term nominal interest rate. The data series for non-military and military spending were obtained from the U.S. BEA. In particular, military spending corresponded to national defence data, whereas non-military spending was obtained from the difference between government consumption expenditures and gross investment data and national defence data. For inflation rate and short-term nominal interest rate, we used the data series that we mentioned above.

In both models, we deflated all variables using their respective deflators. Moreover, we expressed the several variables in log per capita terms. Finally, we detrended all the series using the Hodrick–Prescott filter with a smoothing parameter equal to 1600.

3.2. Prior Distributions of the Parameters

We split the parameters of our models into two groups. The first set was kept fixed. The parameters of this group can be viewed as strict priors, and we set their values in line with previous literature (Galí et al. 2007; Bilbiie et al. 2008). The second group of parameters was estimated using the Bayesian method.

Table 1 shows the fixed parameters in the two sub-samples for both the aggregate government spending model and the disaggregated model. From Panel (a), we note that the share of government expenditure on GDP in S1 was higher than the one in S2. This reflects that fact that the average of public spending decreased over time. Focusing on the disaggregated model, Panel (b) shows that also the shares of non-military spending on GDP (NM_Y) and military spending on GDP (M_Y) decreased from S1 to S2.

Table 1. Fixed parameters for both models. S, Sub-sample.

Parameter	S1 (1954:Q3–1979:Q2)	S2 (1983:Q1–2008:Q2)
(a) Model with Total Government Spending		
β	0.99	0.99
G_Y	0.28	0.18
τ	0.30	0.30
ϕ_g	0.17	0.64
η	0.51	0.71
α	0.75	0.75
σ	2.00	2.00
N	0.25	0.25
(b) Model with Non-Military and Military Expenditures		
β	0.99	0.99
G_Y	0.28	0.18
M_Y	0.10	0.06
NM_Y	0.18	0.12
ϕ_g	0.17	0.64
η	0.51	0.71
τ	0.30	0.30
α	0.75	0.75
σ	2.00	2.00
N	0.25	0.25

In line with Bilbiie et al. (2008), we kept ϕ_g equal to 0.17 in S1 and 0.64 in S2 for both the aggregate government spending model and the disaggregated expenditure model. This implies that there was a greater reliance on deficits to finance an extra public spending unit in S2 than S1. Following Bilbiie et al. (2008), we fixed η equal to 0.51 in the first sub-sample and to 0.71 in the second sub-sample for both the aggregate government expenditure model and the disaggregated spending model. Such values imply a greater persistence of deficits in the second sub-sample.

For the remaining fixed parameters, we used the same values for both sub-samples and in both models. The discount factor (β) corresponded to 0.99, which implies an annual steady state real interest rate of 4%. Moreover, we assumed that, in the steady state, agents spend one-fourth of their time endowment working. Following Bilbiie et al. (2008), we set the inverse of the intertemporal elasticity of substitution (σ) equal to two. The price elasticity of demand for intermediate goods (ε) was chosen such that the mark-up in the steady state equalled 20%. Moreover, in line with Del Negro and Schorfheide (2008), we fixed the probability that prices did not change in a given period (α) at 0.75. Finally, we set the steady state tax rate (τ) equal to 0.3. Together with the assumption that the steady-state share of debt was zero, these last two parameters pinned down lump-sum transfers in the steady state.

Table 2 displays the prior distributions of the endogenous parameters estimated with Bayesian techniques for both models in S1 and S2. We start by describing our prior assumptions on the share of non-asset holders. In line with the findings by Bilbiie et al. (2008), for both models, we assumed that (λ) was gamma distributed and had a higher prior mean in S1 than S2.

Table 2. Priors of endogenous parameters for both models.

Parameter	Prior Distribution	Prior Mean		Prior St. Dev.	
	(a) Model with Total Government Spending				
		S1	S2	S1	S2
ρ^R	Beta	0.65	0.65	0.10	0.10
r_π	Gamma	1.50	1.50	0.10	0.10
r_y	Gamma	0.10	0.10	0.05	0.05
λ	Gamma	0.50	0.30	0.01	0.01
	(b) Model with Non-Military and Military Expenditure				
		S1	S2	S1	S2
ρ^R	Beta	0.65	0.65	0.10	0.10
r_π	Gamma	1.50	1.50	0.10	0.10
r_y	Gamma	0.10	0.10	0.05	0.05
λ	Gamma	0.50	0.30	0.01	0.01

Notes: In the above table, S1 denotes the first sub-sample, whereas S2 indicates the second sub-sample.

Turning to the parameters of the monetary policy rule, we chose a pretty general and agnostic approach by assuming the same prior distributions in both sub-samples and for both models. Our priors were in line with the values found by Smets and Wouters (2007). In particular, we assumed that the interest rate smoothing parameter was beta distributed with prior mean and standard deviation corresponding to 0.65 and 0.10, respectively. The prior for the coefficient on inflation was assumed to have a gamma distribution with mean equal to 1.5 and standard deviation equal to 0.1. Moreover, we assumed that the coefficient on output was gamma distributed with mean equal to 0.10 and standard deviation equal to 0.05.

Table 3 shows the priors of the stochastic processes. The distribution for these parameters was the same in both models and sub-samples. In line with Smets and Wouters (2007), we assumed that the persistence parameters of the $AR(1)$ processes were beta distributed with means equal to 0.70 and standard deviations equal to 0.20. Finally, the standard errors of the innovations were assumed to follow inverse-gamma distributions with mean equal to 0.01 and infinite degrees of freedom.

Table 3. Priors of shock processes for both models.

Parameter	Prior Distribution	Prior Mean		Prior St. Dev.	
	(a) Model with Total Government Spending				
		S1	S2	S1	S2
ρ^G	Beta	0.70	0.70	0.20	0.20
ρ^π	Beta	0.70	0.70	0.20	0.20
σ_G	Inverse-Gamma	0.01	0.01	$Inf.$	$Inf.$
σ_π	Inverse-Gamma	0.01	0.01	$Inf.$	$Inf.$
σ_R	Inverse-Gamma	0.01	0.01	$Inf.$	$Inf.$
	(b) Model with Non-Military and Military Expenditure				
		S1	S2	S1	S2
ρ^{NM}	Beta	0.70	0.70	0.20	0.20
ρ^M	Beta	0.70	0.70	0.20	0.20
ρ^π	Beta	0.70	0.70	0.20	0.20
σ_{NM}	Inverse-Gamma	0.01	0.01	$Inf.$	$Inf.$
σ_M	Inverse-Gamma	0.01	0.01	$Inf.$	$Inf.$
σ_π	Inverse-Gamma	0.01	0.01	$Inf.$	$Inf.$
σ_R	Inverse-Gamma	0.01	0.01	$Inf.$	$Inf.$

Notes: In the above table, S1 denotes the first sub-sample, whereas S2 indicates the second sub-sample.

3.3. Posterior Estimates of the Parameters

In both models and in both sub-samples, for the group of parameters estimated with the Bayesian method, firstly, we estimated the mode of the posterior distribution by maximising the log posterior function, which combined the priors with the likelihood function given by the data. Secondly, we used the Metropolis–Hastings algorithm to obtain the full posterior distribution.[3] Our samples included 1,000,000 draws, and we dropped the first 250,000 of them. The acceptancerates for the total government spending model corresponded to 35% in S1 and 33% in S2, whereas for the model with disaggregated public spending, the components in S1 and S2 were equal to 32% and 33%, respectively. In order to test the stability of the samples, we used the diagnostic test of Brooks and Gelman (1998). We also used other diagnostic tests for our estimates, including the Monte Carlo Markov Chain (MCMC) univariate diagnostics and the multivariate convergence diagnostics. In terms of parameters identification, we performed the test of Iskrev (2010).[4] Such a test shows that all the parameters for both models and in both sub-samples were identifiable in the neighbourhood of our estimates. Finally, we tested for the possibility of the misspecification of our DSGE model. In line with Albonico et al. (2019), we estimated the DSGE-VAR counterparts (in the spirit of Del Negro and Schorfheide 2004) for the models with aggregate government spending, as well as disaggregated non-military and military expenditures in both sub-samples. Overall, our results indicated that, in both sub-samples, the benchmark models outperformed the different DSGE-VAR models.[5]

Tables 4 and 5 report the posterior means for the parameters of both models for S1 and S2 with a 90% confidence interval.

Table 4. Estimated posteriors of endogenous parameters for both models.

Parameter	Posterior Mean	Confidence Interval		Posterior Mean	Confidence Interval	
	S1 (1954:Q3–1979:Q2)			*S2 (1983:Q1–2008:Q2)*		
(a) Model with Total Government Spending						
ρ^R	0.3240	0.2576	0.3894	0.3961	0.3362	0.4557
r_π	1.5330	1.3677	1.6937	1.4920	1.3314	1.6513
r_y	0.1396	0.0363	0.2355	0.1286	0.0340	0.2237
λ	0.4484	0.4390	0.4559	0.2898	0.2743	0.3051
(b) Model with Non-Military and Military Expenditures						
ρ^R	0.2419	0.1647	0.3208	0.3664	0.2969	0.4362
r_π	1.5194	1.3634	1.6816	1.4835	1.3201	1.6416
r_y	0.1183	0.0290	0.2009	0.1252	0.0300	0.2142
λ	0.4488	0.2998	0.5384	0.2901	0.2745	0.3053

---

[3] All the estimations were done with Dynare (http://www.dynare.org/).

[4] All the relative figures are reported in Appendix D together with prior and posterior distributions of the parameters estimated with Bayesian methods.

[5] In Appendix F, Tables A1 and A2 compare the different DSGE-VAR models against the benchmark models, reporting their marginal log densities and Bayes factors.

Table 5. Estimated posteriors of shock processes for both models.

Parameter	Posterior Mean	Confidence Interval		Posterior Mean	Confidence Interval	
	S1 (1954:Q3–1979:Q2)			S2 (1983:Q1–2008:Q2)		
(a) Model with Total Government Spending						
ρ^G	0.8231	0.7340	0.9116	0.7628	0.6653	0.8607
ρ^π	0.9629	0.9305	0.9980	0.9580	0.9223	0.9966
σ_G	0.4954	0.4390	0.5520	0.3155	0.2819	0.3492
σ_π	0.2270	0.1624	0.2927	0.2921	0.1976	0.3900
σ_R	1.3924	1.1659	1.6141	1.2582	1.0998	1.4162
(b) Model with Non-Military and Military Expenditures						
ρ^{NM}	0.6152	0.4861	0.7413	0.8049	0.7192	0.8934
ρ^M	0.9291	0.8830	0.9785	0.8394	0.7552	0.9236
ρ^π	0.9601	0.9264	0.9975	0.9564	0.9196	0.9962
σ_{NM}	0.5104	0.4501	0.5688	0.3273	0.2919	0.3624
σ_M	0.9652	0.8502	1.0741	0.8604	0.7671	0.9534
σ_π	0.2101	0.1482	0.2689	0.2894	0.1936	0.3869
σ_R	1.4603	1.2293	1.6907	1.2815	1.1146	1.4454

We start by describing the estimates of the share of non-asset holders (λ). From Table 4, we observe that asset market participation differed considerably across periods. More specifically, for the model with aggregate government spending, the share of consumers who did not smooth consumption by trading in assets was estimated as 0.45 in S1 and as 0.29 in S2. Similar values were found for the model with disaggregated public spending components. These results imply that access to asset markets widened with the important institutional changes in the early 1980s. As we will discuss below, this result had important implications for the several fiscal policy shocks.

Focusing on the estimated parameters for monetary policy, we note that for the model with aggregate government spending in both sub-samples, the nominal interest responded more strongly to inflation than output changes. Our finding was in line with Andrés et al. (2009). Interestingly, we found that the interest smoothing parameter had a larger value in S2 than S1. The estimates for these parameters showed a similar value for the model with disaggregated government spending.

A number of observations are worth making regarding the estimated exogenous processes. In the model with aggregate government spending, we found that the expenditure shock volatility (σ_G) was much larger in S1 than S2. Similarly, government spending shocks were more persistent in S1 than S2. Regarding the shocks to monetary policy, the inflation target shock was more volatile in S2 than S1, whereas the nominal interest rate shock had a higher volatility in the first sub-sample. Such results confirm a stronger central bank response to inflation in the second sub-period.

Focusing on the model with non-military and military expenditures, we noted remarkable differences across the two sub-samples and between the two components. Firstly, we noted that the volatilities of the government spending components were larger in the first sub-sample. Secondly, we found that civilian spending shocks were more persistent in S2, whereas the opposite occurred to military expenditure shocks. Thirdly, our results showed that σ_M was almost double of σ_{NM} in both S1 and S2. Such findings confirmed that military spending shocks were much more volatile than civilian shocks. Similarly, military expenditure shocks were more persistent than civilian spending shocks in both sub-samples.

4. Analysing the Effects of Different Public Spending Shocks on the Economy

In this section, we show the impulse responses by assuming a 1% increase in total government, civilian and military expenditures. More specifically, we set the values of the several parameters equal to their mean estimates of their posterior distributions. This strategy allowed us to compare the effects of several public spending shocks on the economy effectively.[6]

4.1. Model with Aggregate Government Spending

Figure 1 plots the impulse responses to a positive government spending shock. We observed that such a shock was more persistent in the first sub-sample. This result was in line with the studies by Fatás and Mihov (2003) and Perotti (2005).

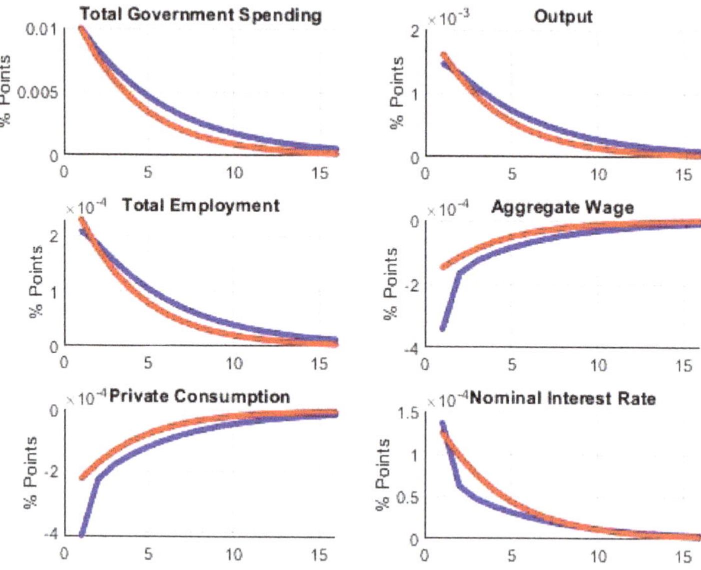

Figure 1. Total government spending shock. Notes: Simulated 1% increase in total government spending. Parameters are set according to their estimated values. The blue lines indicate the responses of the estimated model for S1, whereas the red lines denote the responses of the estimated model in S2.

Our results indicate that, on the shock impact, output increased by 0.15% in S1 and 0.16% in S2. However, from the fourth quarter onwards, we noted a smaller increase in GDP during the post-financial liberalisation period than in S1. Our findings were in line with Albonico et al. (2017), who found that in recent years, and especially during the Great Recession, the discretionary fiscal stimulus has played a negligible role in stabilising the U.S. economy.

From Figure 1, we note that, in both sub-samples, an increase in government spending induced an increase in hours worked. This occurred because both non-asset and asset holders increased their labour supply due to the negative wealth effect induced by the increase in taxation. Aggregate wages fell in response to the shock because the shift in labour supply dominated the shift in labour demand.

Moreover, the nominal interest rate increased. As a consequence, private consumption decreased. Such a finding confirmed the predictions of standard neoclassical models in which higher government spending tends to depress the consumption of asset holders. The reason was the negative wealth effect resulting from the induced increase in the tax burden. Such an effect was strengthened by the increase

---

[6]   In Appendix E, we report the estimated IRFs and their relative error bands for all three public spending shocks in both sub-samples.

in the nominal interest rate. A more aggressive monetary policy implies a higher real interest rate and, in turn, lowered the incentive of asset holders to postpone consumption.

Interestingly, we found that private consumption had a larger fall in S1 than S2. This is explained by the higher persistence of the government spending shock in the first sub-sample that increased the present discounted value of taxes and the wealth effect on asset holders.

4.2. Model with Non-Military and Military Expenditures

Figures 2 and 3 show the impulse responses to non-military and military spending shocks, respectively.

We start by describing the effects of a 1% increase in non-military spending (Figure 2). We observed that the persistence of the shock was much lower in S1 than S2. Moreover, our results showed that, on impact, output increased by 0.13% in the first sub-sample and by 0.10% in the second sub-sample. Similarly, hours worked increased in both S1 and S2.

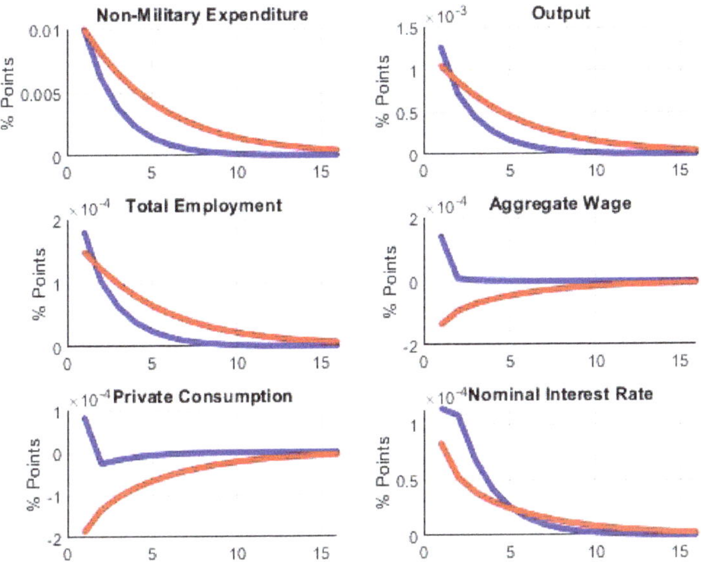

Figure 2. Non-military spending shock. Notes: Simulated 1% increase in non-military spending. Parameters are set according to their estimated values. The blue lines indicate the responses of the estimated model for S1, whereas the red lines denote the responses of the estimated model in S2.

Interestingly, we noted that the responses of aggregate wage and private consumption were very different across the two sub-samples. In particular, we observed an increase in these two variables in S1, whereas they both fell in S2. Therefore, our results showed the crowding-in effect before the 1980s and the crowding-out effect thereafter. The reason for the crowding-in effect in S1 was the strong enough rise in the real wage. Such an increase induced a rise in the consumption of non-asset holders, which more than offset the fall in consumption of asset holders. The increase in the aggregate wage crucially depended on the interaction between labour demand and supply. On the one hand, a positive civilian spending shock increased the demand for goods and, in turn, affected labour demand. The firms that could not change their prices and had to adjust their quantities hence shifted labour demand at a given wage. On the other hand, labour supply shifted for two different reasons. Firstly, non-asset holders would work more as tax burden increased. Secondly, asset holders also increased labour supply for a given wage: this was due both to the wealth effect and to intertemporal substitution.

The lower persistence of the civilian spending shock in S1 implied a lower wealth effect on asset holders, and in turn, the shift in labour demand dominated the shift in labour supply. Accordingly, the real wage increased enough to raise aggregate consumption. Since the opposite effects occurred in the second sub-sample, we observed crowding-out on private consumption. Finally, we note that the nominal interest rate increased more in the first sub-sample, weakening the positive effect of the civilian spending shock on consumption.

We now turn to the effects of a 1% increase in military spending. As we can observe in Figure 3, the persistence of this shock was higher in S1 than S2. Interestingly, we note that the positive effect on output implied by these shocks was lower compared to the increased civilian spending for both sub-samples (0.04% in S1 and 0.05% in S2).

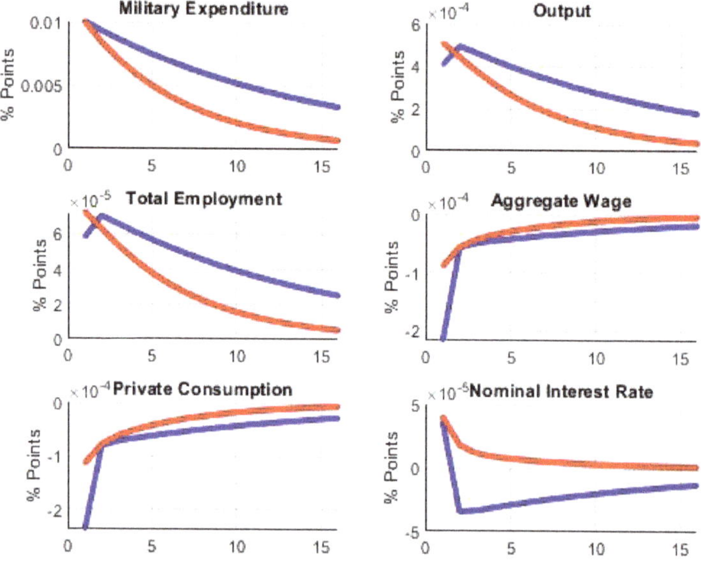

Figure 3. Military spending shock. Notes: Simulated 1% increase in military spending. Parameters are set according to their estimated values. The blue lines indicate the responses of the estimated model for S1, whereas the red lines denote the responses of the estimated model in S2.

Moreover, it is possible to observe that in both S1 and S2, hours worked increased in response to the shock due to the negative wealth effect associated with the increase in taxation. Our results indicated a larger fall in the aggregate wage during the first sub-sample. As a consequence, private consumption dropped more substantially in S1 than S2.

From these results, it is evident that there were important differences between the effects of civilian and military spending. In the pre-1980 period, an increase in civilian expenditure induced a crowding-in effect on private consumption for the U.S. economy. On the contrary, military spending shocks caused a systematic fall in private consumption. Moreover, we note that the civilian spending had a more positive impact on output than military expenditure for both sub-samples.[7]

5. Robustness Analysis: Different Assumptions about the Taylor Rule

In this section, we investigate the role of monetary policy in the presence of the shocks to total government, non-military and military spending. In particular, we provide a counterfactual analysis in which the central bank has a more aggressive monetary policy. More specifically, we assumed that in the Taylor rule (21), the parameters measuring the response of the policy rate to output (r_y) and inflation (r_π), as well as the interest rate smoothing parameter (ρ^R) assumed values that were double those estimated by our models.

Figure 4 shows the responses for both output and consumption in the case of an increase in total government, non-military and military spending, respectively. The black lines represent the responses of output and consumption in the presence of the actual monetary policy, whereas the green lines show the IRFs for the same variables in the presence of a more aggressive monetary policy.

As we explained in the previous section, a more aggressive monetary policy implies a higher nominal interest rate that strengthened household incentives to postpone consumption. As a consequence, private consumption and output were lower. In fact, the top panels of Figure 4 show that in the case of total government spending, for the first sub-sample, both output and consumption were lower in the presence of a more aggressive monetary policy (on the shock impact, 0.01% lower than in the benchmark case). In the second sub-sample, the same effects with similar magnitudes can be observed.

The mid panels of Figure 4 show a more striking difference in the responses of consumption and output to an increase in non-military spending. In S1, although in the presence of the actual monetary policy, private consumption increased, when a more aggressive monetary policy was in operation, the crowding-out effect emerged. In turn, this implies that output in the counterfactual scenario was lower than in the actual case by 0.02%. These effects are less pronounced in the second sub-sample. Finally, the bottom panels of Figure 4 show that different monetary policies had negligible effects in the case of an increase in military spending.

---

[7] In order to further assess the different contribution of fiscal spending shocks on aggregate output, we also performed the forecast error variance decomposition for 1, 4, 10, and 30 quarters ahead (Albonico et al. 2019). Our results indicated that fiscal spending shocks had larger contributions on GDP during the post-financial liberalisation period. Moreover, we found that non-military spending shocks contributed to output changes more than military spending shocks.

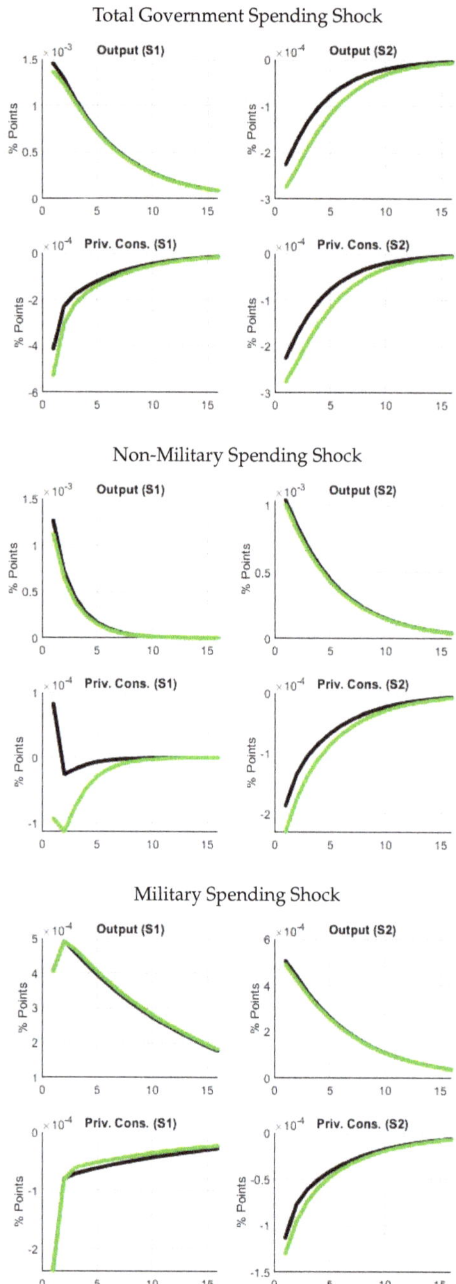

Figure 4. Alternative assumptions on the Taylor rule. Notes: In the above graphs, the black lines denote the IRFsin the presence of the actual U.S. monetary policy, whereas the green lines indicate the IRFs associated with the counterfactual monetary policy.

6. Conclusions

In this paper, the impact of total government, non-military and military spending shocks on the U.S. economy was assessed. We accounted for the established evidence that public spending shocks have changed substantially in the post-1980s. Therefore, we estimated our DSGE model with recent Bayesian techniques for two sample periods: 1954:3–1979:2 and 1983:1–2008:2. Our new Keynesian DSGE model featured limited asset market participation as a potential institutional explanation for different degrees of fiscal policy effectiveness. Therefore, our model allowed us to relate the differences in the transmission of public spending shocks to important financial changes in the U.S. economy.

Our results suggested that asset market participation increased noticeably in the post-1980s, in line with previous evidence in the economic literature. Moreover, we found that an exogenous increase in total government spending led to a higher output, but decreased consumption. Our findings also indicated that, in the first sub-sample, an increase in non-military spending induced a crowding-in effect on consumption. On the contrary, positive shocks to military spending tended to depress private consumption. We also found that military spending shocks had a less positive effect on output than civilian spending shocks in both sub-samples. Finally, we assessed the role of monetary policy in the presence of different public spending shocks. Our findings suggested that a more aggressive monetary policy tended to lower private consumption and output.

Overall, our results indicated that the U.S. economy seemed to benefit from increases in non-military spending. On the other hand, the military Keynesianism hypothesis, which still has many supporters in the U.S., can be at least questionable. The policy implications that can be drawn from our analysis suggested that switching government priorities in favour of supplying civilian goods and services, rather than financing federal defence spending, should foster the U.S. economy.

As future work, it will be intriguing to extend this work by considering a Markov switching rational expectation new-Keynesian model in order to analyse in more detail the change in volatility of fiscal spending shocks in the pre- and post-financial liberalisation periods.

Author Contributions: The work was equally divided between the two co-authors.

Funding: This work was supported by the Department of Political Science, University of Perugia.

Acknowledgments: We thank the editor, the three anonymous referees and Francesco Ravazzolo for their useful comments and suggestions that improved this work.

Conflicts of Interest: The authors declare no conflict of interest.

Appendix A. Maximization Problems of the Model

From the asset holders utility maximization problem, we obtain the following FOCs for $C_{A,t}$ and $L_{A,t}$:

$$\lambda_t = -\frac{L_{A,t}^{\varphi}}{\left(C_{A,t}L_{A,t}^{\varphi}\right)^{\sigma}}\frac{1}{P_t} \tag{A1}$$

$$\frac{\varphi C_{A,t}L_{A,t}^{\varphi-1}}{\left(C_{A,t}L_{A,t}^{\psi}\right)^{\sigma}} = -\lambda_t\left[(1-\tau)W_t\right] \tag{A2}$$

Putting (A1) into (A2), we obtain the labour decision equation:

$$\frac{C_{A,t}}{L_{A,t}} = \frac{(1-\tau)}{\varphi}\frac{W_t}{P_t} \tag{A3}$$

The FOC for $B_{A,t+1}$ is:

$$\lambda_t\frac{1}{R_t} = \lambda_{t+1}\beta \tag{A4}$$

Putting (A1) into (A5), we obtain the Euler equation:

$$\frac{1}{R_t} = \beta \left(\frac{C_{A,t}}{C_{A,t+1}}\right)^{\sigma} \left(\frac{L_{A,t+1}}{L_{A,t}}\right)^{\varphi(1-\sigma)} \frac{P_t}{P_{t+1}} \tag{A5}$$

Thus:

$$R_t^{-1} = \beta E_t \left[\Lambda_{t,t+1}\right]$$

where:

$$\Lambda_{t,t+s} = \beta^s \left(\frac{C_{A,t}}{C_{A,t+s}}\right)^{\sigma} \left(\frac{L_{A,t+s}}{L_{A,s}}\right)^{\varphi(1-\sigma)} \frac{P_t}{P_{t+s}} \tag{A6}$$

This is the stochastic discount factor.

From the non-asset holders utility maximization problem, we obtain the following FOCs for $C_{N,t}$ and $L_{N,t}$:

$$\lambda_t = \frac{L_{N,t}^{\varphi}}{\left(C_{N,t} L_{N,t}^{\varphi}\right)^{\sigma}} \frac{1}{P_t} \tag{A7}$$

$$\frac{\varphi C_{N,t} L_{N,t}^{\varphi-1}}{\left(C_{N,t} L_{N,t}^{\varphi}\right)^{\sigma}} = \lambda_t \left[(1-\tau) W_t\right] \tag{A8}$$

Putting (A8) into (A9) gives the labour decision equation:

$$\frac{C_{N,t}}{L_{N,t}} = \frac{(1-\tau)}{\varphi} \frac{W_t}{P_t} \tag{A9}$$

Given the following production function for intermediate goods:

$$Y_t(i) = N_t(i) - F, \tag{A10}$$

we can write real profits as:

$$O_t(i) \equiv \left[\frac{P_t(i)}{P_t}\right] Y_t(i) - \left[\frac{W_t}{P_t}\right] N_t(i) \tag{A11}$$

A firm i sets $P(i)$ in order to solve the following problem:

$$\max_{\{P_t^*(i)\}} E_t \sum_{s=0}^{\infty} \alpha^s \Lambda_{t,t+s} \left[P_t^*(i) Y_{t,t+s}(i) - W_{t+s} Y_{t,t+s}(i)\right]$$

$$s.t : Y_t(i) = \left(\frac{P_t^*(i)}{P_t}\right)^{-\varepsilon} Y_t$$

that is:

$$\max_{\{P_t^*(i)\}} E_t \sum_{s=0}^{\infty} \alpha^s \Lambda_{t,t+s} \left[P_t^*(i) \left(\frac{P_t^*(i)}{P_t}\right)^{-\varepsilon} Y_t - W_t \left(\frac{P_t^*(i)}{P_t}\right)^{-\varepsilon} Y_t\right]$$

The FOC is given by:

$$E_t \sum_{s=0}^{\infty} \alpha^s \Lambda_{t,t+s} \left[P_t^*(i) - \frac{\varepsilon}{\varepsilon-1} W_{t+s}\right] = 0 \tag{A12}$$

Appendix B. Steady States

The Euler equation in the steady state gives:

$$R = \frac{1}{\beta} \tag{A13}$$

In the steady state, from the FOC of the price setting in the intermediate goods firm's problem, we have for the real wage:

$$\frac{W}{P} = \frac{\varepsilon - 1}{\varepsilon} \tag{A14}$$

we can rewrite (A14) as:

$$\frac{W}{P} = \frac{Y}{N} \frac{1 + F_Y}{1 + \mu} \tag{A15}$$

The ratio of profits to output is given by:

$$O_Y \equiv \frac{\mu - F_Y}{1 + \mu} \tag{A16}$$

We assume, in the steady state, that:

$$N_N = N_A = N \tag{A17}$$

Because of preference homogeneity, we need to ensure that steady-state consumption shares are also equal across groups. This can be seen comparing the two labour decision equations evaluated in the steady state:

$$\frac{C_A}{L} = \frac{1 - \tau}{\varphi} \frac{W}{P} = \frac{C_N}{L} \tag{A18}$$

implying:

$$C_A = C_N = C \tag{A19}$$

The steady-state coefficients needed for our log-linear approximation above are fully determined as:

$$(1 - \tau) \frac{W}{P} \frac{N}{Y} = (1 - \tau) \frac{1 + F_Y}{1 + \mu} \tag{A20}$$

$$\frac{C_N}{Y} = (1 - \tau) \frac{1 + F_Y}{1 + \mu} - T_Y \tag{A21}$$

$$T_Y = G_Y - \tau \tag{A22}$$

$$\frac{C_A}{Y} = (1 - \tau) \frac{1}{1 - \lambda} \left(1 - \lambda \frac{1 + F_Y}{1 + \mu} \right) - T_Y \tag{A23}$$

We thus achieve equalization of steady-state consumption shares by making an assumption on technology. Specifically, we ensure that asset income in the steady state is zero. This requires assuming that the fixed cost of production is characterised by:

$$F_Y = \mu \tag{A24}$$

Substituting in (A22) gives:

$$\frac{C_A}{Y} = \frac{C_N}{Y} = 1 - \tau - T_Y = 1 - G_Y \tag{A25}$$

We want to find hours in steady state. Given the equalization of hours and consumption between the two groups and normalizing $P = 1$, the intratemporal optimality condition implies:

$$(1 - \tau) WN - T = \frac{(1 - \tau)}{\varphi} W (1 - N) \tag{A26}$$

dividing by Y and using (A20) and the expression for the fixed cost, we obtain the following expression for the steady-state hours:

$$\frac{N}{1-N} = \frac{1}{\varphi}\frac{1-\tau}{1-G_Y} \tag{A27}$$

Given τ and G_Y, we chose the steady state N to match average hours worked. From (A27), this implies a unique value for φ.

Appendix C. The Log-Linearized Model

Below, we show the log-linearized equations of our model around the non-stochastic steady state. We denote by small letters the log deviation of a variable from its steady-state value, while for any variable X_t, X stands for its steady-state value and X_Y its steady-state share in output, X/Y.

The log-linearized Euler equation for asset-holders is given by:

$$c_{A,t} = E_t c_{A,t+1} - \frac{1}{\sigma}\left(r_t - E_t\pi_{t+1}\right) + \left(\frac{1}{\sigma}-1\right)\left(1+\frac{T_Y}{1-G_Y}\right)\left(E_t n_{A,t+1} - n_{A,t}\right) \tag{A28}$$

The log-linearization of the labour decision equation for asset holders is given by:

$$\frac{N}{1-N}n_{A,t} = w_t - c_{A,t} \tag{A29}$$

The log-linearized labour decision equation for non-asset holders is equal to:

$$\frac{N}{1-N}n_{N,t} = w_t - c_{N,t} \tag{A30}$$

The consumption for non-asset holders is obtained log-linearizing their budget constraint and is given by:

$$(1-G_Y)\,c_{N,t} = (1-\tau)\,(w_t + n_{N,t}) - T_Y t_t \tag{A31}$$

From the last two relations, we obtain a reduced-form labour supply for non-asset holders:

$$n_{N,t} = \frac{\varphi}{1+\varphi}\left[\frac{-T_Y}{1-G_Y+T_Y}\right](w_t - t_t) \tag{A32}$$

The log-linearized expression for aggregate hours is given by:

$$n_t = \lambda n_{N,t} + (1-\lambda)\,n_{A,t} \tag{A33}$$

The log-linearized expression for aggregate consumption is given by:

$$c_t = \lambda c_{N,t} + (1-\lambda)\,c_{A,t} \tag{A34}$$

The log-linearized aggregate production function is given by:

$$y_t = (1+F_Y)\,n_t \tag{A35}$$

We note that the share of the fixed cost F in the steady-state output governs the degree of increasing returns to scale. The log-linearized new-Keynesian Phillips curve is given by:

$$\pi_t = \beta E_t\pi_{t+1} + \frac{(1-\alpha)\,(1-\alpha\beta)}{\alpha}w_t \tag{A36}$$

In both models of aggregate government spending and disaggregated non-military and military components, the log-linearization of the budget constraint around a steady state with zero debt and a balanced primary budget gives the following expression:

$$\beta b_{t+1} = b_t + G_Y g_t - T_T t_t - \tau y_t \tag{A37}$$

Moreover, in the model with disaggregated non-military and military spending, we have that:

$$g_t G_Y = N M_Y n m_t + M_Y m_t \tag{A38}$$

The log-linearized structural primary deficit is given by:

$$d_{s,t} = G_Y g_t - T_Y t_t \tag{A39}$$

Finally, the log-linearized goods market clearing can be written as:

$$y_t = g_t G_Y + c_t \left(1 - G_Y\right) \tag{A40}$$

Appendix D. Diagnostic Tests

Appendix D.1. Prior and Posterior Distributions

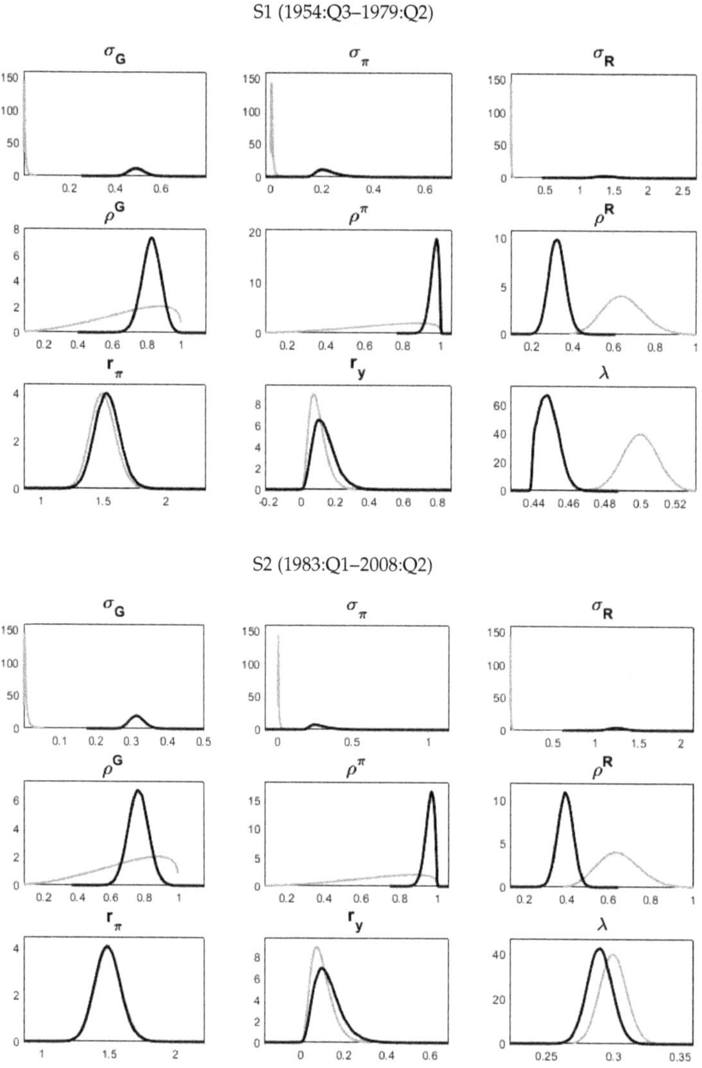

Figure A1. Total government spending model. Notes: In the above graphs, the grey lines represent the prior distributions, whereas the black lines correspond to the posterior distributions.

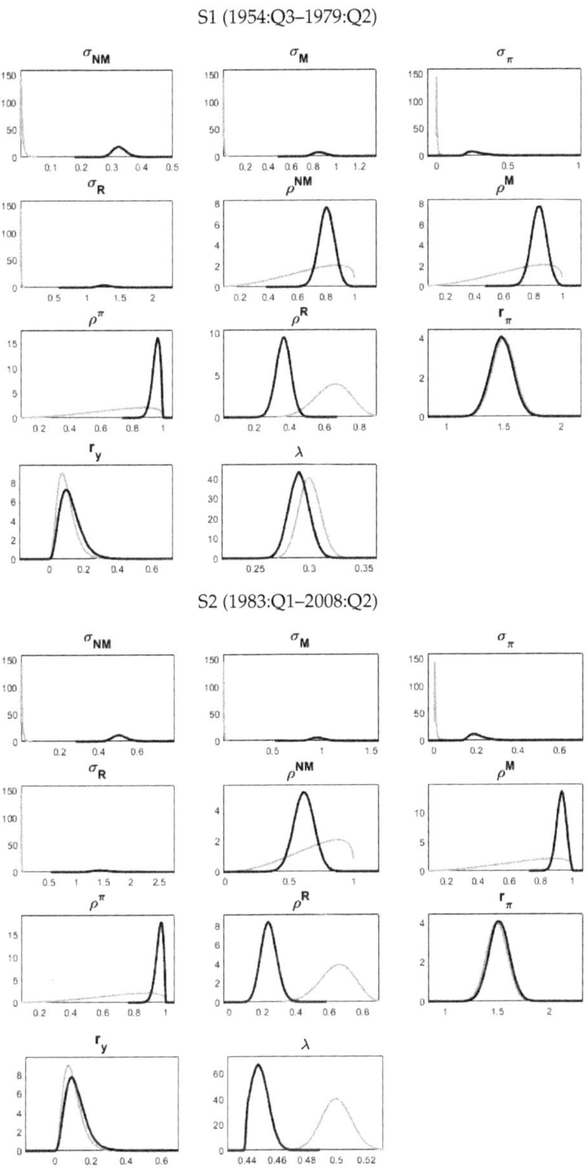

Figure A2. Non-military and military spending model. Notes: In the above graphs, the grey lines represent the prior distributions, whereas the black lines correspond to the posterior distributions.

Appendix D.2. Monte Carlo Markov Chain Univariate Diagnostics

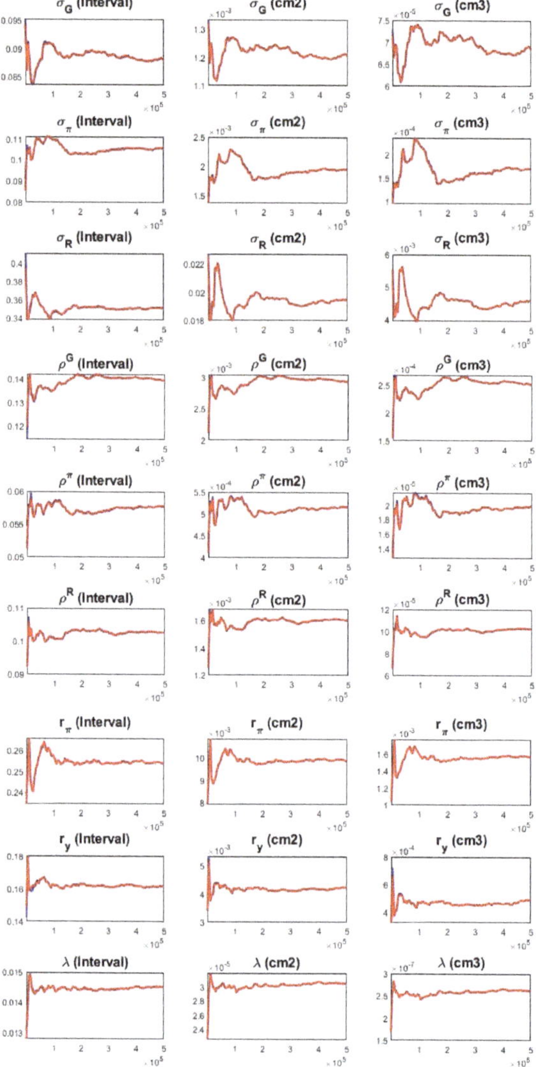

Figure A3. Total government spending model: S1 (1954:Q3–1979:Q2). Notes: In the above graphs, the blue lines represent the 80% interval range based on the pooled draws from all sequences, whereas the red lines indicate the mean interval based on the draws of the individual sequences. The first column shows the convergence diagnostics for the 80% interval. The second and the third column with labels denote an estimate of the same statistics for the second and third central moments.

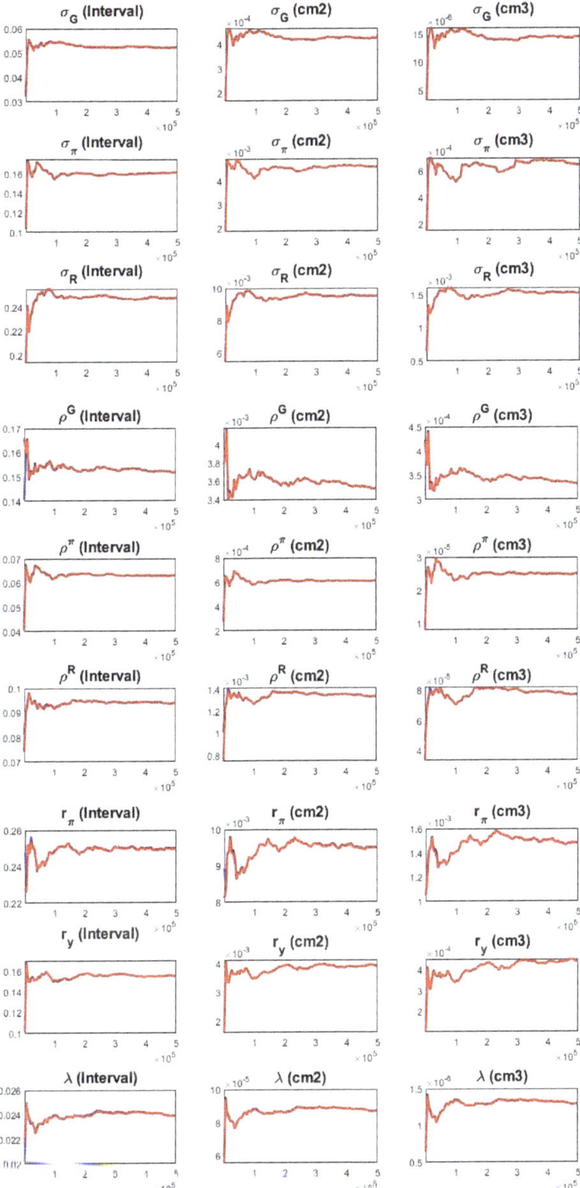

Figure A4. Total government spending model, S2 (1983:Q1–2008:Q2). Notes: In the above graphs, the blue lines represent the 80% interval range based on the pooled draws from all sequences, whereas the red lines indicate the mean interval based on the draws of the individual sequences. The first column shows the convergence diagnostics for the 80% interval. The second and the third column with labels denote an estimate of the same statistics for the second and third central moments.

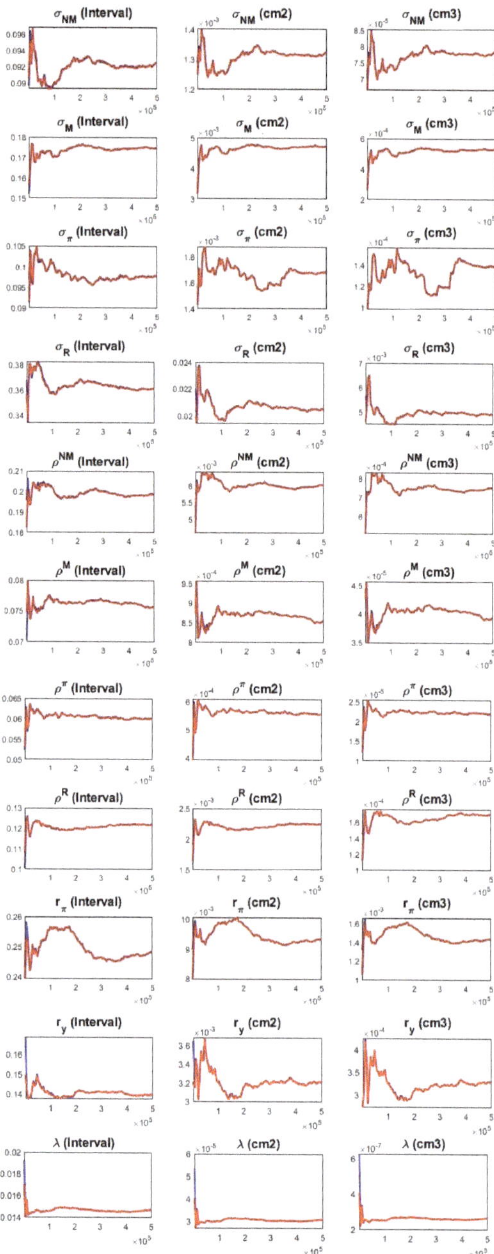

Figure A5. Non-military and military spending model: S1 (1954:Q3–1979:Q2). Notes: In the above graphs, the blue lines represent the 80% interval range based on the pooled draws from all sequences, whereas the red lines indicate the mean interval based on the draws of the individual sequences. The first column shows the convergence diagnostics for the 80% interval. The second and the third column with labels denote an estimate of the same statistics for the second and third central moments.

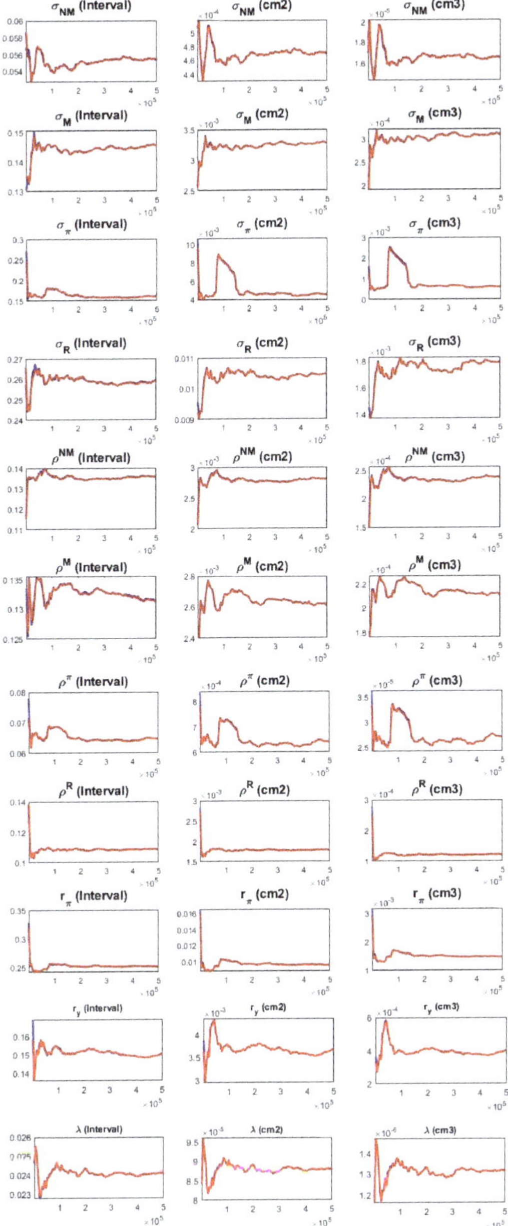

Figure A6. Non-military and military spending model: S2 (1983:Q1–2008:Q2). Notes: In the above graphs, the blue lines represent the 80% interval range based on the pooled draws from all sequences, whereas the red lines indicate the mean interval based on the draws of the individual sequences. The first column shows the convergence diagnostics for the 80% interval. The second and the third column with labels denote an estimate of the same statistics for the second and third central moments.

Appendix D.3. Multivariate Convergence Diagnostics

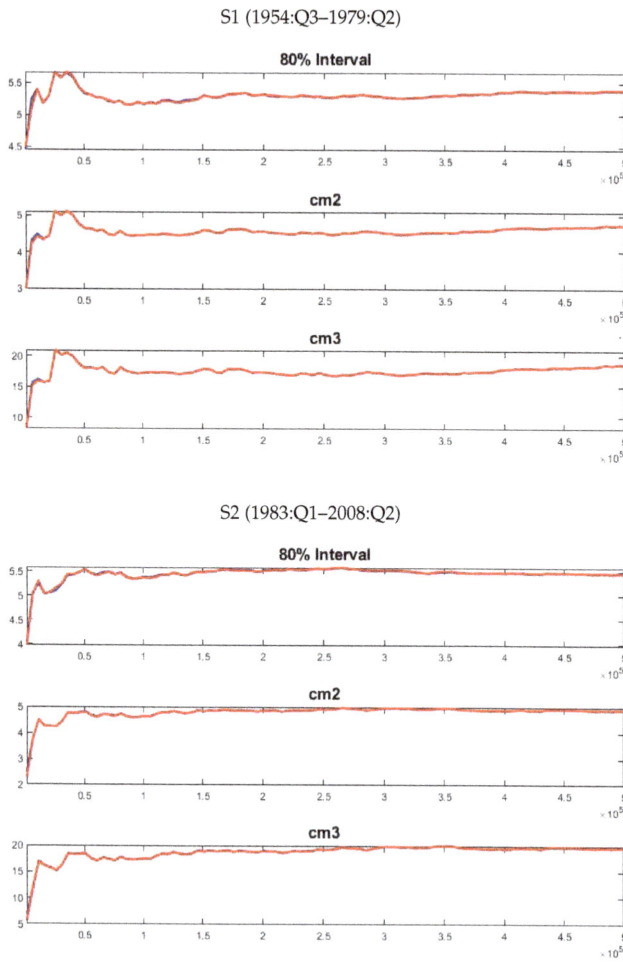

Figure A7. Total government spending model. Notes: In the above graphs, the diagnostics is based on the range of the posterior likelihood function.

S1 (1954:Q3–1979:Q2)

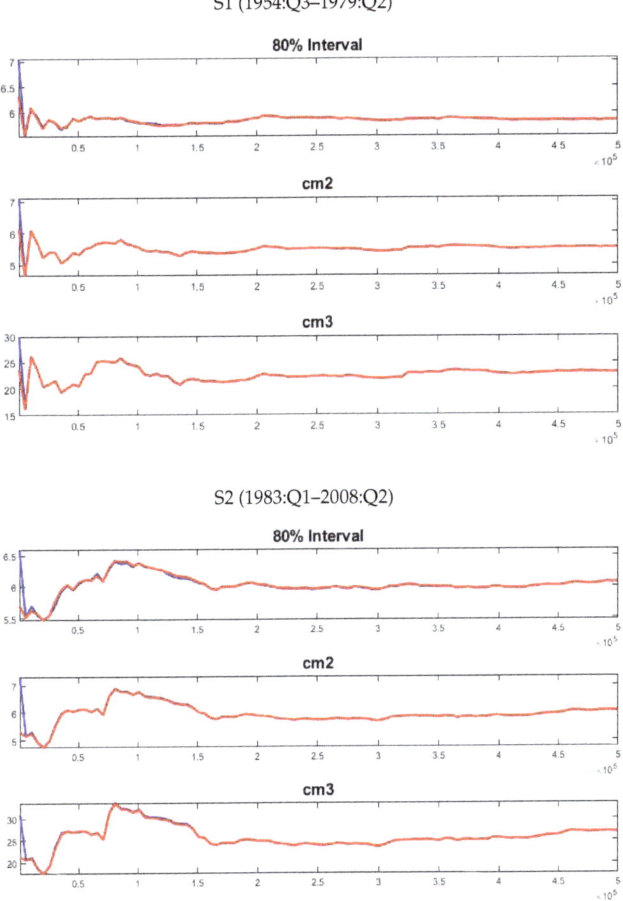

S2 (1983:Q1–2008:Q2)

Figure A8. Non-military and military spending model. Notes: In the above graphs, the diagnostics is based on the range of the posterior likelihood function.

Appendix D.4. Smoothed Shocks

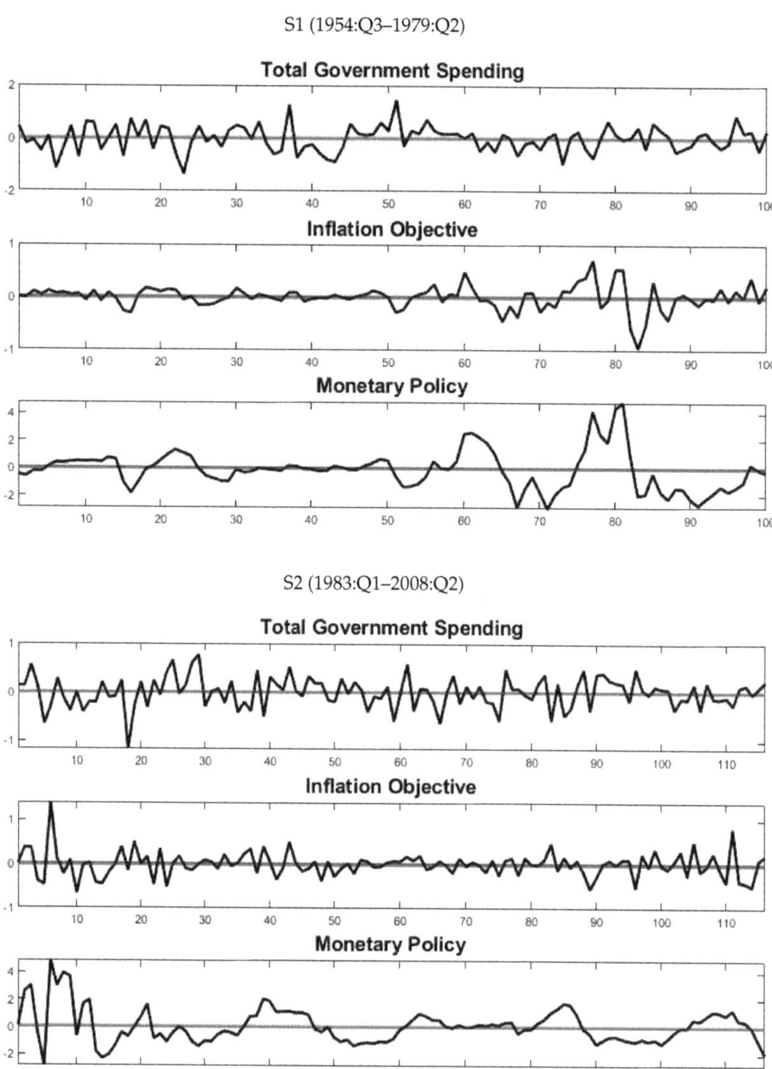

Figure A9. Total government spending model. Notes: In the above graphs, the black line represents the estimate of the smoothed structural shocks.

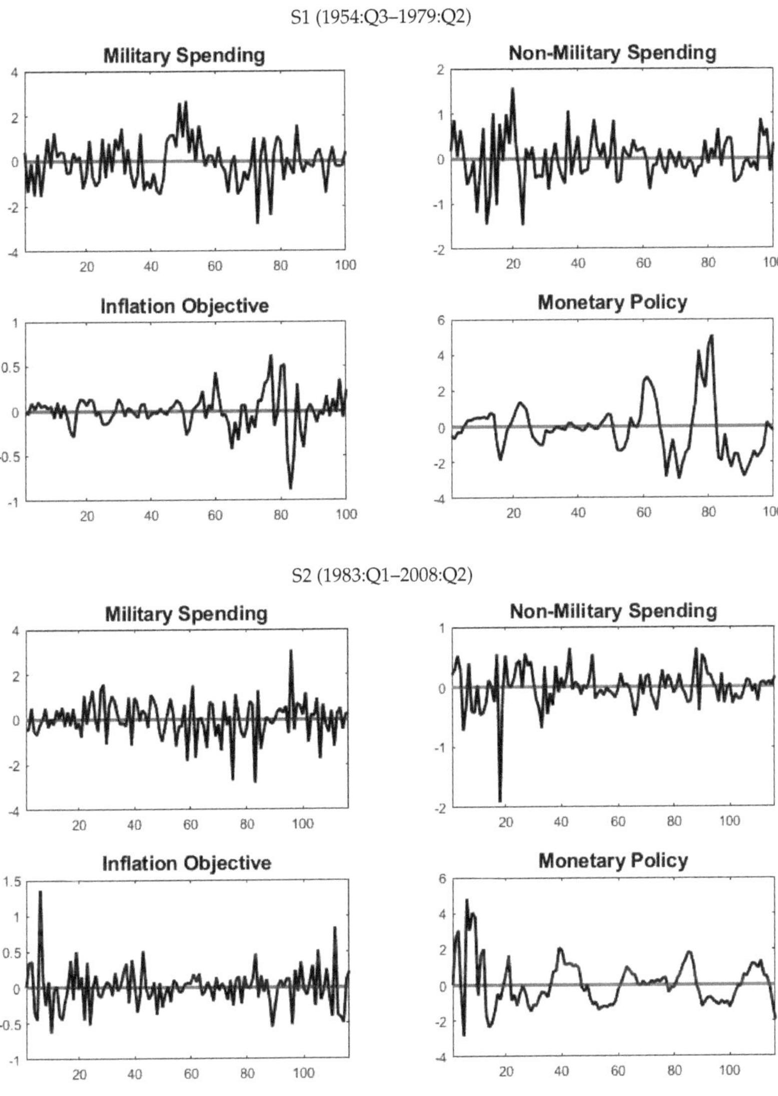

Figure A10. Non-military and military spending model. Notes: In the above graphs, the black line represents the estimate of the smoothed structural shocks.

Appendix D.5. Historical and Smoothed Variables

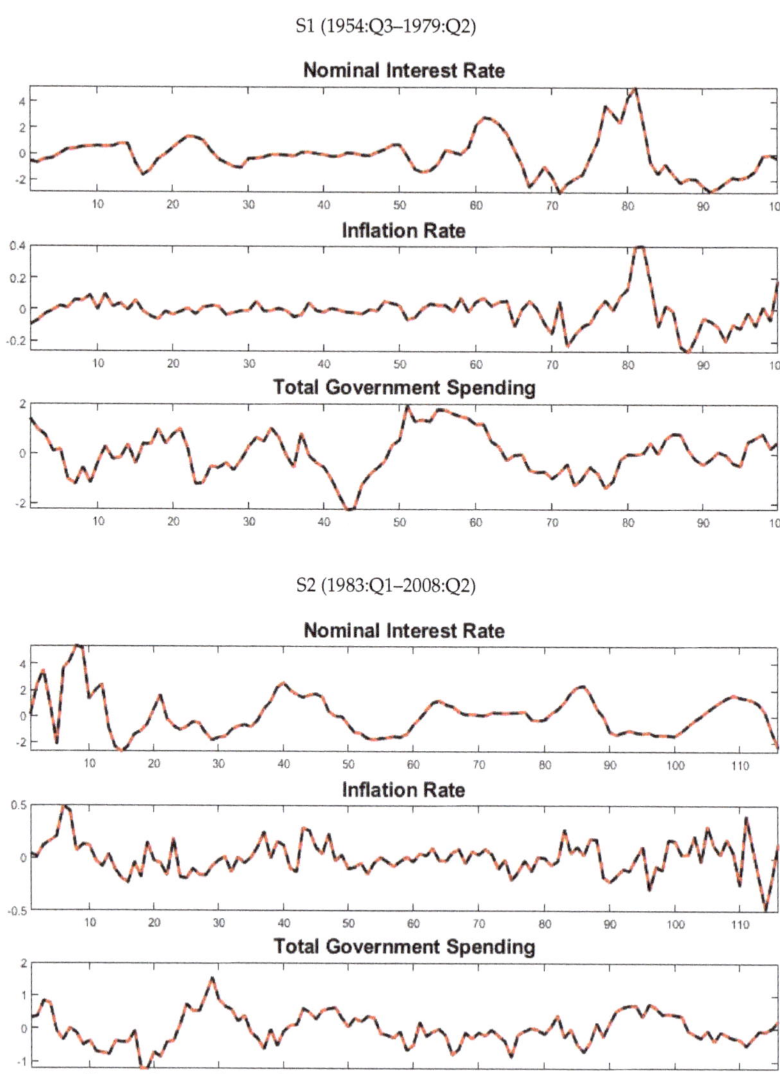

Figure A11. Total government spending model. Notes: In the above graphs, the dotted black lines indicate the observed data. The red lines indicate the estimates of the smoothed variables.

S1 (1954:Q3–1979:Q2)

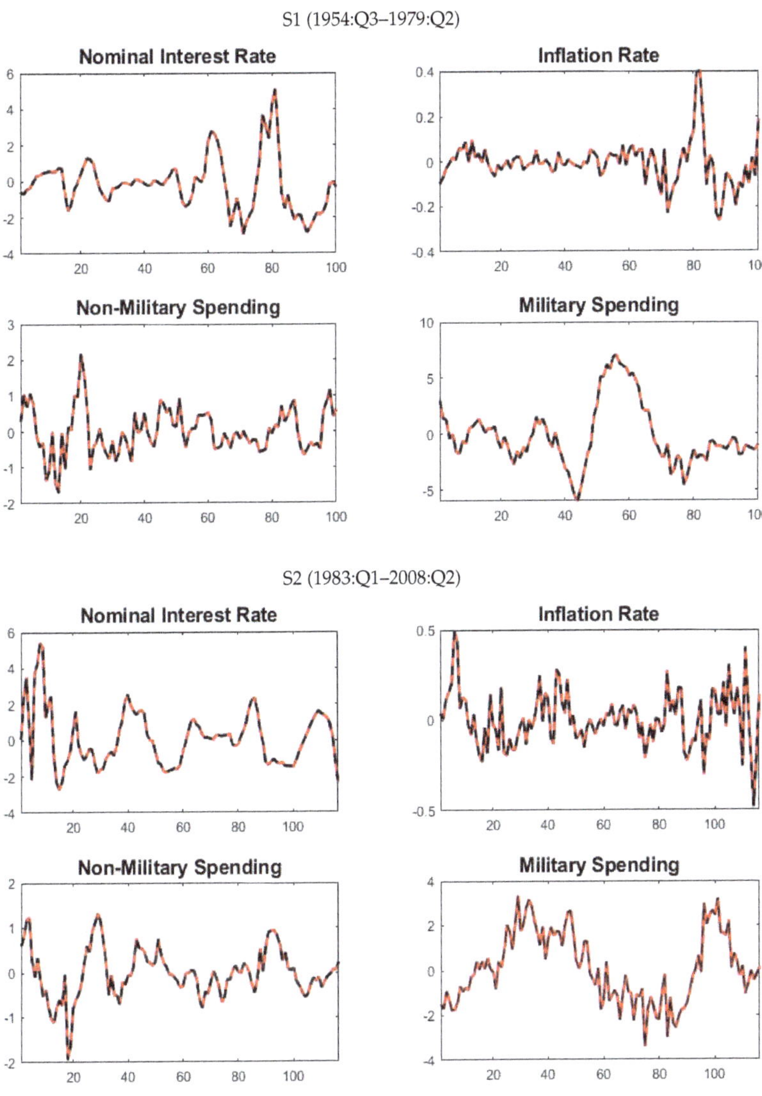

S2 (1983:Q1–2008:Q2)

Figure A12. Non-military and military spending model. Notes: In the above graphs, the dotted black lines indicate the observed data. The red lines indicate the estimates of the smoothed variables.

Appendix D.6. Parameters' Identification

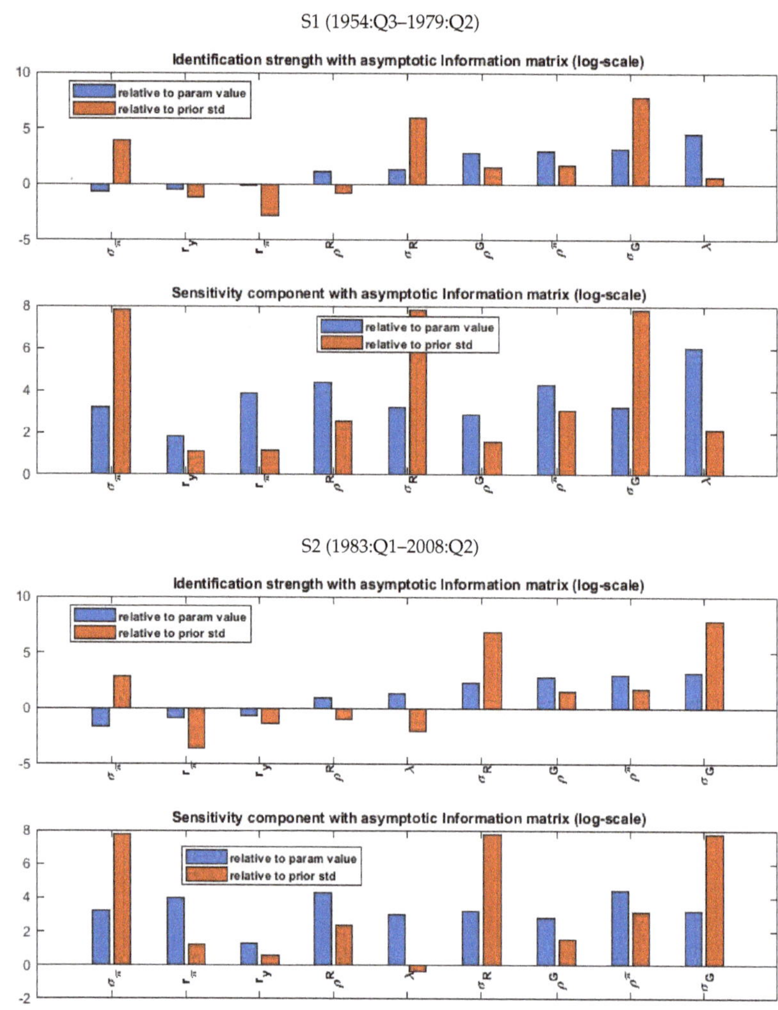

Figure A13. Total government spending model. Notes: In the above graphs, blue bars indicate the identification strength of the parameters based on their prior means, whereas orange bars denote the identification strength of the parameters based on their standard deviations.

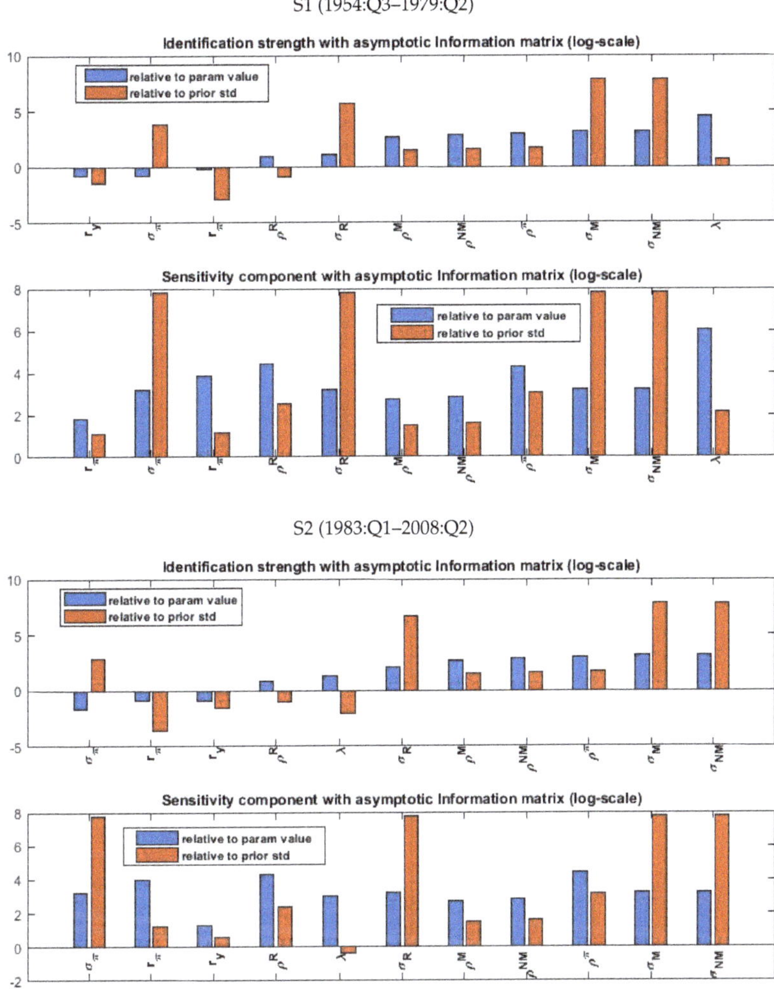

Figure A14. Non-military and military spending model. Notes: In the above graphs, blue bars indicate the identification strength of the parameters based on their prior means, whereas orange bars denote the identification strength of the parameters based on their standard deviations.

Appendix E. Estimated Impulse Response Functions

S1 (1954:Q3–1979:Q2)

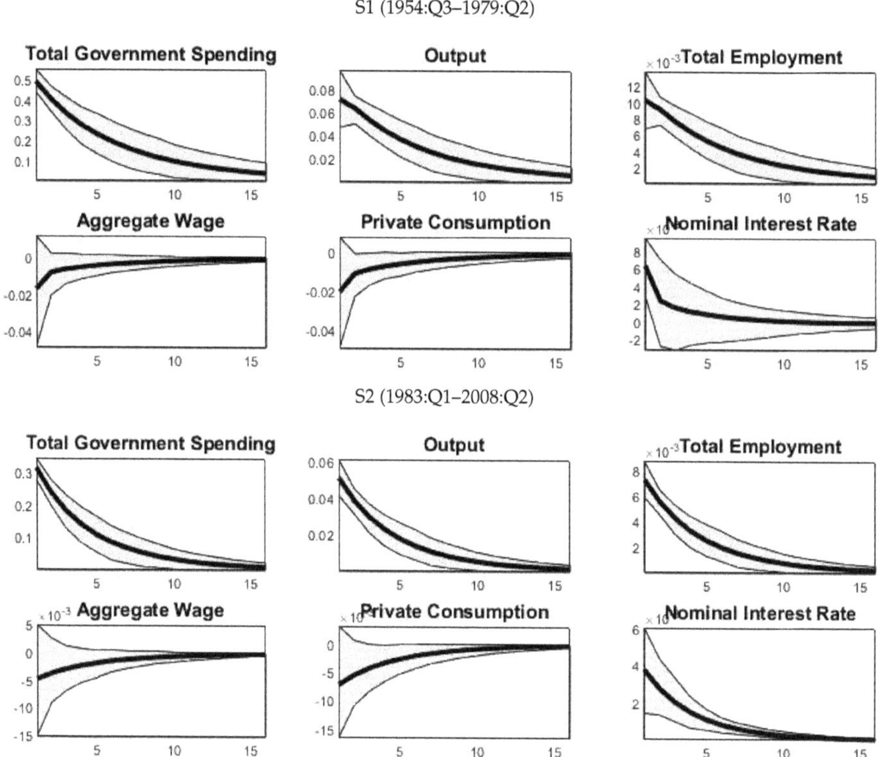

S2 (1983:Q1–2008:Q2)

Figure A15. Total government spending shock. Notes: The above graphs show the responses of the key variables together with their 95% confidence intervals.

S1 (1954:Q3–1979:Q2)

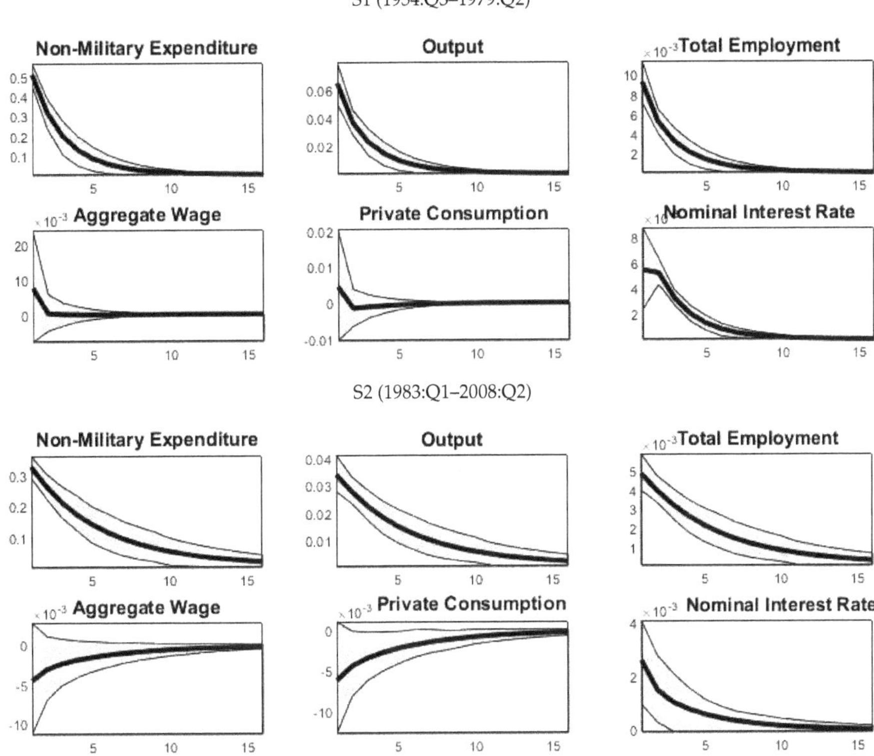

Figure A16. Non-military spending shock. Notes: The above graphs show the responses of the key variables together with their 95% confidence intervals.

S1 (1954:Q3–1979:Q2)

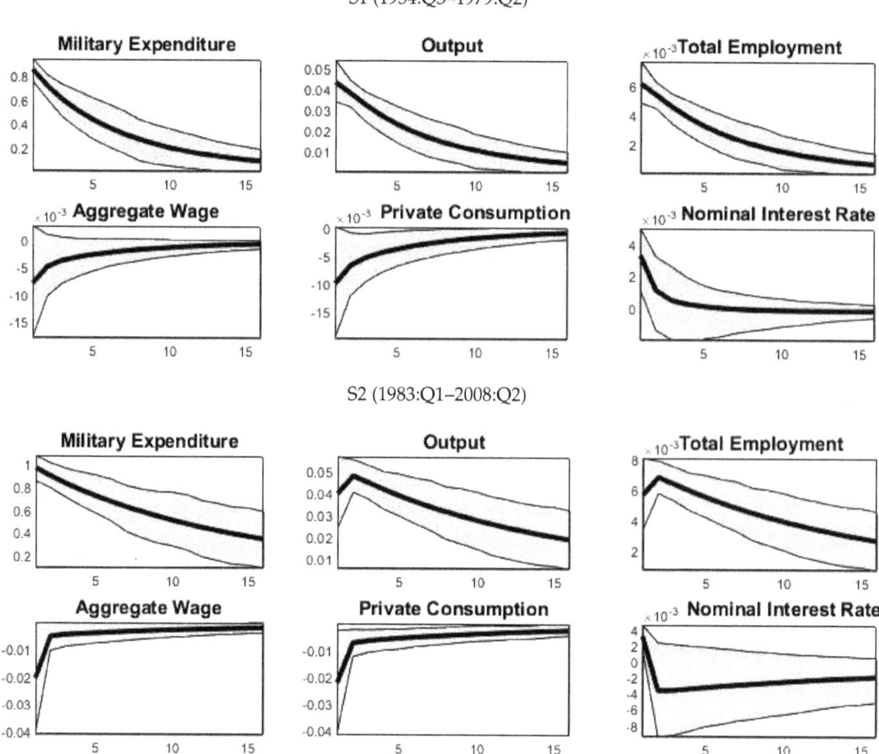

Figure A17. Military spending shock. Notes: The above graphs show the responses of the key variables together with their 95% confidence intervals.

Appendix F. Benchmark Model vs. DSGE-VARs

Table A1. Comparison between the benchmark model and DSGE-VARs: model with total government spending.

	Sub-Sample 1	
	Marginal Log Density	**Bayes Factor vs. Benchmark Model**
DSGE-VAR (1)	−189.714	exp[27.449]
DSGE-BVAR(2)	−175.595	exp[13.331]
DSGE-BVAR (3)	−170.572	exp[8.308]
DSGE-BVAR (4)	−171.844	exp[9.579]
Benchmark Model	−162.264	exp[0.000]
	Sub-Sample 2	
	Marginal Log Density	**Bayes Factor vs. Benchmark Model**
DSGE-VAR (1)	−156.199	exp[−10.742]
DSGE-BVAR (2)	−154.106	exp[−12.835]
DSGE-BVAR (3)	−156.258	exp[−10.684]
DSGE-BVAR (4)	−171.844	exp[4.902]
Benchmark Model	−166.941	exp[0.000]

Notes: As in Bekiros and Paccagnini (2014), the DSGE-VARs are estimated with different numbers of lags (from 1–4). The tightness parameter is set equal to 0.5.

Table A2. Comparison between the benchmark model and DSGE-VARs: model with non-military and military expenditures.

	Sub-Sample 1	
	Marginal Log Density	**Bayes Factor vs. Benchmark Model**
DSGE-VAR (1)	−372.712	exp[46.058]
DSGE-BVAR (2)	−368.905	exp[42.252]
DSGE-BVAR (3)	−368.800	exp[42.146]
DSGE-BVAR (4)	−361.313	exp[34.659]
Benchmark Model	−326.653	exp[0.000]
	Sub-Sample 2	
	Marginal Log Density	**Bayes Factor vs. Benchmark Model**
DSGE-VAR (1)	−347.561	exp[36.952]
DSGE-BVAR (2)	−329.899	exp[19.290]
DSGE-BVAR (3)	−336.235	exp[25.626]
DSGE-BVAR (4)	−326.873	exp[16.264]
Benchmark Model	−310.609	exp[0.000]

Notes: As in Bekiros and Paccagnini (2014), the DSGE-VARs are estimated with different numbers of lags (from 1–4). The tightness parameter is set equal to 0.5.

References

Albonico, Alice, Alessia Paccagnini, and Patrizio Tirelli. 2017. Great recession, slow recovery and muted fiscal policies in the U.S.. *Journal of Economic Dynamics and Control* 81: 140–61. [CrossRef]

Albonico, Alice, Alessia Paccagnini, and Patrizio Tirelli. 2019. Limited asset market participation and the euro area crisis: An empirical dsge model. *Economic Inquiry* 57: 1302–23. [CrossRef]

Ambler, Steve, and Alain Paquet. 1996. Fiscal spending shocks, endogenous government spending, and real business cycles. *Journal of Economic Dynamics and Control* 20: 237–56. [CrossRef]

Andrés, Javier, J. David López-Salido, and Edward Nelson. 2009. Money and the natural rate of interest: Structural estimates for the united states and the euro area. *Journal of Economic Dynamics and Control* 33: 758–76. [CrossRef]

Baxter, Marianne, and Robert G. King. 1993. Fiscal policy in general equilibrium. *The American Economic Review* 83: 315–34.

Beidas-Strom, Samya, and Marco Lorusso. 2019. Do They Hurt? Macroeconomic Effects of Reforms on Three Diverse Oil Exporters: Russia, Saudi Arabia and the UK. IMF Working papers, Forthcoming.

Bekiros, Stelios D., and Alessia Paccagnini. 2014. Bayesian forecasting with small and medium scale factor-augmented vector autoregressive DSGE models. *Computational Statistics & Data Analysis* 71: 298–323.

Bilbiie, Florin O., Andre Meier, and Gernot J. Muller. 2008. What accounts for the changes in U.S. fiscal policy transmission? *Journal of Money, Credit and Banking* 40: 1439–70. [CrossRef]

Blanchard, Olivier, and Roberto Perotti. 2002. An empirical characterization of the dynamic effects of changes in government spending and taxes on output. *The Quarterly Journal of Economics* 117: 1329–68. [CrossRef]

Bohn, Henning. 1998. The behavior of us public debt and deficits. *The Quarterly Journal of Economics* 113: 949–63. [CrossRef]

Brooks, Stephen P., and Andrew Gelman. 1998. General methods for monitoring convergence of iterative simulations. *Journal of Computational and Graphical Statistics* 7: 434–55.

Calvo, Guillermo A. 1983. Staggered prices in a utility-maximizing framework. *Journal of Monetary Economics* 12: 383–98. [CrossRef]

Christiano, Lawrence, Martin Eichenbaum, and Sergio Rebelo. 2011. When is the government spending multiplier large? *Journal of Political Economy* 119: 78–121. [CrossRef]

Coenen, Günter, Roland Straub, and Mathias Trabandt. 2012. Fiscal policy and the great recession in the euro area. *American Economic Review* 102: 71–76. [CrossRef]

Corsetti, Giancarlo, André Meier, and Gernot J. Müller. 2012. Fiscal stimulus with spending reversals. *Review of Economics and Statistics* 94: 878–95. [CrossRef]

Del Negro, Marco, and Frank Schorfheide. 2004. Priors from general equilibrium models for vars. *International Economic Review* 45: 643–73. [CrossRef]

Del Negro, Marco, and Frank Schorfheide. 2008. Forming priors for dsge models (and how it affects the assessment of nominal rigidities). *Journal of Monetary Economics* 55: 1191–208. [CrossRef]

Enders, Zeno, Gernot J. Müller, and Almuth Scholl. 2011. How do fiscal and technology shocks affect real exchange rates?: New evidence for the united states. *Journal of International Economics* 83: 53–69. [CrossRef]

Fatás, Antonio, and Ilian Mihov. 2001. *The Effects of Fiscal Policy on Consumption and Employment: Theory and Evidence.* London: Centre for Economic Policy Research, vol. 2760.

Fatás, Antonio, and Ilian Mihov. 2003. The case for restricting fiscal policy discretion. *The Quarterly Journal of Economics* 118: 1419–47. [CrossRef]

Forni, Lorenzo, Libero Monteforte, and Luca Sessa. 2009. The general equilibrium effects of fiscal policy: Estimates for the euro area. *Journal of Public economics* 93: 559–85. [CrossRef]

Galí, Jordi, David Lopez-Salido, and Javier Valles. 2007. Understanding the effects of government spending on consumption. *Journal of the European Economic Association* 5: 227–70. [CrossRef]

Galí, Jordi, and Roberto Perotti. 2003. Fiscal policy and monetary integration in europe. *Economic Policy* 18: 533–72. [CrossRef]

Iskrev, Nikolay. 2010. Local identification in dsge models. *Journal of Monetary Economics* 57: 189–202. [CrossRef]

Kormilitsina, Anna, and Sarah Zubairy. 2018. Propagation mechanisms for government spending shocks: A Bayesian comparison. *Journal of Money, Credit and Banking* 50: 1571–616. [CrossRef]

Leeper, Eric M., Todd B. Walker, and Shu-Chun S. Yang. 2010. Government investment and fiscal stimulus. *Journal of Monetary Economics* 57: 1000–12. [CrossRef]

Linnemann, Ludger, and Andreas Schabert. 2006. Productive government expenditure in monetary business cycle models. *Scottish Journal of Political Economy* 53: 28–46. [CrossRef]

Lorusso, Marco, and Luca Pieroni. 2017. The effects of military and non-military government expenditures on private consumption. *Journal of Peace Research* 54: 442–56. [CrossRef]

Perotti, Roberto. 2005. Estimating the Effects of Fiscal Policy in OECD Countries. *Proceedings.* Available online: https://econpapers.repec.org/article/fipfedfpr/y_3a2005_3ax_3a9.htm (accessed on 15 July 2019). [CrossRef]

Pieroni, Luca, Giorgio d'Agostino, and Marco Lorusso. 2008. Can we declare military keynesianism dead? *Journal of Policy Modeling* 30: 675–91. [CrossRef]

Rabanal, Pau, and Juan F. Rubio-Ramírez. 2001. Nominal versus Real Wage Rigidities: A Bayesian Approach. Working paper, Federal Reserve Bank of Atlanta, Atlanta.

Ramey, Valerie A., and Matthew D. Shapiro. 1999. Costly Capital Reallocation and the Effects of Government Spending. NBER Working papers, National Bureau of Economic Research, Inc., Cambridge.

Ramey, Valerie A., and Sarah Zubairy. 2018. Government spending multipliers in good times and in bad: Evidence from us historical data. *Journal of Political Economy* 126: 850–901. [CrossRef]

Ramey, Valerie A. 2011. Identifying government spending shocks: It's all in the timing. *The Quarterly Journal of Economics* 126: 1–50. [CrossRef]

Smets, Frank, and Rafael Wouters. 2007. Shocks and frictions in us business cycles: A Bayesian dsge approach. *American Economic Review* 97: 586–606. [CrossRef]

Taylor, John B. 1993. Discretion versus policy rules in practice. *Carnegie-Rochester Conference Series on Public Policy* 39: 195–214.

Journal of
Risk and Financial Management

Article

Unconventional U.S. Monetary Policy: New Tools, Same Channels? [†]

Martin Feldkircher [1,*] and Florian Huber [2]

[1] Oesterreichische Nationalbank (OeNB), A-1090 Vienna, Austria
[2] Salzburg Centre of European Union Studies (SCEUS), A-5020 Salzburg, Austria; florian.huber@sbg.ac.at
* Correspondence: martin.feldkircher@oenb.at; Tel.: +43-1-404-20-5251
† The views expressed in this paper are not necessarily those of the Oesterreichische Nationalbank. We would like to thank Alessandro Galesi, Lukas Reiss, Fabio Rumler and the participants of the 9th International Conference on Computational and Financial Econometrics (CFE 2015) and research seminars at the OeNB and the Vienna University of Business and Economics for helpful comments.

Received: 1 October 2018; Accepted: 25 October 2018; Published: 27 October 2018

Abstract: In this paper, we compare the transmission of a conventional monetary policy shock with that of an unexpected decrease in the term spread, which mirrors quantitative easing. Employing a time-varying vector autoregression with stochastic volatility, our results are two-fold: First, the spread shock works mainly through a boost to consumer wealth growth, while a conventional monetary policy shock affects real output growth via a broad credit/bank lending channel. Second, both shocks exhibit a distinct pattern over our sample period. More specifically, we find small output effects of a conventional monetary policy shock during the period of the global financial crisis and stronger effects in its aftermath. This might imply that when the central bank has left the policy rate unaltered for an extended period of time, a policy surprise might boost output particularly strongly. By contrast, the spread shock has affected output growth most strongly during the period of the global financial crisis and less so thereafter. This might point to diminishing effects of large-scale asset purchase programs.

Keywords: unconventional monetary policy; transmission channel; Bayesian TVP-SV-VAR

JEL Classification: C32; E52; E32

---

1. Introduction

With the onset of the global financial crisis, the U.S. Federal Reserve (Fed) began to lower interest rates to stimulate the economy. Since December 2008, however, the federal funds rate (FFR) is effectively zero, leaving no room for conventional monetary policy to further enhance economic growth. Against the backdrop of lackluster economic conditions and the perceived risks of deflation at that time, the U.S. Fed decided to engage in an "unconventional" monetary policy, which took mostly the form of asset purchases from the private banking and non-banking sector. After three large-scale asset purchase programs (LSAPs), assets on the central bank's balance sheet more than quadrupled since 2007 to about 4500 billion U.S. dollars in February 2015.

While a large body of empirical literature has hitherto investigated how conventional U.S. monetary policy affects the real economy, there is less empirical research on the transmission of quantitative easing (QE). QE implies switching from interest rate targeting steered via reserve management to targeting the quantity of reserves (Fawley and Juvenal 2012). In the USA, the Fed did so by buying longer term securities either issued by the U.S. government or guaranteed by government-sponsored agencies. This should directly put downward pressure on long-term yields in these markets. In addition, financing conditions will ease more generally, since investors selling to the Fed reinvest those proceeds to buy other longer term securities such as corporate bonds and other privately-issued securities (portfolio re-balancing, Joyce et al. 2012). On the back of increased equity prices and heightened loan demand, both private sector wealth and asset growth in the banking sector should tick up, leading to an increase in aggregate demand.

The strength of these transmission channels is likely to depend on the current economic environment. In fact, and considering the transmission of conventional monetary policy, several authors have suggested that the transmission mechanism has changed over time; see, e.g., (Boivin and Giannoni 2006; Boivin et al. 2010; Breitfuß et al. 2018). In a recent contribution, Kastner et al. (2018) found empirical evidence for a change in transmission related to inflation, namely a considerable price puzzle (i.e., an increase in the price level after a monetary policy contraction) in the 1960s, which starts disappearing in the early 1980s. Miranda-Agrippino and Ricco (2017) showed for the USA that price and output puzzles vanish once a robust identification strategy and a rich information set are considered. They also acknowledged that the emergence of such puzzles can indeed depend on the sample period under study. Looking at more recent data, the global financial crisis was a severe rupture of the financial system and could have potentially changed the way monetary policy was conducted. Arguments why a monetary policy shock might have smaller effects during recessions associated with financial crises such as the one in 2008/2009 include balance sheet adjustments and deleveraging in the private sector, which typically takes place after economic boom phases that predate financial crises (Bech et al. 2014). Furthermore, heightened uncertainty might weigh on the business climate and impede investment growth. The works in Aastveit et al. (2017) and Hubrich and Tetlow (2015) investigated monetary policy in times of financial stress or heightened uncertainty and found smaller effects in these periods for the USA. The work in Tenreyro and Thwaites (2016) more generally found that U.S. monetary policy is less effective during recessions. Whether these arguments carry over to unconventional monetary policy is less researched. Recent work actually suggests the opposite. For example, Engen et al. (2015) emphasized the role of quantitative easing in underpinning the commitment of the Fed to be accommodative for a longer period. This signaling channel is more effective when financial markets are impaired and economic conditions characterized by high uncertainty. This reasoning ascribes quantitative easing the greatest effectiveness during the onset of a crisis, contrasting the empirical work on the effectiveness of conventional monetary policy during financial crises. In a recent paper, Wu (2014) corroborated this result attesting the latest asset purchase programs having a smaller effect than the earlier ones.

In this paper, we address these questions within a coherent econometric framework. More specifically, and to cover a broad range of potential transmission channels, we propose a simple Bayesian estimation framework that handles medium- to large-scale models and that allows for drifting parameters and time-varying variances and covariances. Accounting for time variation and including a rich information set enhance the model to yield an appropriate representation of the underlying data. Moreover, since we assume that changes happen gradually, no further assumptions about the number of regimes such as in a Markov-switching framework have to be made. Akin to Baumeister and Benati (2013), we model the asset purchases of the U.S. Fed by assuming a compression of the yield curve. The transmission of the "spread shock" is compared with that of a conventional monetary policy shock.

Our main results can be summarized as follows: First, we find evidence that unconventional monetary policy works mainly via the wealth channel to spur aggregate demand. There is less evidence for the credit/bank lending channel. Second, conventional monetary policy works strongly through expanding assets and deposits of the banking sector, while the impact on consumer wealth growth is more modest. Last, for both shocks, we find a distinct pattern over our sample period. More specifically, we find small output effects of a conventional monetary policy shock during the period of the global financial crisis and stronger effects in its aftermath. This might imply that when the central bank has successfully committed the policy rate to a certain value, an unexpected deviation from that commitment might boost output growth particularly strongly. By contrast, the spread shock has affected output growth most strongly during the period of the global financial crisis, when the Fed launched its first asset purchase program, and less so thereafter. This might point to diminishing effects of large-scale asset purchase programs on real output growth.

The paper is structured as follows. Section 2 introduces the econometric framework and how we identify the monetary policy and the term spread shock. Section 3 investigates the effects and the transmission of the two shocks over time, while Section 4 concludes.

2. Econometric Framework

In this section, we introduce the data, the econometric framework and the identification strategy to investigate the transmission of unconventional and conventional monetary policy. We use a novel approach to estimation based on the work by Lopes et al. (2013) that can handle medium- to large-scale time-varying vector autoregressions with stochastic volatility (TVP-SV-VAR).

2.1. Data

Our analysis is based on variables typically employed in monetary vector autoregressions and on a quarterly frequency. The time period we consider spans from 1984Q1 to 2015Q1, and the variables comprise real GDP growth (Δgdp), consumer price inflation (Δp), the federal funds rate (i_s) and the term spread (sp) defined as the yield on 10-year-government bonds minus the federal funds rate. In addition to these standard variables, we include several variables that should allow us to gauge the importance of different channels for monetary policy transmission. These are growth in net household and non-profit organizations' wealth (Δwealth), growth in commercial banks' assets and deposits (Δbanks_assets, Δbanks_deposits) and the net interest rate margin (nim) of large U.S. banks. Growth rates are calculated as log-differences and are thus in quarter-on-quarter terms.[1]

2.2. The TVP-SV-VAR Model with a Cholesky Structure

In what follows, we draw on a new approach to estimate a TVP-SV-VAR. This approach differs from standard estimation by recasting the VAR as a system of unrelated regressions and imposing a recursive structure on the model a priori.

We collect the data in an $m = 8 \times 1$ vector:

$$y_t = (\Delta\text{gdp}_t, \Delta\text{p}_t, \Delta\text{wealth}_t, i_{s,t}, \Delta\text{banks\_assets}_t, \Delta\text{banks\_deposits}_t, \text{sp}_t, \text{nim}_t)'.$$

Now, we assume the individual elements of y_t to be described by a set of equations, with the first equation $i = 1$ given by:

$$y_{1t} = c_{1t} + \sum_{j=1}^{p} b_{1j,t} y_{t-j} + e_{1t} \tag{1}$$

$$e_{1t} \sim \mathcal{N}(0, \lambda_{1t}) \tag{2}$$

---

[1] Data on real GDP growth (GDPC96), CPI inflation (CPALTT01USQ661S), the effective federal funds rate (FEDFUNDS) calculated as the quarterly average of daily rates, 10-year-government bond yields to proxy long-term interest rates (IRLTLT01USQ156N), net worth of households and nonprofit organizations resembling consumer wealth (TNWBSHNO) deflated by the personal income deflator (PCECTPI) and net interest rate margins for large U.S. banks (USG15NIM) are from the Fred database, https://research.stlouisfed.org/fred2/. Data on commercial banks' assets (FL764090005.Q, FL474090005.Q), deposits (FL763127005.Q, FL764110005.Q FL763131005.Q, FL763135005.Q, FL762150005.Q) are from the financial accounts database of the Federal Reserve System, https://www.federalreserve.gov/releases/z1/current/. By and large, all transformed data are stationary according to an augmented Dickey–Fuller test.

and for $i = 2, \ldots, m$:

$$y_{it} = c_{it} + \sum_{s=1}^{i-1} a_{is,t} y_{st} + \sum_{j=1}^{p} b_{ij,t} y_{t-j} + e_{it} \tag{3}$$

$$e_{it} \sim \mathcal{N}(0, \lambda_{it}) \tag{4}$$

where c_{it} $(i = 1, \ldots, m)$ denotes a constant and $b'_{ij,t}$ $(j = 1, \ldots, p)$ are m-dimensional coefficient vectors associated with the $p = 2$ lags of y_t in each equation. The triangular structure is imposed on the contemporaneous coefficients. More specifically, the $a_{is,t}$ denote coefficients associated with the first $i - 1$ elements of y_t with $a_{1s,t} = 0$ for $s = 1, \ldots, i - 1$. Finally, e_{it} is a normally distributed error with time-varying variance given by λ_{it}. Note that all coefficients in Equations (1)–(4) are allowed to vary over time.

We assume that $a_{is,t}$ evolves according to:

$$a_{is,t} = a_{is,t-1} + u_{it} \text{ for } i = 2, \ldots, m. \tag{5}$$

u_{it} is a standard white noise error term with variance σ_i^2. Equation (5) implies that the parameters associated with the contemporaneous terms are following a random walk.

Let us define an mp-dimensional vector $b_{it} = (b_{i1,t}, \ldots, b_{ip,t})'$. Similarly to Equation (5), we assume that b_{it} follows the subsequent law of motion:

$$b_{it} = b_{it-1} + v_{it}. \tag{6}$$

with v_{it} being a vector white noise error with the variance-covariance matrix equal to Q_i. Finally, the λ_{it}s follow:

$$h_{it} = \mu_i + \rho_i(h_{i,t-1} - \mu_i) + \eta_{it} \text{ for } i = 1, \ldots, m, \tag{7}$$

where $h_{it} = \log(\lambda_{it})$ denotes the log-volatility, μ_i is the mean of the log-volatility and $\rho_i \in (-1, 1)$ the autoregressive parameter. η_{it} is the zero-mean error term with variance ς_i^2. Several studies have shown that it is important to allow for both changes in residual variances and parameters. Assuming constant error variances, while they are in fact time-varying, could lead to misleading parameter estimates of the VAR.[2] Moreover, changes in the economic environment can affect how monetary policy transmits to the real economy. In other words, previous literature suggested that the volatility of economic shocks also tends to influence real activity (Bloom 2009; Fernández-Villaverde et al. 2011).

The reason why the log-volatility process is assumed to be stationary in contrast to the non-stationary state equation of the autoregressive parameters is mainly due to the fact that a random walk assumption for the log-volatility would imply that it is unbounded in the limit, hitting any lower or upper bound with probability one. In practice, however, the differences between a stationary and non-stationary state equation are negligible since the data are not really informative about the specific value of ρ_i.[3]

The model given by Equations (1)–(4) can be recast in a more compact form by collecting all contemporaneous terms on the left-hand side:

$$A_t y_t = c_t + \sum_{j=1}^{p} B_{jt} y_{t-j} + e_t \tag{8}$$

---

[2] See, for example, Cogley and Sargent (2005), who in response to the criticism raised by Sims (2001), extended their TVP framework put forward in Cogley and Sargent (2002) to allow for stochastic volatility.

[3] In fact, experimenting with stationary state equations for a_{it} and b_{it} leaves our results qualitatively unchanged.

where A_t denotes an $m \times m$ lower triangular matrix with diagonal $diag(A_t) = \iota_m$ and the typical non-unit/non-zero element given by $-a_{sj,t}$. Here, we let ι_m be an m-dimensional unit vector. In what follows we collect free elements of A_t in an $m(m-1)/2$ vector a_t. c_t is an $m \times 1$ vector of constants, and $B_{jt} = (b'_{1j,t}, \ldots, b'_{mj,t})'$ denotes an $m \times m$ dimensional coefficient matrix to be estimated. The m-dimensional error vector has zero mean and a diagonal time-varying variance-covariance matrix given by $\Lambda_t = diag(\lambda_{1t}, \ldots, \lambda_{mt})$. Equation (8) resembles the structural TVP-SV-VAR model put forth in Primiceri (2005). The lower triangular nature of A_t is closely related to a recursive identification scheme, which assumes a natural ordering of variables. In fact, we use the ordering as the variables appear in y_t. However, note that we do not identify the shocks based on this Cholesky decomposition. Rather, we impose the triangular structure due to computational reasons only, while identification of the shocks will be based on sign restrictions discussed in Section 2.4. These are two isolated steps, and the a priori Cholesky decomposition does not interfere with identification based on sign restrictions, which re-weights orthogonalized errors (that we directly obtain from the estimation stage of the model) and selects those that fulfill the postulated sign restrictions. Our structural analysis will thus be unaffected by the triangular structure imposed on the model. For an excellent overview on sign restrictions, see Fry and Pagan (2011). In Section 3.5, we show that estimates based on a different ordering yield virtually the same impulse response functions.

In the absence of specific assumptions on A_t, the model in Equation (8) is not identified. Thus, researchers usually estimate the reduced form imposing restrictions that originate from theory ex-post.[4] The reduced form of the TVP-SV-VAR is given by:

$$y_t = d_t + \sum_{j=1}^{p} F_{jt} y_{t-j} + u_t \tag{9}$$

with $d_t = A_t^{-1} c_t$, $F_j = A_t^{-1} B_j$ and $u_t = A_t^{-1} e_t$. The reduced form errors u_t are normally distributed with the variance covariance matrix given by $\Sigma_t = A_t^{-1} \Lambda_t (A_t^{-1})'$. It can easily be seen that the matrix A_t establishes contemporaneous links between the variables in the system.

To emphasize the distinct features of our estimation strategy, it is worth mentioning how this model is traditionally estimated. Typically, one would start with the complete system of reduced form equations given in Equation (9) and obtain reduced form parameter estimates by employing Gibbs sampling coupled with a data augmentation scheme (Cogley et al. 2005; Primiceri 2005). This approach to estimation comes along with a significant computational burden. To be more precise, if as in our case, $m = 8$ and the number of lags is set to $p = 2$, the algorithms outlined in Carter and Kohn (1994) and Frühwirth-Schnatter (1994) require the inversion of a $k \times k$ variance-covariance matrix at each point in time. In our case, $k = m(mp + 1)$ would be $k = 136$, rendering estimation with the traditional algorithms cumbersome.[5]

Following Lopes et al. (2013), we impose a Cholesky structure a priori, estimate the structural form in an equation-by-equation fashion and use the estimated coefficients to solve Equation (8) to finally obtain Equation (9). Using an equation-by-equation approach decreases the computational burden significantly, by first reducing the dimension of the matrices that have to be inverted. More specifically, while the inversion of a $k \times k$ matrix requires $m^3(mp + 1)^3$ operations using Gaussian elimination, we reduce this to $m(mp + 1)^3$, which is a marked gain as compared to full-system estimation. Second, and more importantly, equation-by-equation estimation can make full use of parallel computing. Recently, Carriero et al. (2015) suggested a related estimation strategy, which imposes a triangular structure on the errors rather than the contemporaneous coefficients related to the dependent variable.

---

[4]   For notable exceptions, see, among others, Sims and Zha (1998) and Baumeister and Hamilton (2015).

[5]   Another strand of the literature proposes factor augmented VARs (FAVARs) with drifting parameters and stochastic volatility (Korobilis 2013). While FAVARs provide a flexible means of reducing the dimensionality of the estimation problem at hand, they could also lead to problems with respect to identification and structural interpretation of the underlying shocks.

While this approach is invariant to the ordering of the variables, it prohibits parallel computing, and hence, computational gains are more limited.

2.3. Bayesian Inference

We use a Bayesian approach and impose tight priors on the variance-covariance structure in the various state equations, which describe the law of motion for the parameters.

General Prior Setup and Implementation

Following Primiceri (2005) and Cogley et al. (2005), we impose a normally distributed prior on the free elements of the initial state A_t, which are collected in a vector a_0 and on $b_0 = vec(B_{j0})$:

$$a_0 \sim \mathcal{N}(\underline{a}_0, \underline{V}_a), \tag{10}$$

$$b_0 \sim \mathcal{N}(\underline{b}_0, \underline{V}_b), \tag{11}$$

where $\underline{a}_0$ and $\underline{b}_0$ are prior mean matrices and $\underline{V}_a$ and $\underline{V}_b$ are prior variance-covariance matrices. We follow common practice (Primiceri 2005) and use a training sample of $\underline{T} = 30$ quarters to scale the priors. We set the prior mean for a_0 and b_0 equal to the OLS estimate based on this training sample. The prior variance-covariance matrices are specified such that $\underline{V}_a = 4 \times \hat{V}_a$ and $\underline{V}_b = 4 \times \hat{V}_b$, with $\hat{V}_a$ and $\hat{V}_b$ being the variances of the OLS estimator.[6]

The priors on the variance-covariances in the state Equations (5) and (6) are of the inverted Wishart form:

$$S \sim \mathcal{IW}(\underline{v}_S, \underline{S}), \tag{12}$$

$$Q \sim \mathcal{IW}(\underline{v}_Q, \underline{Q}), \tag{13}$$

with S denoting the variance-covariance matrix of a_t. This matrix is block-diagonal with each block corresponding to the m equations of the system. The degree of freedom parameters are denoted by $\underline{v}_S$ and $\underline{v}_Q$, and the corresponding prior scaling matrices are labeled as $\underline{S}$ and $\underline{Q}$. In principle, we set $\underline{v}_S = \underline{v}_Q = \underline{T}$ and $\underline{S} = k_S^2 \times \hat{V}_a$, with k_S being a scalar parameter controlling the tightness on the propensity of a_t to drift. We set $k_S^2 = 0.01$ after having experimented with a grid of different values. The results remain qualitatively unchanged as long as the prior is not set too loose, placing much prior mass on regions of the parameter space, which imply explosive behavior of the model. We use the same hyperparameters for the prior on Q, i.e., $\underline{v}_Q = \underline{T}$ and $\underline{Q} = k_b^2 \times \hat{V}_b$ with $k_b^2 = 0.01$. Again, this choice is based on experimenting with a grid of values ruling out hyperparameter choices that imply excessively explosive behavior of the model.

We impose the following prior setup on the parameters of Equation (7):

$$\mu_i \sim \mathcal{N}(\underline{\mu}_i, \underline{V}_\mu) \tag{14}$$

$$\frac{\rho_i + 1}{2} \sim Beta(\gamma_0, \gamma_1) \tag{15}$$

$$\varsigma_i^2 \sim \mathcal{G}(1/2, 1/2B_\sigma). \tag{16}$$

Finally, we follow Kastner and Frühwirth-Schnatter (2013) and set $\underline{\mu}_i = 0$ and $\underline{V}_\mu = 10$, implying a loose prior on the level of the log-volatility. The prior on ρ_i is set such that much prior mass is centered on regions for ρ_i close to unity, providing prior evidence for the non-stationary behavior of h_{it}. Thus, we set $\gamma_0 = 25$ and $\gamma_1 = 1.5$. For the non-conjugate Gamma prior on ς_i^2, we set B_σ equal to

---

[6]   Since we estimate the model on an equation-by-equation basis, $\hat{V}_a$ and $\hat{V}_b$ are block diagonal matrices.

one. The Appendix contains a brief sketch of the Markov Chain Monte Carlo (MCMC) algorithm to estimate the model.

2.4. Structural Identification

To identify a U.S. monetary policy shock and a shock to the term spread, we use a set of sign restrictions put directly on the impulse responses.[7] More specifically, we identify a "monetary policy" or "term spread" shock by singling out from a set of generated responses those that comply with our a priori reasoning about how the economy typically responds to either of the shocks. The restrictions refer to the directional movements of impulse responses on impact and are outlined in Table 1.

Table 1. Identification via sign restrictions.

Shock	Channel							Aggregate Demand	
	i_s	sp	Δwealth	nim	Δbanks_assets	Δbanks_deposits	Δp		Δgdp
Monetary Policy	↓	↑	↑	↑	↑	↑	↑		↑
Term Spread	0	↓	↑	↓	demand ↑/supply ↓ = ?	↑	↑		↑

Notes: All restrictions are imposed on impact only. For the sake of completeness and unrelated to the identification scheme, note that we set all coefficients in the interest rate equation to zero for the first eight quarters, assuming that the interest rates do not respond to either shocks. By this, we mimic an extended period of the interest rate tied to the zero lower bound (Baumeister and Benati 2013).

We look at two shocks related two monetary policy and three broad transmission channels.[8] We assume that an expansionary conventional monetary policy shock works via an unexpected lowering of the short-term interest rate. The most direct way lower interest rates feed into the economy is via the "interest rate/investment" channel. The decrease in the policy rate lowers the user cost of capital, thereby spurring investment and real GDP growth (Ireland 2005). In addition, aggregate demand can also increase through a boost to "consumption wealth", as advocated in Ludvigson et al. (2002). Following a monetary expansion, equity prices are likely to tick up since the price of debt instruments rises in parallel with the reduction of the short-term rate, making them less attractive for investors (Ireland 2005). This leads to an increase in consumer wealth, which might boost consumption spending and aggregate demand (Ludvigson et al. 2002).

The cut in short-term interest rates has also bearings on the financial side of the economy. We assume an increase in the term spread in response to a decrease of the policy rate. This can be motivated by an imperfect pass-through along the term structure, implying that long-term interest rates do not follow the decrease in short-term interest rates one-to-one (Baumeister and Benati 2013).[9] Trailing the term spread, net interest rate margins of banks tend to increase (Adrian and Shin 2010). This affects asset and deposit growth of the banking sector along two dimensions. First, the decrease

---

[7] There is a huge literature on the identification of conventional monetary policy shocks, but a consensus seems so far out of reach. Alternatively, one could use recursive identification, such as heavily used in the early literature; see, e.g., (Christiano et al. 2005). Recursive identification got criticized recently because of the stark underlying assumptions about the information set of the respective central bank and the unrealistic timing of the shocks, especially when also dealing with financial data. Since then, a number of authors proposed the use of external instruments, based on either the narrative approach (Romer and Romer 2004) or high frequency information (Gertler and Karadi 2015; Miranda-Agrippino and Ricco 2017). However, also, this literature came under criticism, since as pointed out by Hamilton (2018), Fed announcements provide not only information about a policy action, but about the Fed's assessment of future economic conditions, and these effects are not easily separated. An approach to separate these effects is provided in Miranda-Agrippino (2016) and Nakamura and Steinsson (2018).

[8] One aspect of monetary policy that we do not capture directly is forward guidance. There is a fast-growing literature assessing the effects of forward guidance; see, e.g., McKay et al. (2016), who present a theoretical model in which the power of forward guidance is highly sensitive to the assumption of complete markets. More recently, Nakamura and Steinsson (2018) provided an external instrument that measures also changes in the path of future interest rates in response to Fed announcements, which allows one to capture forward guidance effects empirically.

[9] More specifically, an unexpected monetary expansion can be expected to drive up inflation and therefore inflation expectations. This in turn implies long-rates to decrease less strongly than short rates, causing a widening of the yield curve (Benati and Goodhart 2008).

in the long-term rate (even if less pronounced than that of short-rates) makes taking a loan cheaper, implying that the demand for loans is strengthened by the policy-induced decrease of the short-term rate. This effect is amplified by an improvement of balance sheets of households and firms on the back of the policy-induced rise of asset prices, which increases the demand for loans by those that were previously excluded from access to credit ("balance-sheet channel"). Second and since net interest rate margins increase, generating new loans becomes more attractive for banks (compared to faring excessive reserves with the Fed). Thus, the supply for loans is stimulated as well. As a consequence, deposit growth is assumed to tick up. The newly-generated loans will increase deposits mechanically since for each newly-issued loan, the bank creates a deposit of the same amount. On top of that, the increase of reservable deposits created by the monetary expansion will reduce the amount of managed liabilities banks need to fund their loans. This might be passed on to their clients by lowering loan rates and increasing loan supply (Bernanke and Blinder 1988; Black et al. 2007). We summarize these developments under a broad "credit and bank lending channel". Naturally, aggregate demand is positively affected by loan growth, which leads to more investment and consumption.

Second, we investigate a shock to the term spread. Since the purchases of longer term securities have significantly lowered longer term yields, as demonstrated, e.g., in Doh (2010), Gagnon et al. (2011), Krishnamurthy and Vissing-Jorgensen (2011) and Hamilton and Wu (2012), assuming a reduction of the term spread can be thought of as a way to model the effects of quantitative easing within a standard monetary VAR framework. In contrast to a conventional expansionary monetary policy shock, asset purchases by the central bank will trigger a decrease in the term spread. As with the monetary policy shock, a shock to the term spread will trigger an increase in equity prices since yields on debt securities decline. An increase in consumer wealth, coupled with eased finance conditions, should spur economic activity and inflation. That asset purchase programs had an effect on consumer confidence through signaling has been emphasized in Engen et al. (2015) and Wu (2014). While we can investigate the signaling channel implicitly by tracing the effectiveness of unconventional monetary policy through periods of different financial and economic conditions, we cannot model this transmission mechanism explicitly by including a suitable control variable. Looking at the financial side of the economy, the reduction of the term spread triggers a decrease in net interest margins of commercial banks: since the cost of funding (the short-term interest rate) is unaltered and tied to the zero lower bound, the revenues of lending (approximated by the long-term interest rate) decrease. As in Adrian and Shin (2010), this implies an inward shift of the supply curve of credit and is likely to contain new lending. This effect, however, might be offset by a stronger demand for lending, since lower long-term rates make it more attractive to take a loan. Since a priori, we do not know which of these effects is likely to dominate, we leave the signs on growth in bank assets unrestricted. Next and in line with the assumption about the monetary policy shock, we assume an initial increase in banks' deposits. This increase is rather mechanical since the proceeds of the asset purchase will be deposited in the investors' bank accounts, raising deposits of the banking sector, and might be rather short-lived, as pointed out in Butt et al. (2014).[10]

Last and to mimic the zero lower bound environment, we will hold the response of the short-term interest rate constant at zero for eight quarters (Baumeister and Benati 2013). Note that this is unrelated to identification of the shock, for which restrictions are only binding on impact. The Appendix provides further details on the technical implementation of the sign restrictions and the zero restriction on the short-term interest rate for the spread shock.

---

[10] In the case that the Fed purchases assets directly from the banking sector, the proceeds would be charged to the banks' reserve balances with the Fed, leaving deposits untouched. The positive restriction on deposit growth is warranted since part of the Fed's purchases directly concern the private non-banking sector.

3. Empirical Results

In this section, we investigate the transmission of the monetary policy and the term spread shock, examine whether overall effects vary over time and establish that both shocks mattered historically in determining fluctuations in the time series considered in this paper. We start by briefly summarizing the movements of the two identified shocks over time. This should yield further confidence regarding the appropriateness of the proposed restrictions to recover the shocks. Figure 1 shows the structural shocks, the left panel relating to the term spread shock and the middle panel to the monetary policy shock. For completeness, we also show the evolution of the actual federal funds rate and the term spread in the right panel.

Looking at the term spread shock first, we have indicated three distinct time periods by red vertical bars, namely the start of the Clinton debt buyback program (Q1 2000–Q4 2001), which was in many ways similar to an LSAP, and the start of LSAPs I–III (Q4 2008, Q4 2010 and Q3 2012; see (Dunne et al. 2015)). The figure shows that negative surprises to the term spread indeed coincide with these periods. There is also a pronounced negative shock visible in the last quarter of 2003 in which the term spread started to decrease sharply (see the right panel, Figure 1).

The monetary policy shock is shown in the middle panel. For comparison, we also plot a monetary policy shock series based on the narrative approach put forward in Romer and Romer (2004), extended to cover the period up until Q4 2008.[11] Both shocks identified the same monetary policy cycle, and the correlation between the series amounted to about 0.6.

3.1. How Do Term Spread and Monetary Policy Shocks Affect Output Growth and Inflation?

In this section, we examine through which channels both shocks affect aggregate demand and CPI inflation. To this end, we report impulse response functions in Figures 2 and 3 and a related forecast error variance decomposition in Table 2. Since we use a time-varying framework, the reported impulse responses showed how the economy would react to a hypothetical shock at a specific point in time. This holds equally true for sample periods where actually no monetary policy/spread shock occurred.[12] Both shocks were normalized to a 100 basis point (bp) reduction, either of the policy rate (monetary policy shock) or the term spread (spread shock). Results are shown for real GDP growth, inflation, wealth growth and banking sector variables.

The top panel of Figure 2 lists results for real output growth: on the left-hand side in response to the conventional monetary policy shock and on the right-hand side in reaction to the term spread shock. Note that we have opted for slicing the time-varying impulse responses by fixing time periods of interest to show accompanying credible sets (50% in dark blue and 68% in light blue). These periods relate to the global financial crisis, namely the pre-crisis period (Q1 1991–Q3 2007), the crisis period (Q4 2007–Q2 2009) and its aftermath (Q3 2009–Q1 2015).[13]

---

[11] To be precise, the narrative shock is transformed to quarterly frequency by simply averaging over the corresponding months. The monetary policy shock corresponds to the smoothed structural shocks. In general, residuals of the VAR are more volatile due to the inherent iid assumption, which is why we opted for smoothing the shocks, facilitating visual comparison to the more persistent narrative shocks.

[12] All results are based on 500 draws from the full set of 15,000 posterior draws that have been collected after a burn-in phase of 15,000 draws.

[13] These are based on the National Bureau of Economic Research (NBER) dating of recessions, available at http://www.nber.org/cycles.html. The full history of impulse responses over time and for all variables is available from the authors upon request.

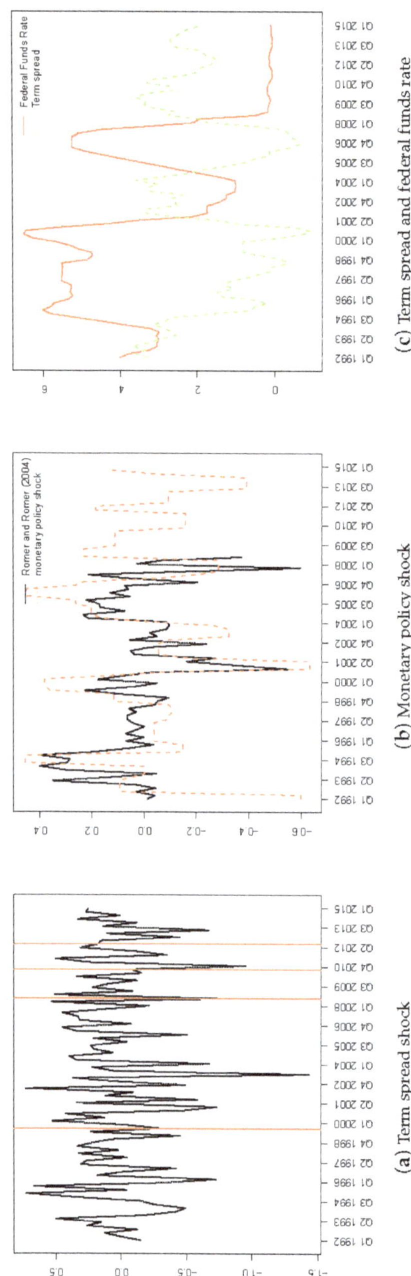

(a) Term spread shock

(b) Monetary policy shock

(c) Term spread and federal funds rate

Figure 1. Term spread and monetary policy shock. Notes: The plot in the left panel shows the identified term spread shock. Vertical bars refer to the launch of the Clinton debt buyback program and the three LSAP programs. The middle panel shows the monetary policy shock along with the narrative monetary policy shock of Romer and Romer (2004). The right panel shows the evolution of the term spread and the federal funds rate (realized data).

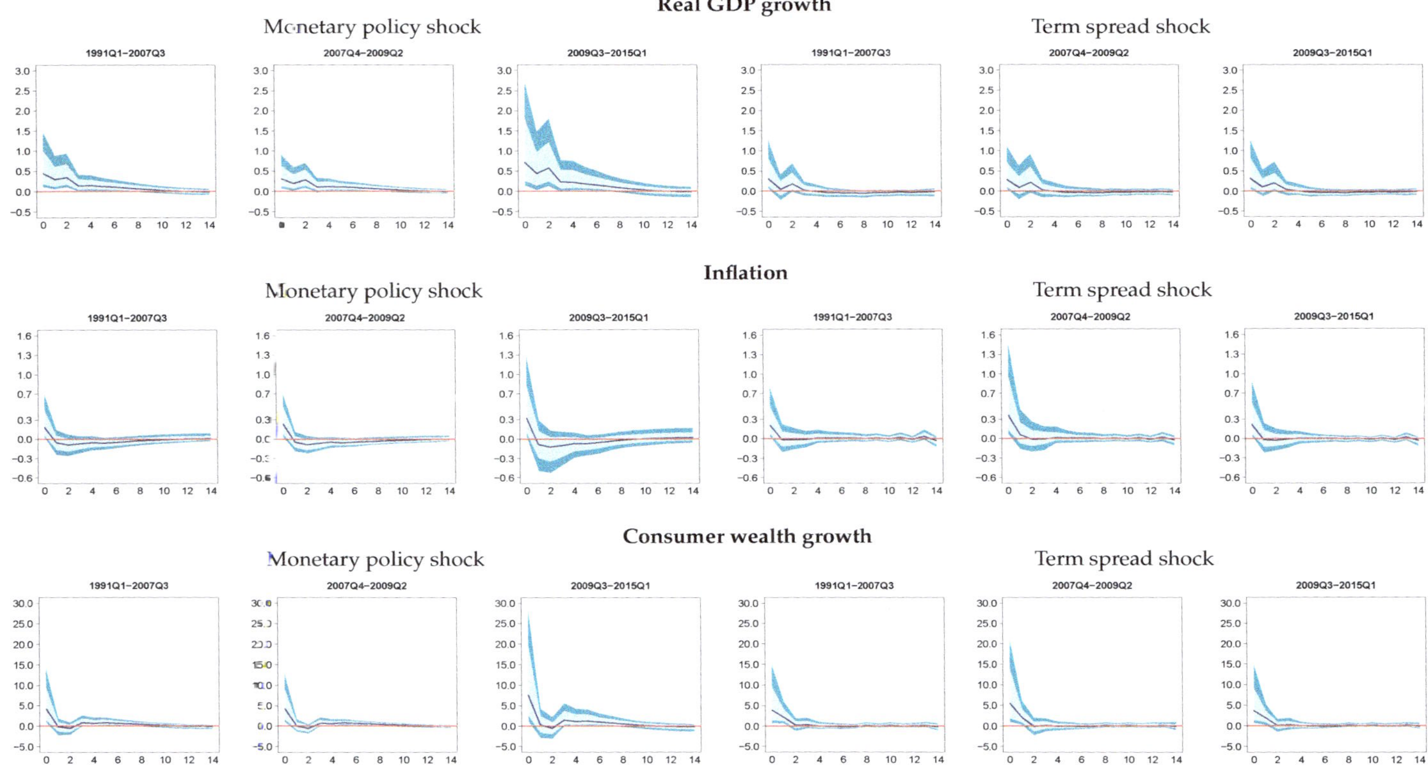

Figure 2. Impulse response functions. Notes: Posterior median responses to an expansionary monetary policy shock (−100 bp) and shock to the term spread (−100 bp) along with 50% (dark blue) and 68% (light blue) credible bounds. Results shown as averages over three periods, pre-crisis from 1991Q1–2007Q3, global financial crisis from 2007Q4–2009Q2 and its aftermath from 2009Q3–2015Q1.

Table 2. Forecast error variance decomposition.

	Monetary Policy Shock			
	1991Q1–2007Q3	2007Q4–2009Q2	2009Q3–2015Q1	1991Q1–2015Q1
Real GDP growth	0.10	0.10	0.08	0.10
Inflation	0.06	0.04	0.04	0.06
Consumer wealth growth	0.07	0.08	0.07	0.07
Short-term interest rate	0.07	0.07	0.06	0.07
Banks' deposit growth	0.10	0.10	0.09	0.10
Banks' asset growth	0.13	0.11	0.10	0.12
Term spread	0.11	0.13	0.10	0.11
Net interest rate margin	0.08	0.09	0.07	0.08
	Term Spread Shock			
	1991Q1–2007Q3	2007Q4–2009Q2	2009Q3–2015Q1	1991Q1–2015Q1
Real GDP growth	0.08	0.07	0.07	0.08
Inflation	0.10	0.05	0.08	0.09
Consumer wealth growth	0.13	0.08	0.10	0.12
Short-term interest rate	0.12	0.06	0.09	0.11
Banks' deposits	0.11	0.08	0.10	0.11
Banks' assets	0.11	0.09	0.10	0.11
Term spread	0.12	0.06	0.09	0.11
Net interest rate margin	0.17	0.10	0.12	0.15

The table shows a forecast error variance decomposition after 20 quarters based on the posterior; simple averages over the time periods considered.

Looking at the unexpected lowering of the policy rate first, we find positive and tightly estimated responses up until eight quarters, indicating rather persistent effects on output growth. This holds true throughout the sample periods considered. The size of the effects, however, varies with the period under consideration. More specifically, the 100-bp decrease in the policy rate accelerates real GDP growth on impact by around 0.3–0.4 percentage points prior to and during the crisis. In the aftermath of the global financial crisis, this effect increases markedly to about 0.7 percentage points.[14] To put our results into perspective, we compare the cumulative responses with established findings of the literature, which are mainly based on pre-crisis data. In cumulative terms, the responses prior to the crisis point to an increase in real GDP by 1.8%, whereas previous findings indicate peak level effects of about 0.3%–0.6%; see, e.g., (Bernanke et al. 1997; Leeper et al. 1996; Uhlig 2005). In a more recent paper, Gorodnichenko (2005) reported a peak effect in real GDP of approximately 0.8%. See Coibion (2012) for an excellent and more comprehensive summary of the relevant literature.

Responses of output growth to the lowering of the term spread are depicted on the right-hand side of the top panel of Figure 2. The term spread shock accelerates real GDP growth throughout the sample period. Our estimates are broadly in line with those provided in Baumeister and Benati (2013), who report an annualized impact response of about 2% for 2010. Compared to findings on the conventional monetary policy shock, however, the effects of the term spread shock are rather short-lived and peter out after one to two quarters. This finding is in contrast to Inoue and Rossi (2018), who proposed identifying conventional and unconventional monetary policy shocks in a unified manner by modeling an exogenous shift of the whole term structure. Their results imply similar effects of conventional on unconventional monetary policy on both output growth and inflation. In Table 2, we present a forecast error variance decomposition. At the 20-quarter forecast horizon, the monetary policy shock explains about 20%–30% more forecast error variance than the spread shock.

The middle panel of Figure 2 shows impulse responses of consumer price inflation. Both shocks drive up inflation by about 0.2–0.3 percentage points on impact, as we have ruled out a price puzzle by assumption. Adjustment of inflation turns negative in response to lowering the policy rate,

---

[14] Responses are to be interpreted as the reaction of a variable to a hypothetical 100-bp monetary policy/term spread shock independent of the actual value of the FFR during that period.

while effects are positive and then quickly converge to zero in response to the spread shock. The spread shock accounts for a larger part of forecast error variance throughout the sample period. Summing up, we find that both shocks accelerate output growth and drive up inflation. While the effects of a conventional monetary policy shock on output growth are rather persistent and tightly estimated, the effects of the term spread shock are short-lived. Responses of CPI inflation are accompanied by wide credible sets for both shocks.

3.2. The Transmission of Monetary Policy and Term Spread Shocks

In this section, we analyze the potential transmission mechanisms starting with the wealth channel. In the bottom panel of Figure 2, we depict responses for consumer wealth growth. Looking at the conventional monetary policy shock first, we find positive responses of consumer wealth throughout most of the sample period. These effects, however, are very short-lived and peter out immediately after impact. By contrast, the reduction of the term spread spurs wealth growth throughout the sample periods, and effects tend to be slightly more persistent compared to responses to the monetary policy shock discussed before. In terms of forecast error variance and with the exception of the period of the global financial crisis, the term spread shock explains about 1.5–2-times as much variance as the monetary policy shock. Taken at face value, the results reveal the wealth channel as an important facet of the transmission mechanism through which unconventional monetary policy can affect aggregate demand. In terms of persistence, the channel seems less important when monetary policy is conducted by steering short-term interest rates. This result is in line with Ludvigson et al. (2002), who attest the wealth channel having only a minor role in the transmission of conventional monetary policy to consumption.

Next, we investigate the bank lending/credit channel. Figure 3 shows the responses of growth in assets and deposits of commercial banks, as well as net interest rate margins and Table 2 the corresponding forecast error variance decomposition.

The impact response of asset growth to a conventional monetary policy shock is shown in the top panel of the figure. A loosening of monetary policy spurs asset growth for all three time periods considered; responses are tightly estimated; and the effects tend to be very persistent. Next, we look at the growth of deposits depicted in the middle panel of Figure 3. Albeit that for both shocks, we have assumed an immediate acceleration of deposit growth, the effects of the term spread immediately peter out after one quarter, while responses to the conventional monetary policy shock are rather persistent and mostly tightly estimated. That is, the impact of the term spread shock on asset and deposit growth is negligible, while we find tightly estimated responses to the conventional monetary policy shock. This impression is broadly confirmed by a forecast error variance decomposition, shown in Table 2. At the 20-quarter forecast horizon, the spread shock accounts for 11% of both the error variance of banks' asset and deposit growth. Shares of explained variance in banks' deposit growth are comparable to that explained by the spread shock. Shares related to banks' asset growth explained by the monetary policy shock are somewhat higher. Strong and persistent effects of a conventional monetary policy shock on asset and deposit growth and a large share of explained forecast error variance reveal an important role for the credit/bank lending channel for monetary policy transmission. By contrast, this channel seems less important in the case that the stimulus comes from lowering the term spread.

For completeness, we show responses of net-interest rate margins in the bottom panel of Figure 3. An unexpected decrease of the policy rate triggers an increase in net interest rate margins, probably driven by an imperfect pass through of the policy rate change to the long end of the yield curve. After four quarters, effects start hovering around zero and are accompanied by wide credible sets. Responses to the term spread shock show a different pattern: net interest rate margins decrease in response to a lowering of the term spread. These effects are very persistent for all three time periods considered. Naturally, and since net interest margins follow the term spread, the term spread shock explains considerably more forecast error variance as the conventional monetary policy shock. This holds true throughout the sample period.

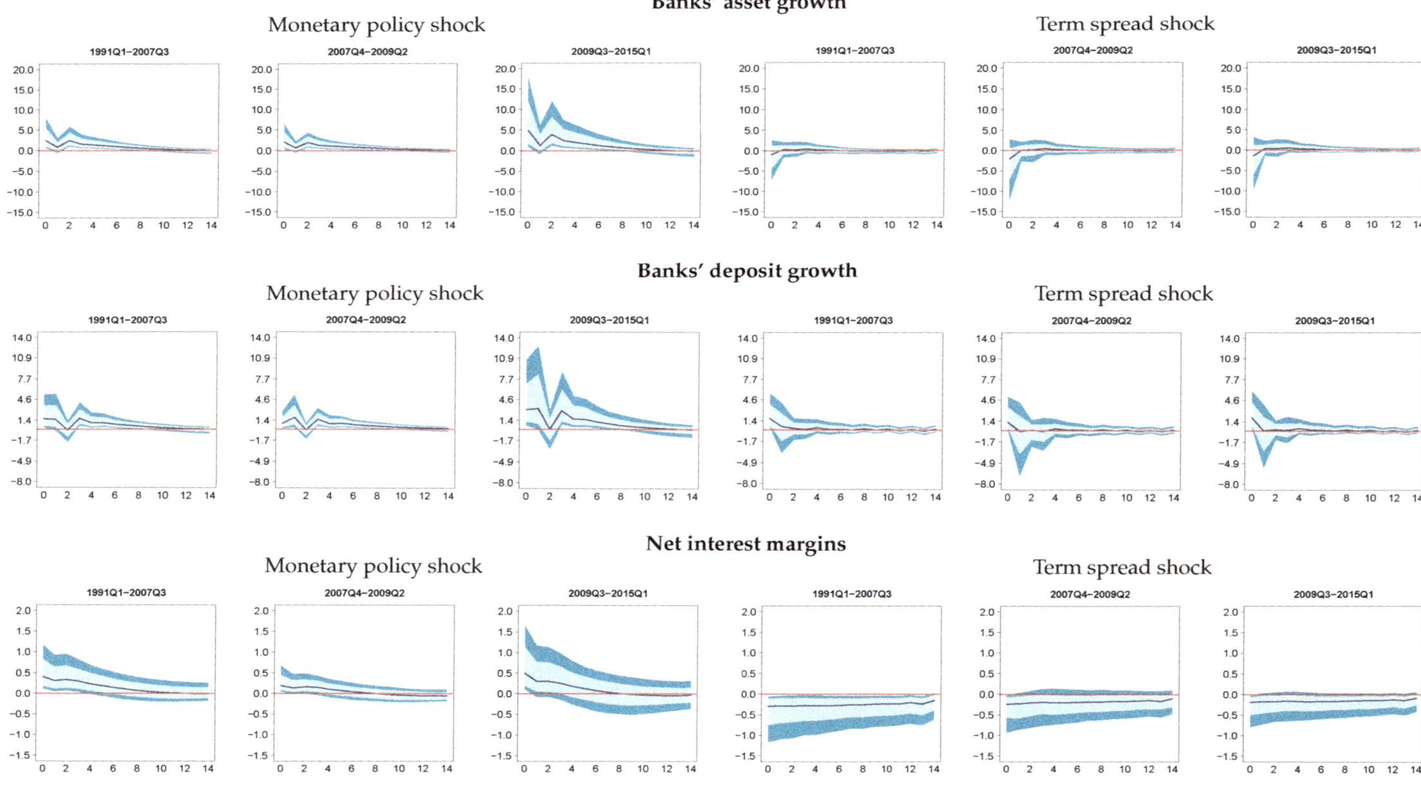

Figure 3. Impulse response functions. Notes: Posterior median responses to an expansionary monetary policy shock (−100 bp) and shock to the term spread (−100 bp) along with 50% (dark blue) and 68% (light blue) credible bounds. Results shown as averages over three periods, pre-crisis from 1991Q1–2007Q3, global financial crisis from 2007Q4–2009Q2 and its aftermath from 2009Q3–2015Q1.

Summing up, positive effects on output growth seem to be driven by an expansion of asset and deposit growth of the banking sector, lending empirical support for the importance of the credit/bank lending channel in case stimulus comes from lowering the policy rate. By contrast, the spread shock has no significant effect on asset and deposit growth. Rather, positive (and short-lived) effects on output growth are triggered by an acceleration of consumer wealth growth.

3.3. Do Effects Vary over Time?

Having established through which channels both shocks transmit to the real economy, we now investigate more closely their overall effects. The strength of both shocks might depend on the specific economic environment when the shock is carried out. For example, Jannsen et al. (2014) found strong effects of monetary policy during recessions associated with financial crises, which holds especially true for the recent global financial crisis. They attribute their finding to the particular effectiveness of the credit/bank lending channel in a recession, as advocated in Bernanke and Gertler (1995). Others find the opposite, namely that monetary policy is less effective in times of heightened uncertainty (Aastveit et al. 2017; Bech et al. 2014). Considering the term spread shock, recent empirical research hints at diminishing effectiveness of the LSAP programs; see, e.g., (Wu 2014).

So far, results reported in Figures 2 and 3 have indicated changes in the strength of the shocks' impacts on the variables considered in this study. However, these results might be driven by the normalization of the shocks to 100 basis points, which is achieved by dividing through the impact response of the short-term interest rate and the term spread (both which have diminished strongly, since the period the FFR is technically zero). To investigate this further, we report the ratio of the cumulative response after 20 quarters to the one standard deviation shock on impact, with the standard deviation varying over the sample. These "elasticities" are thus free of the normalization effect and show the responsiveness of a given variable in cumulative terms to the two shocks on impact over the sample period.

Elasticities shown in Figure 4 reveal a very systematic pattern over time. Stimulus from conventional monetary policy is less effective during the period of the global financial crisis compared to prior to the crisis. This is particularly so in terms of output growth for which the elasticity reaches its trough over the whole sample period during the crisis. Hence, we qualitatively corroborate the findings of Bech et al. (2014), Aastveit et al. (2017), Hubrich and Tetlow (2015), who attributed smaller effects of monetary policy during financial crises to balance sheet adjustments and the deleveraging of the private sector. on the one hand, and heightened uncertainty weighing on the business climate, on the other hand. Strikingly, elasticities in the aftermath of the crisis do not simply revert back to their pre-crisis values. The responsiveness of all variables except net interest rate margins evens peaks during the aftermath of the crisis. This finding is certainly less related to the episode of the crisis and its long-lasting consequences for the economy. Rather, the specific monetary environment with the policy rate bound at zero seem to drive this result. Taken at face value, our finding implies that monetary policy is particularly effective if the policy rate is altered after it has been committed to a particular value for a prolonged time.

Elasticities related to the term spread shock spike for most variables during the crisis and during the period from 2000–2001. In the latter period, the Clinton debt buyback program took place, which was in many ways similar to an LSAP. See Greenwood and Vayanos (2010) for an in-depth analysis of the buyback program and its effect on the Treasury yield curve. This time pattern holds in particular true for inflation, consumer wealth and growth in bank's assets and deposits. The effects of lowering the term spread on output growth have also diminished after the launch of the first LSAP. Our findings thus ascribe the latter to LSAPs' smaller effects on the macroeconomy than the first programs, corroborating the results of Wu (2014) and Engen et al. (2015). The work in Engen et al. (2015) explicitly attributed the stronger effects of the earlier programs to the fact that they have been implemented at times when market conditions were highly strained, and a signal of commitment to accommodative policy over a longer horizon—such as the launch of quantitative easing—would be most effective.

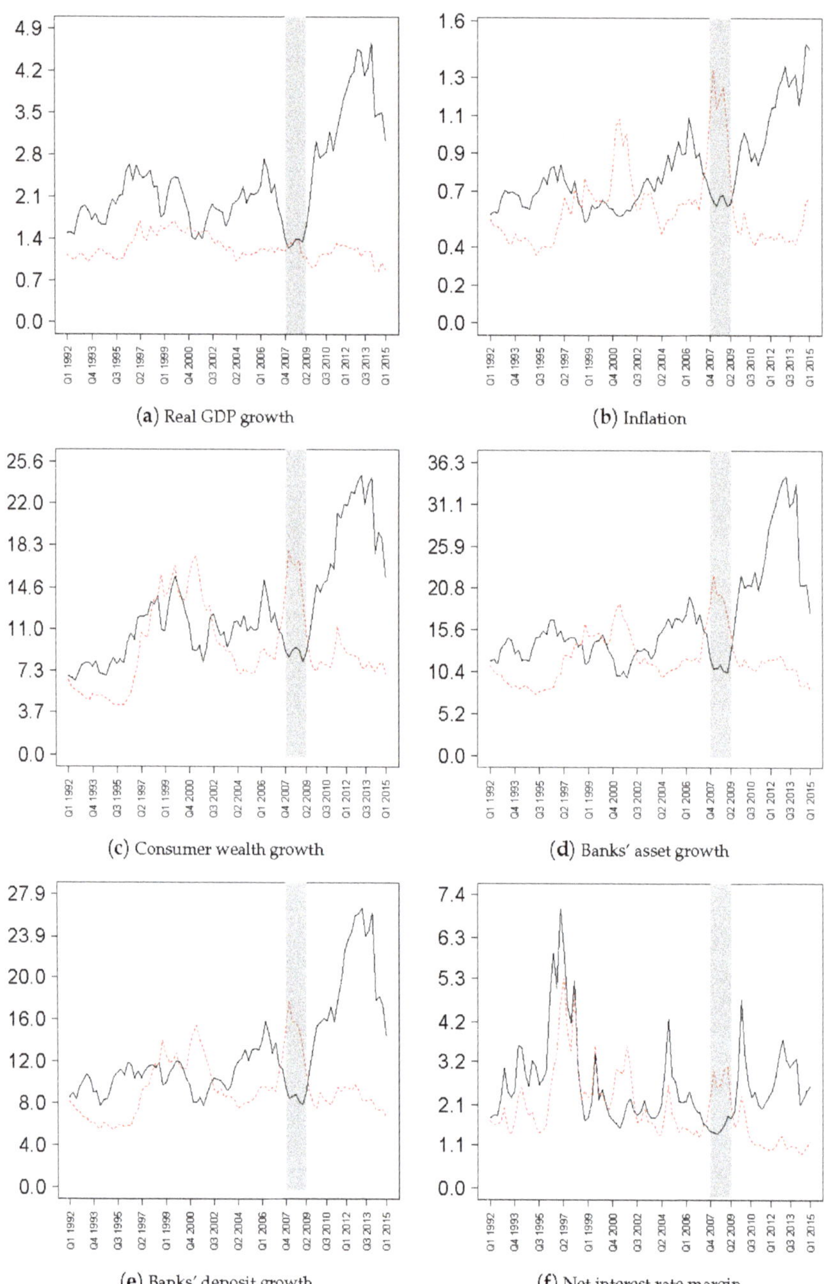

Figure 4. Elasticity of cumulative response to the size of shock on impact. Notes: The figure shows the ratio of the cumulative response of particular variable to the impact shock of the conventional monetary policy shock (black, solid line) and the spread shock (red, dashed line). Elasticities are in absolute terms. The shaded grey area indicates the period of the recession associated with the global financial crisis.

Summing up, we find that monetary policy effectiveness in boosting aggregate demand decreases significantly in the run-up of the global financial crisis. In the aftermath of the crisis, however, a hypothetical monetary policy shock would lead to strong effects on output growth and inflation. The opposite holds true for the spread shock, which is particularly stimulating during the period of the crisis when the Fed's engagement in quantitative easing served as an important signal to longer term accommodative monetary policy. In the aftermath of the crisis, the effectiveness of the hypothetical spread shock declines.

3.4. Did Term Spread and Monetary Policy Shocks Matter Historically?

Last, we examine the contribution of both shocks in explaining deviations from trend growth in the variables under consideration. These are depicted in Figure 5. We would expect higher contributions of the monetary policy shock prior to the global financial crisis and increasing contributions of the spread shock thereafter. The historical decomposition of most time series actually corroborates this presumption. More specifically, monetary policy shocks explain larger shares of movements in real GDP growth, inflation and banks' asset growth prior to and after the global financial crisis. However, the ratio of monetary policy to spread shock contribution declined significantly from end-2008 to the end of our sample. Even more visible are contributions related to the term spread, banks' deposit growth, consumer wealth growth and net interest margins, for which the spread shock explains a considerably larger part of movements than the monetary policy shock in the aftermath of the crisis.

Summing up, a historical decomposition analysis revealed that the monetary policy shock can explain movements in real GDP growth and inflation to a comparably larger extent than the spread shock throughout the sample period. By contrast, the spread shock explains movements in the term spread, consumer wealth growth, banks' deposit growth and net interest margins to a comparably larger extent. For all variables considered, the importance of the spread shock has increased significantly since end-2008, the period in which the first LSAP was launched. This finding is in line with our expectations and thus leads to further confidence in the statistical framework used in this study.

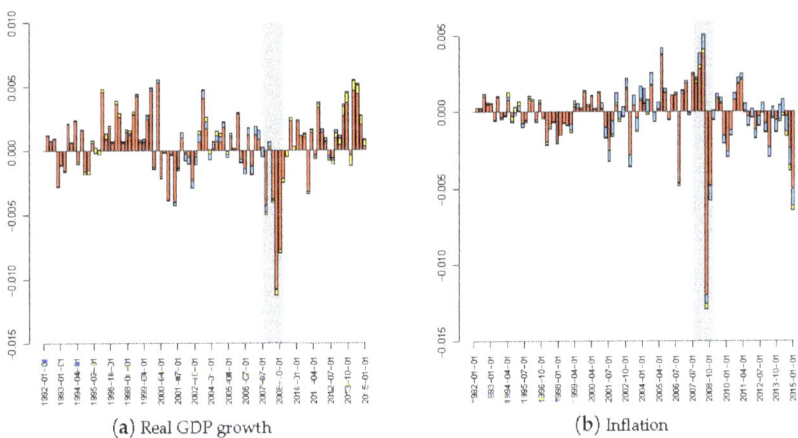

(a) Real GDP growth   (b) Inflation

Figure 5. *Cont.*

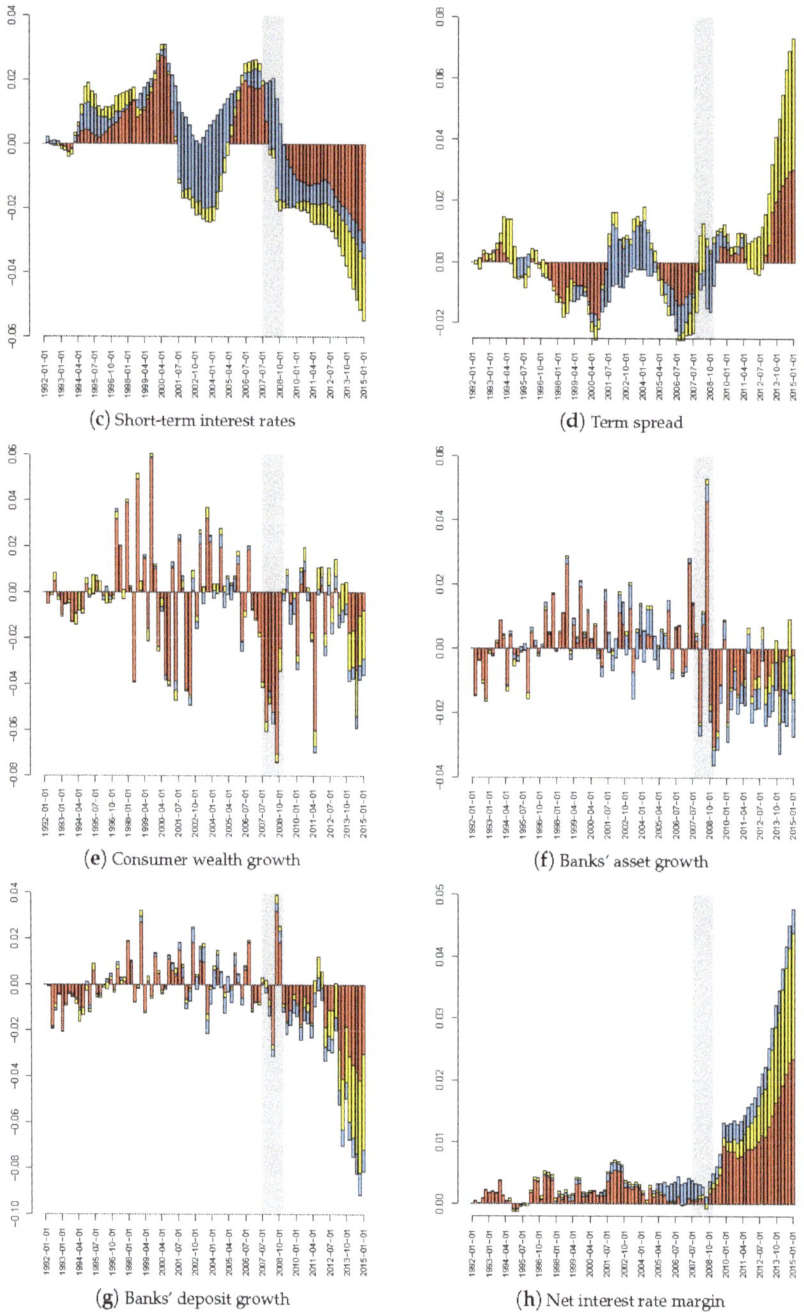

Figure 5. Historical decomposition of time series. Notes: Historical decomposition of time series based on the posterior median. The overall contribution of all shocks except the term spread and monetary policy shock in red. Contributions of the monetary policy shock and the term spread shock in blue and yellow, respectively. The shaded grey area indicates the period of the recession associated with the global financial crisis.

3.5. Robustness and Extensions

In this section, we investigate the robustness of our results. We do this by first looking at another measure of banks' asset growth taking a broader definition of the banking sector, by including investment growth as a further variable to the system and last by imposing different orderings of the variables to demonstrate that our estimates remain qualitatively unaffected.

First, since the shadow banking sector has expanded rapidly over the last decade in the USA, it has been argued that focusing on commercial banks' assets might yield an incomplete assessment of monetary policy transmission; see, e.g., (Adrian et al. 2010; Nelson et al. 2018). Hence, we substitute commercial banks' assets with assets of the shadow banking sector and re-run the analysis outlined in Section 3. Shadow banks are defined as financial intermediaries that conduct functions of banking without access to central bank liquidity and, in the definition following Nelson et al. (2018), comprise finance companies, issuers of asset-backed securities and funding corporations.[15] In a nutshell, credit intermediation through the shadow banking system is comparable to credit intermediation of a traditional bank with wholesale investors at the deposit end, and at the loan origination end are finance companies and traditional banks.

Figure 6 shows impulse responses of asset growth, deposit growth and real GDP growth. Overall, results on real activity are nearly unaffected by inclusion of shadow assets, albeit the uncertainty of the estimates is slightly more elevated especially in the most recent part of our sample. While the shape of asset and deposit growth responses is very similar to our baseline estimates, including shadow assets yields stronger responses in terms of overall magnitudes. This holds true for all time periods considered, for both shocks and for both variables. However, these stronger magnitudes are estimated with much uncertainty and hence do not translate into overall stronger responses of real GDP growth. The responses of the other variables are very similar to the results of our baseline estimation. This is also evident from Table 3, top panel, which lists correlations of median impulse responses with the baseline model. The fact that we get very similar results of asset responses to both shocks contrasts the findings of Nelson et al. (2018), who reported a decrease of commercial banks' assets and an increase of shadow assets in response to a contractionary monetary policy shock. Note that we have not restricted the responses of asset growth, and our results are hence purely data driven. They might differ from those of Nelson et al. (2018) since we use a richer framework in terms of included variables and covered transmission channels.

Second, and as pointed out in Stein (2012), a reason why the effects of asset purchase programs might have diminished over time are smaller effects via investment spending. In principle, a decrease in longer term borrowing costs for firms should boost investment spending. If, however, borrowing costs are further reduced by additional asset purchase programs, firms might simply pay back short-term debt and issue more and less expensive long-term debt. In that case, there is no additional impetus to the economy via investment spending. To investigate this in more depth, we re-run our analysis with gross fixed investment growth as an additional variable. We also modify the characterization of the two shocks provided by the restrictions in Table 1. Here, we add further restrictions saying that investment growth ticks up in response to both, a conventional monetary policy expansion and a shock to the term spread. Figure 7 shows the elasticity of the cumulative response with respect to the initial size of the shock.

---

15   Data on shadow assets (FL504090005.Q, FL674090005.Q, FL614090005.Q) are from the financial accounts database of the Federal Reserve System, http://www.federalserver.gov/releases/z1/about.htm.

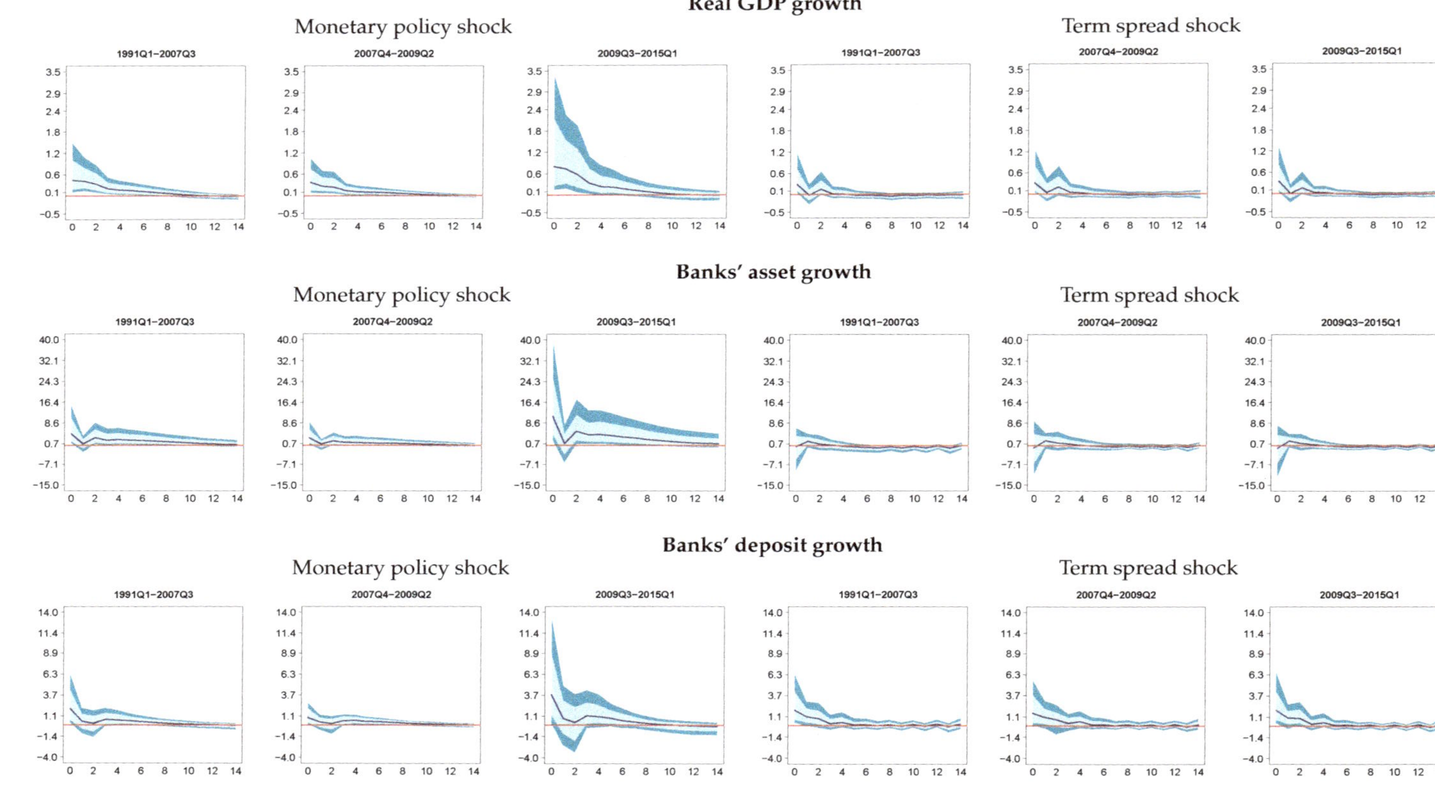

Figure 6. Impulse responses with shadow assets. Notes: Posterior median responses to an expansionary monetary policy shock (-100 bp) and shock to the term spread (-100 bp) along with 50% (dark blue) and 68% (light blue) credible bounds. Results shown as averages over three periods, pre-crisis from 1991Q1–2007Q3, global financial crisis from 2007Q4–2009Q2 and its aftermath from 2009Q3–2015Q1. Results based on inclusion of assets of the shadow banking sector instead of commercial banks' assets.

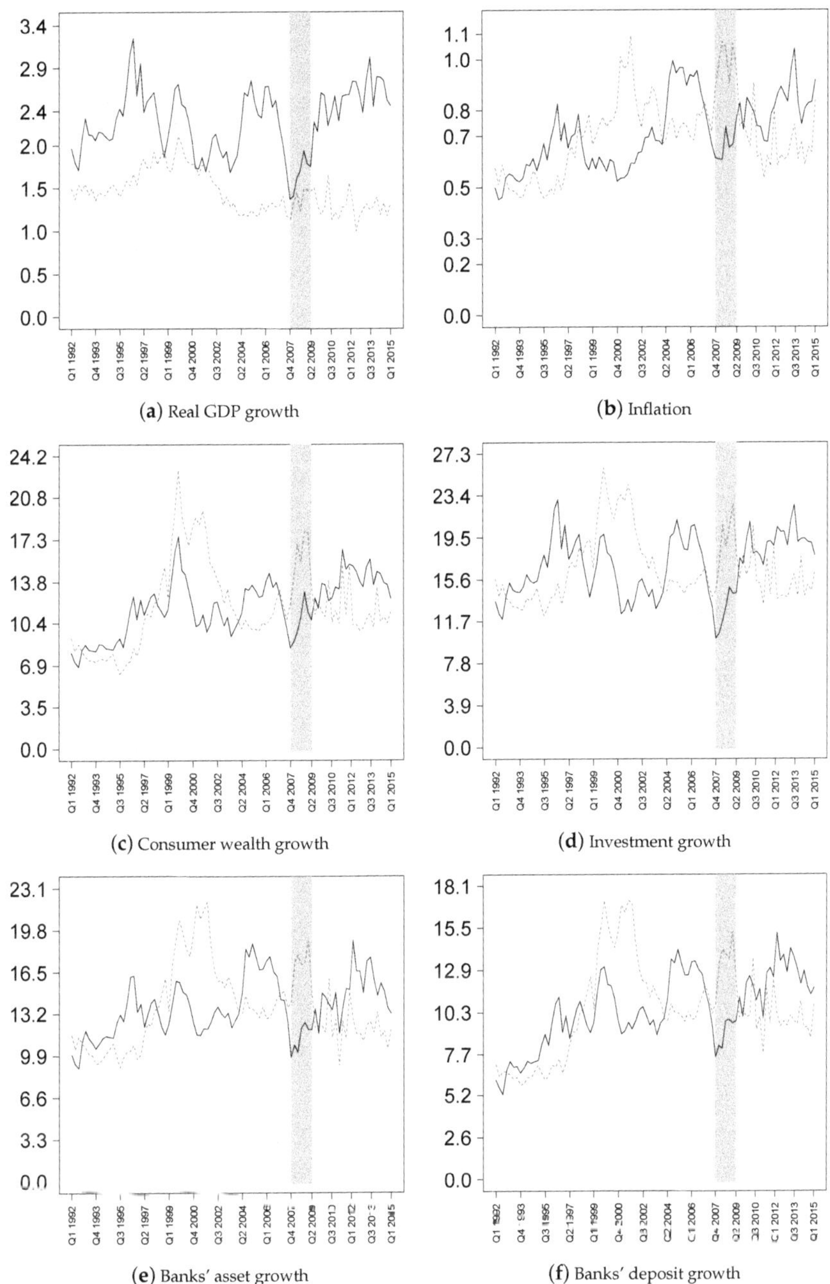

Figure 7. Elasticity of cumulative response to size of shock on impact; investment growth included. Notes: The figure shows the ratio of the cumulative response of a particular variable to the impact shock of the conventional monetary policy shock (black, solid line) and the spread shock (red, dashed line). Elasticities are in absolute terms. The shaded grey area indicates the period of the recession associated with the global financial crisis.

Looking at investment growth points indeed to a smaller elasticity in the aftermath of the crisis compared to the crisis period itself. The pattern of the other variables is consistent with our baseline estimates, stronger effects during the crisis and smaller impacts in the aftermath regarding the term spread shock, while the opposite holds true for the monetary policy shock. In general, including investment growth has rendered elasticities more volatile in the aftermath of the crisis. This is due to the fact that with the additional restrictions imposed, it is harder to find rotation matrices fulfilling the complete set of identifying assumptions. More specifically, while impulse responses of our baseline estimate are typically based on 250–300 rotation matrices each ten quarters we sample them, the number of successfully sampled matrices decreases to about 150 per sampling point when including investment growth. Considering impulse responses (available from the authors upon request), the inclusion of investment growth leaves our results broadly unchanged.

Last and to add further confidence to our results, we change the ordering of the variables for our estimation setup. For the baseline ordering, we put real GDP growth first, followed by inflation, wealth, short-term interest rates, banks' deposits and assets, the term spread and net interest rate margins. This ordering is motivated in Christiano et al. (1996) and states that output cannot be contemporaneously affected by inflation, consumer wealth and the policy rate. Results of the baseline ordering are compared to results under 10 randomly chosen orderings. As stressed before and since we rely on an explicit identification of the shocks via sign restrictions, the ordering of the variables should not affect our results qualitatively. This is evident in the bottom panel of Table 3, which shows average correlations of median impulse responses under the baseline and the 10 permuted orderings. In fact, correlations are in almost all cases virtually unity. These small differences can be well attributed to sampling error.

Table 3. Correlation of median impulse responses.

| | Correlation of Shadow Assets with Baseline | | | | | |
| | Monetary policy shock | | | Term spread shock | | |
	1991Q1–2007Q3	2007Q4–2009Q2	2009Q3–2015Q1	1991Q1–2007Q3	2007Q4–2009Q2	2009Q3–2015Q1
Real GDP growth	0.976	0.969	0.968	0.984	0.979	0.948
Inflation	0.957	0.991	0.914	0.963	0.950	0.938
Wealth	0.996	0.998	0.997	0.995	0.996	0.994
Short-term interest rate	0.994	0.999	0.978	1.000	0.999	1.000
Banks' deposits	0.775	0.658	0.768	0.930	0.694	0.810
Banks' assets	0.934	0.956	0.926	0.497	0.457	0.625
Term spread	0.999	0.999	0.996	0.990	0.978	0.988
Net interest rate margin	0.996	0.994	0.994	0.930	0.694	0.786
	Average Correlation of Different Cholesky Orderings with Baseline					
	Monetary policy shock			Term spread shock		
	1991Q1–2007Q3	2007Q4–2009Q2	2009Q3–2015Q1	1991Q1–2007Q3	2007Q4–2009Q2	2009Q3–2015Q1
Real GDP growth	0.999	0.995	0.999	0.998	0.997	0.990
Inflation	0.998	0.998	0.995	0.996	0.998	0.995
Wealth	0.999	0.999	0.999	1.000	1.000	0.999
Short-term interest rate	0.999	0.989	1.000	1.000	1.000	1.000
Banks' deposits	0.998	0.993	0.998	0.998	0.984	0.986
Banks' assets	0.998	0.997	0.999	0.999	0.997	0.961
Term spread	1.000	0.996	1.000	0.999	0.997	1.000
Net interest rate margin	1.000	0.998	0.999	0.987	0.954	0.837

Notes: The table shows the correlation of median impulse responses to the conventional and unconventional monetary policy shocks, over three selected horizons. Correlations in the top panel refer to those of a model using assets of the shadow banking sector instead of commercial banks' assets with estimates of the baseline model. Correlations in the bottom panel refer to estimates using 10 randomly-permuted Cholesky orderings and the baseline model.

4. Conclusions

In this paper, we have analyzed the effects and transmission of conventional and unconventional monetary policy in the USA. For that purpose, we have proposed a medium- to large-scale model that allows parameters to drift and residual variances to change over time. Our main results remain qualitatively unaffected when considering an alternative measure for banking sector assets, including investment growth as a further transmission channel and using different Cholesky orderings in the estimation stage of the model. These can be summarized as follows:

First, we discuss the monetary policy shock. The rate cut has positive and rather persistent effects on output growth. These are driven by an expansion of asset and deposit growth of the banking sector and thus by a broad credit/bank lending channel. By contrast and in line with previous findings (see, e.g., (Ludvigson et al. 2002)), the wealth channel appears less important for the transmission of conventional monetary policy in the USA. A forecast error variance decomposition lends further support to these findings. More importantly though, we find a pronounced and distinct pattern of monetary policy effectiveness over time. More specifically, our results point to comparably modest effects on output growth in response to a hypothetical and unexpected lowering of the policy rate during the period of the global financial crisis. In this sense, our results corroborate the findings of a recent strand of the literature stating that monetary policy is weak in recessions associated with either high economic uncertainty or more generally financial crises; see, e.g., (Aastveit et al. 2017; Bech et al. 2014; Hubrich and Tetlow 2015; Tenreyro and Thwaites 2016). There is less empirical work on the effectiveness of monetary policy in the aftermath of the global financial crisis, a period in which the main U.S. policy rate was effectively zero. Our results show the strongest responsiveness of the economy to a hypothetical monetary policy shock during that period. From the perspective of a policymaker, this seems less relevant in practical terms, since obviously, the policy rate cannot enter negative territory. However, it is rather the fact that the policy rate has not changed for an extended time than the level at which the policy rate stood that drives this result. If changes in the policy rate are rare, volatility associated with a monetary policy shock is low, and a deviation from the commitment can provide a particularly strong boost to output growth. Note, however, that a central bank's loss function typically consists of other additional targets such as price stabilization, and hence, our finding does not directly translate into a policy recommendation to deviate from a commitment. Still, it suggests that effects of a correction of the monetary policy stance after an extended period of unchanged monetary policy might have large macroeconomic effects.

Second, and looking at the term spread shock, we find positive, but short-lived effects on output and consumer price growth. These work mainly through the consumer wealth channel and via steering inflation, while there is less evidence of impetus via banks' asset and deposit growth. Effects of the term spread shock show also a distinct pattern over time. More specifically, we find that the term spread shock impacts most strongly the output growth during the period of the global financial crisis and less so in its aftermath. Taken at face value, this result implies that the effectiveness of the Fed's unconventional monetary policy measures has abated since the early programs. Smaller effects in the most recent period stem from a decrease in stimulus of consumer wealth and a smaller responsiveness of inflation. These might be attributed to an implicit signaling channel, which is particularly effective when financial markets are impaired and economic conditions are characterized by high uncertainty (Engen et al. 2015). In addition, we show that effects of quantitative easing on investment growth have diminished over time providing, thereby less stimulus for overall GDP growth.

Author Contributions: Conceptualization, M.F. and F.H.; methodology, F.H.; software, F.H.; validation, M.F., F.H.; formal analysis, M.F. and F.H.; investigation, M.F.; resources, M.F.; data curation, M.F.; writing—original draft preparation, M.F.; writing—review and editing, F.H.; visualization, M.F.; supervision, M.F. and F.H.; project administration, M.F.

Funding: This research received no external funding.

Conflicts of Interest: The authors declare no conflict of interest.

Appendix A. Structural Identification

To implement the sign restrictions technically, note that Equation (8) can be written as:

$$A_t y_t = c_t + \sum_{j=1}^{p} B_{jt} y_{t-j} + \Lambda_t^{0.5} v_t, \tag{A1}$$

where $\Lambda = \Lambda_t^{0.5} \Lambda_t^{0.5}$ and $v_t \sim \mathcal{N}(0, I_m)$ is a standard normal vector error term. Multiplication from the left by $\Lambda_t^{-0.5}$ yields:

$$\tilde{A}_t y_t = \tilde{c}_t + \sum_{j=1}^{p} \tilde{B}_{jt} y_{t-j} + v_t \tag{A2}$$

with $\tilde{A}_t = \Lambda_t^{-0.5} A_t$, $\tilde{c}_t = \Lambda_t^{-0.5} c_t$ and $\tilde{B}_{jt} = \Lambda_t^{-0.5} B_{jt}$.

It can be shown that left multiplying Equation (A2) with an $m \times m$-dimensional orthonormal matrix R with $R'R = I_m$ leaves the likelihood function untouched. This implies that impulse responses are set-identified. To implement the sign restrictions approach, we simply draw R using the algorithm outlined in Rubio-Ramírez et al. (2010) until the impulse response functions satisfy a given set of sign restrictions to be chosen by the researcher. This has to be done for each draw from the posterior, which in our application boils down to 500 draws randomly taken from the full set of 15,000 posterior draws. To speed up computation, we do not search for each point in time a new rotation matrix. Instead, we look for new rotation matrices after 10 quarters and check whether the restrictions are fulfilled throughout the sample. These leaves us with 11 time periods for which we look for new rotation matrices. For each of these time points, we recovered 250–300 rotation matrices that fulfilled our restrictions. There was no visible time pattern over the amount of sign restrictions recovered throughout our sample period.

To impose the additional restriction that the short-term interest rate reacts sluggishly with respect to an unconventional monetary policy shock, we construct the following deterministic rotation matrix (Baumeister and Benati 2013):

$$S = \begin{pmatrix} I_{m-2} & 0_{m-2 \times 2} \\ 0_{2 \times m-2} & U \end{pmatrix} \tag{A3}$$

with:

$$U = \begin{pmatrix} \cos(\vartheta) & -\sin(\vartheta) \\ \sin(\vartheta) & \cos(\vartheta) \end{pmatrix}. \tag{A4}$$

The rotation angle is defined as:

$$\vartheta = \tan^{-1}([\tilde{A}_t R']_{ij} / [\tilde{A}_t R']_{ii}). \tag{A5}$$

Here, the notation $[\tilde{A}_t R']_{ij}$ selects the i, j-th element of the impact matrix, corresponding to the contemporaneous response of variable the short-term interest rate (variable i) to an unconventional monetary policy shock (variable j). Multiplying the impact matrix with U from the right yields a new impact matrix that satisfies the set of sign restrictions specified in Section 2.4 and the zero impact restriction described above.

Since we assume that the central bank is constrained by the zero lower bound, we zero-out the structural coefficients of the monetary policy rule for the first eight quarters after the shock hit the economy. This procedure, however, is subject to the Lucas critique because economic agents are not allowed to change their behavior accordingly. However, the findings in Baumeister and Benati (2013) suggest that the differences between the results obtained by manipulating the structural coefficients or by manipulating the historical structural shocks to keep the interest rate at the zero lower bound are quite similar. Moreover, manipulating the structural shocks gives rise to additional shortcomings like the fact that this approach ignores the impact of agents expectations about future changes in the policy rate. In addition, the systematic component of monetary policy implies that the short-term interest rate reacts to different shocks. However, the unsystematic part, by construction, offsets this behavior, and the corresponding shocks would no longer originate from a white noise process.

Appendix B. A Brief Sketch of the Markov Chain Monte Carlo Algorithm

Since we impose a Cholesky structure on the model a priori and estimate the system equation-by-equation, our Markov chain Monte Carlo (MCMC) algorithm consists of the following three steps:

1. Sample $a^T = (a_1, \ldots, a_T)'$ and $b^T = (b_1, \ldots, b_T)'$ using the algorithm of Carter and Kohn (1994).
2. Sample the variances of Equations (5) and (6) using Gibbs steps by noting that the conditional posteriors are again of inverted Wishart form.
3. Sample $h^T = (h_1, \ldots, h_T)'$ and the corresponding parameters of Equation (7) through the algorithm put forth in Kastner and Frühwirth-Schnatter (2013). A brief description of this algorithm is provided in Appendix C.

Step 1 is a standard application of Gibbs sampling in state-space models. In Step 2, we draw the parameters of the corresponding state equations conditional on the states. Step 3 is described in more detail in the Appendix. Finally, note that we sample the parameters of the different equations simultaneously.

Appendix C. Sampling Log-Volatilities

To simulate the full history of log-volatilities for the i-th equation $h_i^T = (h_{i1}, \ldots, h_{iT})'$, we use the algorithm outlined in Kastner and Frühwirth-Schnatter (2013). This algorithm samples h_i^T, all without a loop. This is achieved by rewriting h_i^T in terms of a multivariate normal distribution. Moreover, the parameters of the state equation in Equation (7) are sampled through simple Metropolis–Hastings (MH) or Gibbs sampling steps. To achieve a higher degree of sampling efficiency, we sample the corresponding parameters from the centered parameterization in Equation (7) and a non-centered variant given by:

$$\tilde{h}_{it} = \rho_i \tilde{h}_{it-1} + \epsilon_{it}, \ \epsilon_{it} \sim \mathcal{N}(0,1). \tag{A6}$$

To simplify the exposition, we illustrate the algorithm for the case when $i = 2, \ldots, m$. For $i = 1$, the same steps apply with only minor modifications. Let us begin by rewriting Equation (4) as:

$$e_{it} = c_{it} - \sum_{s=1}^{i-1} a_{is,t} y_{st} - \sum_{j=1}^{p} b_{ij,t} y_{t-j} = \lambda_{it}^{0.5} \epsilon. \tag{A7}$$

Squaring and taking logarithms yield:

$$e_{it}^2 = h_{it} + \ln(u_{it}^2). \tag{A8}$$

Since $\ln(u_{it}^2)$ follows a $\chi^2(1)$ distribution, we use a mixture of Gaussian distribution to render Equation (A8) conditionally Gaussian,

$$\ln(u_{it}^2)|r_{it} \sim \mathcal{N}(m_{it}, s_{it}^2), \tag{A9}$$

where r_{it} is an indicator controlling the mixture component to use at time t with $r_{it} \in \{1, \ldots, 10\}$. m_{it} and s_{it}^2 define the mean and the variance of the mixture components employed.

The mixture indicators allow us to rewrite Equation (A8) as a linear Gaussian state space model:

$$e_{it}^2 = m_{ir,t} + h_{it} + \xi_{it}, \ \xi_{it} \sim \mathcal{N}(0, s_{ir,t}^2). \tag{A10}$$

The algorithm then consists of the following steps.

1. Sample $h_{i,-1}|r_{it},\mu_i,\rho_i,\sigma_{ih},\Psi_{it}$ or $\tilde{h}_{ij,-1}|r_{ij},\rho_i,\sigma_{ih},\Psi_{it}$, all without a loop (AWOL). Here, $\Psi_{it} = (c_{it},a_{is,t},\ldots,a_{ii-1,t},b_{i1,t},\ldots,b_{ip,t})'$ is a vector of stacked coefficients and $h_{i,-1} = (h_{i2},\ldots,h_{iT})'$. Following Rue (2001), $h_{i,-1}$ can be written in terms of a multivariate normal distribution:

$$h_{i,-1} \sim \mathcal{N}(\Omega_{h_i}^{-1}c_i, \Omega_{h_i}^{-1}). \tag{A11}$$

Similarly, the normal distribution corresponding to the non-centered parameterization is given by:

$$\tilde{h}_{i,-1} \sim \mathcal{N}(\tilde{\Omega}_{h_i}^{-1}\tilde{c}_i, \tilde{\Omega}_{h_i}^{-1}). \tag{A12}$$

The corresponding posterior moments are:

$$\Omega_{h_i} = \begin{pmatrix} \frac{1}{s^2_{r_{ij,2}}} + \frac{1}{\sigma^2_{ih}} & \frac{-\rho_i}{\sigma^2_{ih}} & 0 & \cdots & & 0 \\ -\frac{\rho_i}{\sigma^2_{ih}} & \frac{1}{s^2_{r_{i,3}}} + \frac{1+\rho_i}{\varsigma^2_i} & -\frac{\rho_i}{\sigma^2_{ih}} & \ddots & & \vdots \\ 0 & -\frac{\rho_i}{\sigma^2_{ih}} & \ddots & \ddots & & 0 \\ \vdots & & \ddots & \ddots & \frac{1}{s^2_{r_{ij,T-1}}} + \frac{1+\rho_i}{\sigma^2_{ih}} & \frac{-\varsigma_{ij}}{\sigma^2_{ih}} \\ 0 & & \cdots & 0 & -\frac{\rho_i}{\sigma^2_{ih}} & \frac{1}{s^2_{r_{ij,T}}} + \frac{1}{\sigma^2_{ih}} \end{pmatrix} \tag{A13}$$

and:

$$c_i = \begin{pmatrix} \frac{1}{s^2_{r_{ij,2}}}(\tilde{y}^2_{ij,2} - m_{r_{ij,2}}) + \frac{\mu_i(1-\rho_i)}{\sigma^2_{ih}} \\ \vdots \\ \frac{1}{s^2_{r_{ij,T}}}(\tilde{y}^2_{ij,T} - m_{r_{ij,T}}) + \frac{\mu_i(1-\rho_i)}{\sigma^2_{ih}} \end{pmatrix}. \tag{A14}$$

Multiplying by σ^2_{ih} yields the moments for the non-centered parameterization: $\tilde{\Omega}_i = \sigma^2_{ih}\Omega_{h_{ij}}$ and $\tilde{c}_{ij} = \sigma^2_{ih}c_{ij}$. Finally, the initial states of h_i^T, h_{i1} and $\tilde{h}_{i1}$ are obtained from their respective stationary distributions.

2. Obtain the parameters of Equation (7) and Equation (A8). Since we impose a non-conjugate Gamma prior on σ_{ih}, we employ a Metropolis-within-Gibbs algorithm to sample μ_i, ρ_i and σ_i for both parameterizations. For the centered variant, we simulate μ_i and ρ_i with a single Gibbs step, and σ^2_i is sampled through an MH step. For the non-centered parameterization, we sample ρ_i with MH and the other parameters with Gibbs steps.

3. Sample the mixture indicators with inverse transform sampling. Note that we can rewrite Equation (A8) as:

$$e^2_{it} - h_{it} = \tilde{\xi}_{it}, \; \tilde{\xi}_{it} \sim \mathcal{N}(m_{ir,t}, s^2_{it}). \tag{A15}$$

This allows us to compute the posterior probabilities that $r_{it} = j$, which are given by:

$$p(r_{it} = c|\bullet) \propto p(r_{it} = c)\frac{1}{s_{ik}}\exp\left(-\frac{(\tilde{\xi}_{it} - m_{ik})}{2s^2_{r_{it}}}\right), \tag{A16}$$

where $p(r_{it} = c|\bullet)$ are the unnormalized weights associated with the c-th mixture component.

The algorithm simply draws the parameters under both parametrizations and decides ex-post which of the parametrizations to use. This choice depends on the relationship between the variances of Equations (7) and (A8). For more information, see Kastner and Frühwirth-Schnatter (2013) and Kastner (2013).

The sampled log-volatilities are shown in Figure A1.

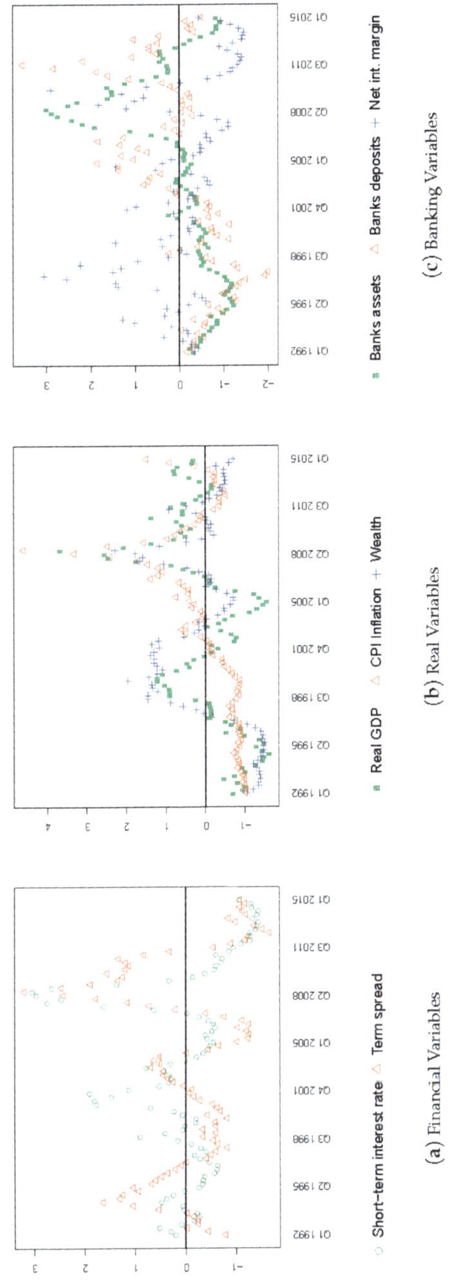

Figure A1. Stochastic volatility over time. Notes: Posterior mean of residual variance over time.

Reduced form volatility of the short-term interest rate and the term spread has increased considerably in the run-up of the global financial crisis, a period during which the Fed has aggressively lowered interest rates. Volatility has spiked around mid-2008 and hence in the midst of the crisis. While the crisis peak of residual variance associated with the short-term interest rate marked also the peak over our sample period, volatility of the term spread peaked in the early 1990s.

The middle panel of Figure A1 shows the volatilities for variables related to the real side of the economy. Residual variance associated with real GDP growth was elevated in the early 2000s and peaked around the same time as the financial variables discussed above. During the early 2000s, the so-called "dot-com bubble" burst, causing the slowing down of the U.S. economy. Stochastic volatility of wealth, which is strongly anchored on movements in stock market prices, naturally was also elevated during that period. In contrast to the volatility of real GDP, residual variance of wealth was pronounced for a longer period during the global financial crisis. Residual variance of CPI inflation started to rise more considerably from the beginning of the 2000s until 2008, a period that was characterized by sound growth in price dynamics in the USA. Residual variance peaked in the aftermath of the crisis and hence a little later than that associated with real GDP growth, when CPI inflation reverted from negative to positive territory.

Last, the bottom panel of Figure A1 shows residual variance for variables related to the banking sector. Residual variance of asset growth of commercial banks was elevated during the early 2000s and the global financial crisis, where it peaked around the same time as residual variance of real GDP growth, short-term interest rates and the term spread. Since 2009, estimated volatility has declined and is considerably smaller in the most recent period in our sample compared to its peak value. Residual variance associated with bank deposits and net interest margins show a slightly different pattern. Bank deposit volatility increased gradually from the beginning of 2004 until 2009, after which it gradually started to decline until the end of our sample period. Volatility associated with net interest margins spiked around 1997 and peaked in late 2009. That is, for both variables, banking deposits and net interest margins, volatility spikes during the global financial crisis occurred slightly later than those of the other variables considered in this study.

References

Aastveit, Knut Are, Gisle James Natvik, and Sergio Sola. 2017. Economic uncertainty and the influence of monetary policy. *Journal of International Money and Finance* 76: 50–67. [CrossRef]

Adrian, Tobias, Emanuel Moench, and Hyun Song Shin. 2010. *Financial Intermediation, Asset Prices, and Macroeconomic Dynamics*. Staff Reports 422. New York: Federal Reserve Bank of New York.

Adrian, Tobias, and Hyun Song Shin. 2010. Financial Intermediaries and Monetary Economics. In *Handbook of Monetary Economics*. Edited by Benjamin. M. Friedman and Michael Woodford. Amsterdam: Elsevier, vol. 3, chp. 12, pp. 601–50.

Baumeister, Christiane, and Luca Benati. 2013. Unconventional Monetary Policy and the Great Recession: Estimating the Macroeconomic Effects of a Spread Compression at the Zero Lower Bound. *International Journal of Central Banking* 9: 165–212.

Baumeister, Christiane, and James D. Hamilton. 2015. Sign restrictions, structural vector autoregressions, and useful prior information. *Econometrica* 83: 1963–99. [CrossRef]

Bech, Morten L., Leonardo Gambacorta, and Enisse Kharroubi. 2014. Monetary Policy in a Downturn: Are Financial Crises Special? *International Finance* 17: 99–119. [CrossRef]

Benati, Luca, and Charles Goodhart. 2008. Investigating time-variation in the marginal predictive power of the yield spread. *Journal of Economic Dynamics and Control* 32: 1236–72. [CrossRef]

Bernanke, Ben S., and Alan S. Blinder. 1988. Credit, Money, and Aggregate Demand. *American Economic Review* 78: 435–9.

Bernanke, Ben S., and Mark Gertler. 1995. Inside the Black Box: The Credit Channel of Monetary Policy Transmission. *Journal of Economic Perspectives* 9: 27–48. [CrossRef]

Bernanke, Ben S., Mark Gertler, and Mark Watson. 1997. Systematic Monetary Policy and the Effects of Oil Price Shocks. *Brookings Papers on Economic Activity* 28: 91–157. [CrossRef]

Black, Lamont, Diana Hancock, and Waynee Passmore. 2007. *Bank Core Deposits and the Mitigation of Monetary Policy*. Technical Report 65. Federal Reserve Board Finance and Economics Discussion Series. Washington: Federal Reserve Board.

Bloom, Nicholas. 2009. The Impact of Uncertainty Shocks. *Econometrica* 77: 623–85.

Boivin, Jean, and Marc P. Giannoni. 2006. Has Monetary Policy Become More Effective? *The Review of Economics and Statistics* 88: 445–62. [CrossRef]

Boivin, Jean, Michael T. Kiley, and Frederic S. Mishkin. 2010. How Has the Monetary Transmission Mechanism Evolved Over Time? In *Handbook of Monetary Economics*. Edited by Benjamin. M. Friedman and Michael Woodford. Amsterdam: Elsevier, vol. 3 , chp. 8, pp. 369–422.

Breitfuß, Sebastian, Martin Feldkircher, and Florian Huber. 2018. Changes in U.S. monetary policy and its transmission over the last century. *German Economic Review*. [CrossRef]

Butt, Nick, Rohan Churm, Michael McMahon, Arpad Morotz, and Jochen Schanz. 2014. *QE and the Bank Lending Channel in the United Kingdom*. Working Paper 511. London: Bank of England.

Carriero, Andrea, Todd E Clark, and Massimiliano Marcellino. 2015. *Large Vector Autoregressions With Asymmetric Priors*. Working Paper Series (2015/759). London: Queen Mary University of London.

Carter, Chris K., and Robert Kohn. 1994. On gibbs sampling for state space models. *Biometrika* 81: 541–53. [CrossRef]

Christiano, Lawrence J., Martin Eichenbaum, and Charles Evans. 1996. The Effects of Monetary Policy Shocks: Evidence from the Flow of Funds. *The Review of Economics and Statistics* 78: 16–34. [CrossRef]

Christiano, Lawrence J., Martin Eichenbaum, and Charles L. Evans. 2005. Nominal rigidities and the dynamic effects of a shock to monetary policy. *Journal of Political Economy* 113: 1–45. [CrossRef]

Cogley, Timothy, Sergei Morozov, and Thomas J. Sargent. 2005. Bayesian fan charts for uk inflation: Forecasting and sources of uncertainty in an evolving monetary system. *Journal of Economic Dynamics and Control* 29: 1893–925. [CrossRef]

Cogley, Timothy, and Thomas J. Sargent. 2002. Evolving Post-World War II U.S. Inflation Dynamics. In *NBER Macroeconomics Annual 2001*. Cambridge: National Bureau of Economic Research, Inc., vol. 16, NBER Chapters, pp. 331–88.

Cogley, Timothy, and Thomas J. Sargent. 2005. Drifts and volatilities: Monetary policies and outcomes in the post wwii us. *Review of Economic Dynamics* 8: 262–302. [CrossRef]

Coibion, Olivier. 2012. Are the Effects of Monetary Policy Shocks Big or Small? *American Economic Journal: Macroeconomics* 4: 1–32. [CrossRef]

Doh, Taeyoung. 2010. The efficacy of large-scale asset purchases at the zero lower bound. *Economic Review* 95: 5–34.

Dunne, Peter, Mary Everett, and Rebecca Stuart. 2015. *The Expanded Asset Purchase Programme—What, Why and How of Euro Area QE*. Quarterly Bulletin Articles. Dublin: Central Bank of Ireland, pp. 61–71.

Engen, Eric M., Thomas T. Laubach, and David Reifschneider. 2015. *The Macroeconomic Effects of the Federal Reserve's Unconventional Monetary Policies*. Finance and Economic Discussion Series 2015-005. Washington: Board of Governors of the Federal Reserve System (U.S.).

Fawley, Brett W., and Luciana Juvenal. 2012. Quantitative easing: Lessons we've learned. *The Regional Economist* 7: 8–9.

Fernández-Villaverde, Jesús, Pablo Guerró-Quintana, Juan F. Rubio-Ramírez, and Martin Uribe. 2011. Risk matters. The real effects of volatility shocks. *American Economic Review* 101: 2530–61. [CrossRef]

Frühwirth-Schnatter, Sylvia. 1994. Data augmentation and dynamic linear models. *Journal of Time Series Analysis* 15: 183–202. [CrossRef]

Fry, Renée, and Adrian Pagan. 2011. Sign restrictions in structural vector autoregressions: A critical review. *Journal of Economic Literature* 49: 938–60. [CrossRef]

Gagnon, Joseph, Matthew Raskin, Julie Remache, and Brian Sack. 2011. The Financial Market Effects of the Federal Reserve's Large-Scale Asset Purchases. *International Journal of Central Banking* 7: 3–43.

Gertler, Mark, and Peter Karadi. 2015. Monetary policy surprises, credit costs, and economic activity. *American Economic Journal: Macroeconomics* 7: 44–76. [CrossRef]

Gorodnichenko, Yuriy. 2005. *Reduced-Rank Identification of Structural Shocks in VARs*. Macroeconomics 0512011. Germany: University Library of Munich.

Greenwood, Robin, and Dimitri Vayanos. 2010. Price Pressure in the Government Bond Market. *American Economic Review* 100: 585–90. [CrossRef]

Hamilton, James D. 2018. *The Efficacy of Large-Scale Asset Purchases When the Short-term Interest Rate is at its Effective Lower Bound.* Brookings Papers on Economic Activity. Washington: Brookings Press.

Hamilton, James D., and Jing Cynthia Wu. 2012. The Effectiveness of Alternative Monetary Policy Tools in a Zero Lower Bound Environment. *Journal of Money, Credit and Banking* 44: 3–46. [CrossRef]

Hubrich, Kirstin, and Robert J. Tetlow. 2015. Financial stress and economic dynamics: The transmission of crises. *Journal of Monetary Economics* 70: 100–15. [CrossRef]

Inoue, Atsushi, and Barbara Rossi. 2018. *The Effects of Conventional and Unconventional Monetary Policy on Exchange Rates.* NBER Working Papers 25021. Cambridge: National Bureau of Economic Research, Inc.

Ireland, Peter N. 2005. *The Monetary Transmission Mechanism.* Working Papers 06-1. Boston: Federal Reserve Bank of Boston.

Jannsen, Nils, Galina Potjagailo, and Maik H. Wolters. 2014. *Monetary Policy during Financial Crises: Is the Transmission Mechanism Impaired?* Kiel: Kiel Institute for the World Economy, mimeo.

Joyce, Michael, David Miles, Andrew Scott, and Dimitri Vayanos. 2012. Quantitative easing and unconventional monetary policy—An introduction. *The Economic Journal* 122: F271–88. [CrossRef]

Kastner, Gregor. 2013. Stochvol: Efficient Bayesian Inference for Stochastic Volatility (sv) Models. R Package Version 0.7-1. Available online: http://CRAN.R-project.org/package=stochvol (accessed on 25 October 2018).

Kastner, Gregor, and Sylvia Frühwirth-Schnatter. 2013. Ancillarity-sufficiency interweaving strategy (asis) for boosting mcmc estimation of stochastic volatility models. *Computational Statistics & Data Analysis* 76: 408–23.

Kastner, Gregor, Florian Huber, and Martin Feldkircher. 2018. Should I stay or should I go? A latent threshold approach to large-scale mixture innovation models. *Journal of Applied Econometrics* arXiv:1607.04532.

Korobilis, Dimitris. 2013. Assessing the Transmission of Monetary Policy Using Time-varying Parameter Dynamic Factor Models. *Oxford Bulletin of Economics and Statistics* 75: 157–79. [CrossRef]

Krishnamurthy, Arvind, and Annette Vissing-Jorgensen. 2011. The Effects of Quantitative Easing on Interest Rates: Channels and Implications for Policy. *Brookings Papers on Economic Activity* 43: 215–87. [CrossRef]

Leeper, Eric M., Christopher A. Sims, and Tao Zha. 1996. What Does Monetary Policy Do? *Brookings Papers on Economic Activity* 27: 1–78. [CrossRef]

Lopes, Hedibert F, Robert E. McCulloch, and Ruey S. Tsay. 2013. *Cholesky Stochastic Volatility Models for High-Dimensional Time Series.* Technical Report. Chicago: University of Chicago, mimeo.

Ludvigson, Sydney, Charles Steindel, and Martin Lettau. 2002. Monetary policy transmission through the consumption-wealth channel. *Economic Policy Review* 8: 117–33.

McKay, Alisdair, Emi Nakamura, and Jón Steinsson. 2016. The Power of Forward Guidance Revisited. *American Economic Review* 106: 3133–58. [CrossRef]

Miranda-Agrippino, Silvia. 2016. *Unsurprising shocks: information, premia, and the monetary transmission.* Technical Report 626, Bank of England Working Paper. London: Bank of England.

Miranda-Agrippino, Silvia, and Giovanni Ricco. 2017. *The Transmission of Monetary Policy Shocks.* Technical Report 657, Bank of England Working Paper. London: Bank of England.

Nakamura, Emi, and Jón Steinsson. 2018. High Frequency Identification of Monetary Non-Neutrality: The Information Effect. *Quarterly Journal of Economics* 133: 1283–330. [CrossRef]

Nelson, Benjamin, Gabor Pinter, and Konstantinos Theodoridis. 2018. Do contractionary monetary policy shocks expand shadow banking? *Journal of Applied Econometrics* 33: 198–211. [CrossRef]

Primiceri, Giorgio E. 2005. Time varying structural vector autoregressions and monetary policy. *The Review of Economic Studies* 72: 821–52. [CrossRef]

Romer, Christina D., and David H. Romer. 2004. A New Measure of Monetary Shocks: Derivation and Implications. *American Economic Review* 94: 1055–84. [CrossRef]

Rubio-Ramírez, Juan F., Daniel F. Waggoner, and Tao Zha. 2010. Structural vector autoregressions: Theory of identification and algorithms for inference. *Review of Economic Studies* 77: 665–96. [CrossRef]

Rue, Håvard. 2001. Fast sampling of gaussian markov random fields. *Journal of the Royal Statistical Society: Series B (Statistical Methodology)* 63: 325–38. [CrossRef]

Sims, Christopher A. 2001. Discussion of Cogley and Sargent 'Evolving Post World War II U.S. Inflation Dynamics'. *NBER Macroeconomics Annual* 16: 373–79.

Sims, Christopher A., and Tao Zha. 1998. Bayesian Methods for Dynamic Multivariate Models. *International Economic Review* 39: 949–68. [CrossRef]

Stein, Jeremy C. 2012. *Evaluating Large-Scale Asset Purchases*. Speech at the Brookings Institution. Washington, D.C.: Brookings Institution.

Tenreyro, Silvana, and Gregory Thwaites. 2016. Pushing on a string: U.S. monetary policy is less powerful in recessions. *American Economic Journal: Macroeconomics* 8: 43–74. [CrossRef]

Uhlig, Harald. 2005. What are the effects of monetary policy on output? Results from an agnostic identification procedure. *Journal of Monetary Economics* 52: 381–419. [CrossRef]

Wu, Tao. 2014. *Unconventional Monetary Policy and Long-Term Interest Rates*. Technical Report WP/14/189, IMF Working Paper. Washington: International Monetary Fund (IMF).

Journal of
Risk and Financial Management

Article

Comparing the Forecasting of Cryptocurrencies by Bayesian Time-Varying Volatility Models

Rick Bohte and Luca Rossini *

School of Business and Economics, Department of Econometrics and Operations Research, Vrije Universiteit Amsterdam, De Boelelaan 1105, 1081 HV Amsterdam, The Netherlands; r.bohte@student.vu.nl
* Correspondence: luca.rossini87@gmail.com

Received: 9 September 2019; Accepted: 14 September 2019; Published: 18 September 2019

Abstract: This paper studies the forecasting ability of cryptocurrency time series. This study is about the four most capitalised cryptocurrencies: Bitcoin, Ethereum, Litecoin and Ripple. Different Bayesian models are compared, including models with constant and time-varying volatility, such as stochastic volatility and GARCH. Moreover, some cryptopredictors are included in the analysis, such as S&P 500 and Nikkei 225. In this paper, the results show that stochastic volatility is significantly outperforming the benchmark of VAR in both point and density forecasting. Using a different type of distribution, for the errors of the stochastic volatility, the student-t distribution is shown to outperform the standard normal approach.

Keywords: Bayesian VAR; cryptocurrency; Bitcoin; forecasting; density forecasting; time-varying volatility

1. Introduction

Nowadays it is more common to handle your affairs online. According to the World Payments Report (Capgemini and BNP Paribas 2017), electronic payments are expected to increase by almost 11% each year worldwide from 2015 to 2020. The world is becoming more online accessible due to innovations and modern technology. Online investing on the open market is due to technology much easier to do, for example there are applications such as eToro, Robinhood and Plus500 where people can invest money with their mobile devices.

In the last decades, a new type of currency is launched on the financial market and has gained importance. In particular, it is a virtual currency of which the main feature is the total absence of any intrinsic value. In 2009, Nakamoto (Nakamoto 2008) documented the creation of the first decentralised cryptocurrency, called Bitcoin. Since its introduction, it has been gaining more attention from the media, the finance industry, and academics. There are several reasons for this interest: Firstly Japan and South Korea have recognised Bitcoin as a legal method of payment (Bloomberg 2017a; Cointelegraph 2017). Second, some central banks are exploring the use of cryptocurrencies (Bloomberg 2017b). Third, the Enterprise Ethereum Alliance was created by a large number of companies and banks to make use of cryptocurrencies and the related technology called blockchain (Forbes 2017). These are just three of the many reasons the interest in cryptocurrencies has spiked. After the introduction of Bitcoin, many cryptocurrencies (around 1000) were created and became a new investment opportunity for trades. Hereafter, a short overlook of the four most important cryptocurrencies is described.

Bitcoin (BTC) is based on decentralisation, which means that it is controlled and owned by its users. This decentralisation is often criticised due to the lack of control over the whole system. Despite this criticism, Bitcoin increased in value from a couple of cents in the beginning (2009) to about 20,000 US dollar at the end of 2017. Ethereum (ETH, Ethereum 2014) is also decentralised and features smart contract functionality. Due to this contractual agreement, there is no possibility of fraud, downtime, third party interference or censorship. The researcher and programmer Vitalik Buterin proposed it in late 2013 and Ethereum went live at the end of July in 2015.

Ripple (XRP, Ripple 2012) is founded by Ryan Fugger in 2004. It is a blockchain network that incorporates both a currency system known as XRP and a payment system. This enables real-time international payments and is therefore currently used by multiple banks. Litecoin (LTC, Litecoin 2014) was created in 2011 by Charles Lee and is based on the same peer to peer protocol used by Bitcoin. It is often considered Bitcoin's rival due to its improvements in transactions; these transactions are significantly faster than Bitcoin. Therefore it could be particularly attractive in certain situations to invest in.

Recently, researchers have started to study cryptocurrencies by applying different models and techniques. However, apart from Catania et al. (2019), a forecasting analysis of cryptocurrencies has not been strongly used and proposed. This paper tries to continue the analysis initialised by Catania et al. (2019) and to improve it by comparing different multivariate models for point and density forecasting of the four most capitalised cryptocurrencies previously described.

To study and forecast the cryptocurrencies, vector autoregressive models and moreover its extension to time-varying volatility have been introduced. Vector autoregressions (VARs) are used in models for empirical macroeconomic applications. VARs were introduced by Sims (1980) and have been widely adopted for forecasting and analysis of macroeconomic variables. The formulation of VARs is simple, however they tend to forecast well and are often used as the benchmark to compare the performance of forecasts among models. Sims and Zha (2006) emphasised the value of volatility modelling for improving efficiency. Accordingly, taking time variation in volatility into account should improve the estimation of a VAR-based model and inference common in analysis of macroeconomic variables. Modelling changes in volatility of VARs should also improve the accuracy of density forecasts. Forecast densities are potentially either too wide or too narrow, due to shifts in volatility. D'Agostino et al. (2013) showed that the combination of time-varying parameters and stochastic volatility improves the accuracy of point and density forecasts. One application of these regressions on a macroeconomic level is investing in assets, stocks and, as the purpose for this paper, in cryptocurrencies, as mentioned above.

VAR models can have many parameters if they include many lags, however using non-data information and turning it into priors is found to greatly improve the forecast performance. In Bayesian estimation algorithms, the stochastic volatility specification is computationally tractable, while in frequentist estimation it is captured with a single model. This is one of the reasons, in this paper, the Bayesian approach is used. Another reason is that the Bayesian approach gives some advantages in parameter uncertainty, computing of probabilistic statements and estimation with many parameters. As a standard procedure, the normal distribution is often used as a distribution of the so called "noise". For this paper, not only the normal distribution, but also the student-t distribution is used for modelling the errors.

A strong improvement of our paper is the introduction of time-varying specifications for multivariate models for better forecasting the cryptocurrencies behaviour. In particular, the use of time-varying volatility jointly with the multivariate time series is of interest for capturing the possible heteroscedasticity of the shocks and non-linearities in the simultaneous relations among the different cryptocurrencies in the models. Moreover, taking into account the time variation in volatility improves the VAR-based estimation and inference that have been shown in the preliminary cryptocurrencies analyses.

Our results show that including time-varying volatility and in particular stochastic volatility provides forecasting gains in terms of point and density forecasting relative to the multivariate autoregressive model. The inclusion of cryptopredictors can lead to better forecasting with respect to the benchmark but not strong improvements with respect to time-varying volatility models with only lags of the cryptocurrencies included. Directional predictability indicates that using stochastic volatility with heavy tails can be used to create profitable investment strategies.

The content of this paper is structured as follows. In Section 2, some literature used as research background is reviewed, especially research in the field of Bayesian VARs and cryptocurrencies. Section 3 describes the data. Section 4 presents our models, estimation methodology and metrics used to assess our results, which are discussed in Section 5 together with the major findings. Finally, Section 6 concludes.

2. Literature Review

Cryptocurrency is becoming a hot topic in academia and outside of it. In particular, in the last years, the interest in cryptocurrencies has exploded from around 19 billion Dollars in February 2018 to around 800 billion Dollars in December 2017, thus much research has been done about this subject. Although Bitcoin is a relatively new currency, there have already been some studies on this topic.

Hencic and Gourieroux (2015) investigated the presence of bubbles in Bitcoin/US Dollar exchange rate by applying a non-causal AR model; the dynamics of the daily Bitcoin/USD exchange rate shows episodes of local trends, which can be modelled and interpreted as speculative bubbles. Cheah and Fry (2015) focused on the same issue; as with many asset classes, they showed that Bitcoin exhibits bubbles. They found empirical evidence that the fundamental price of Bitcoin is zero. The volatility of six major currencies against the volatility of Bitcoin was measured by Sapuric and Kokkinaki (2014), the results indicate a high volatility for Bitcoin exchange rate. Then, Chu et al. (2015) did a statistical analysis of the log-returns of the exchange rate of Bitcoin against the US Dollar and the generalised hyperbolic distribution is shown to give the best fit. Yermack (2015) wondered whether Bitcoin can be considered a real currency on the financial market.

Fernández-Villaverde and Sanches (2016) analysed privately issued fiat currencies, checked the existence of price equilibria and showed that there exists an equilibrium in which price stability is consistent with competing private monies. However, they also concluded that the value of private currencies monotonically converges to zero by equilibrium trajectories. Dyhrberg (2016) showed that the movements of the volatility of Bitcoin has several similarities to gold and the dollar. Bianchi (2018) investigated if there is a relationship between returns on cryptocurrencies and traditional asset classes. There was a mild correlation with some commodities, but not that many macroeconomic variables.

Catania et al. (2018) showed that predicting volatility can be improved by using leverage and time-varying skewness at different forecast horizons. Hotz-Behofsits et al. (2018) used time-varying parameter VAR with t-distributed measurement errors and stochastic volatility to model three cryptocurrencies: Bitcoin, Ethereum and Litecoin. Griffin and Shams (2018) investigated whether the cryptocurrency called Tether is directly manipulating the price of Bitcoin, increasing its predictability. By using algorithms to analyse the data, they found that purchases with Tether go along with sizeable increases in Bitcoin prices.

In 2019, there are more studies done on cryptocurrencies. Muglia et al. (2019) investigated the predictability of the S&P 500 by the movement of Bitcoin, showing that Bitcoin does not have any direct impact on the predictability of the S&P 500. Catania et al. (2019) found that point forecasting is statistically significant for Bitcoin and Ethereum when using combinations of univariate models. They also concluded that density forecasting for all four cryptocurrencies is significant when relying on time-varying multivariate models.

The exercise in this paper is generalised to multivariate models where the four cryptocurrencies are predicted jointly using Bayesian VAR models with stochastic volatility as in Koop and Korobilis (2013). Johannes et al. (2014) predicted stock prices using time-varying parameter and stochastic volatility VAR models and found statistically and economically significant portfolio benefits for an investor who uses models of return predictability.

Many institutions tried to investigate the relationship between Bitcoin and the stock market. An article by Bloomberg (2018) stated that "big investors may be dragging Bitcoin toward Market correlation", thus investors looking for high gains may be attracted to the increasing risk of this cryptocurrency. Stavroyiannis et al. (2019) studied the relation between Bitcoin and the S&P500 and found that it does not hold any of the hedge, diversifier, or safe-haven properties and the intrinsic value is not related to US markets.

There are still no studies that can confirm that Bitcoin is a good stock market predictor. This paper tries to fill the gap, analysing whether Bitcoin, Ethereum, Litecoin and Ripple can be forecasted by its lags and other macroeconomic variables.

3. Data

The data collected for the sample span from 8 August 2015 to 28 February 2019, giving a total of 1301 observations. The data can be seen in Figure 1, which shows a big spike around the end of 2017. Chinn'a "Big Three" exchanges were pending closure around that time; however, the cryptocurrencies were largely buoyed by a bullish sentiment and went up. In December 2017, the peaks were reached and a couple days later they dropped. At this time, cryptocurrencies are mainly considered as an alternative investment, due to the fact that their use for payment is still limited. This can create correlations with other assets in the financial market for at least two main reasons. The first regards investors, who usually allocate wealth in a global portfolio and hedge across investments; the second relates to market sentiments that spread fast among different assets. See the work of Bianchi (2018) for similar arguments.

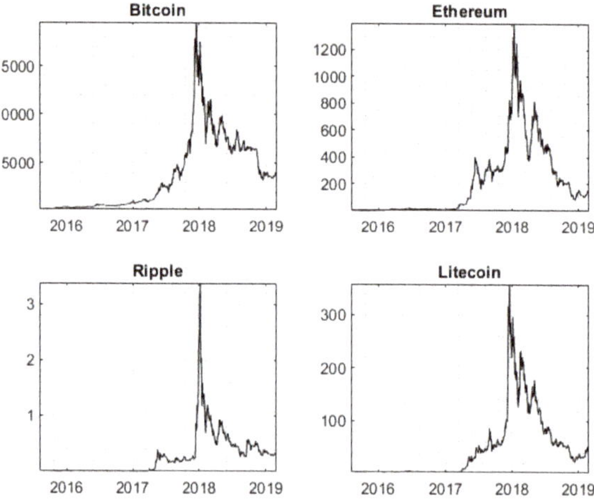

Figure 1. Price of the four cryptocurrencies from 8 August 2015 to 28 February 2019.

In this paper, we consider different cryptopredictors, as described below. The choice of these cryptopredictors is due to the fact that possible correlations between cryptocurrencies and these assets can be created, because Bitcoin and other currencies are considered as an alternative investment and their use as payment is still poor. We use the following list of predictors for cryptocurrencies as stated in Catania et al. (2019) as proxying market sentiments: international stock index prices (the S&P 500, Nikkei 225 and Stoxx Europe 600); commodity prices (gold and silver); interest rates (the 1-month and 10-year US Treasury rates); and the VIX closing price. To study the possible dependence between cryptocurrencies, a transformation is necessary. The percentage daily log returns of cryptocurrencies is computed as follows:

$$y_t = 100 \times \log(S_t/S_{t-1}),$$

where S_t is the price on day t and y_t is the cryptocurrency log return. Table 1 reports the descriptive statistics of the cryptocurrencies. In Figure 2, the transformed data are plotted against time;

as documented in Chu et al. (2015), the cryptocurrencies display high volatility, non-zero skewness, very high kurtosis and several spikes.

Table 1. Descriptive statistics, calculated between 8 August 2015 and 28 February 2019.

Coin	Bitcoin	Ethereum	Ripple	Litecoin
Maximum	22.5119	41.2337	102.7356	51.0348
Minimum	−20.7530	−31.5469	−61.6273	−39.5151
Mean	0.2071	0.4001	0.2781	0.1912
Median	0.2343	−0.0884	−0.3537	0.0000
Std Dev.	3.9543	6.7950	7.4433	5.7424
Skewness	−0.2624	0.4898	3.0179	1.2631
Kurtosis	7.8178	7.6368	42.6234	15.3417

Ripple has the highest volatility due to the highest kurtosis. Litecoin has also a high volatility but not that high compared to Ripple. The other two (Bitcoin and Ethereum) are compared to the aforementioned cryptocurrencies less volatile, however the kurtosis is still far away from the normal distribution, which has a kurtosis of three. Another interesting statistic is the skewness; Bitcoin is the only one with a negative skewness. This indicates that the tail is at the left side of the distribution, so the probability of lower values than the mean is higher than the normal distribution, which has a skewness of zero. With a positive skewness, this is the case for the other cryptocurrencies, the opposite is true. As before, Ripple has the highest skewness, which indicates that Ripple has the highest probabilities of higher values than its mean.

In Figure 2, the transformation of daily log returns is shown. This gives some more insight into the cryptocurrencies. Ripple is the most volatile crypto, the descriptive statistics of which are also indicated. In addition, Ethereum stands out in the first half and after that it is more stable, which means that it is less volatile. Bitcoin is the most stable crypto according to Figure 2.

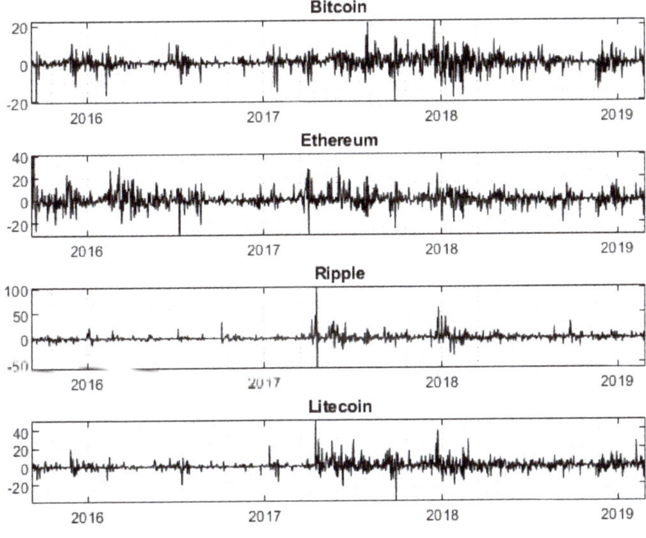

Figure 2. Daily log returns of the four cryptocurrencies.

The crypto market is open 24/7, however the predictor variables are not. For this reason, the data have to be adapted to use for forecasting. The procedure is simple; when the market is closed, for a variable, the previous value of that variable is used. This gives a return of zero, however this is the best way since the variable is actually not changing for a day. Figure 3 shows the plots of the predictor variables.

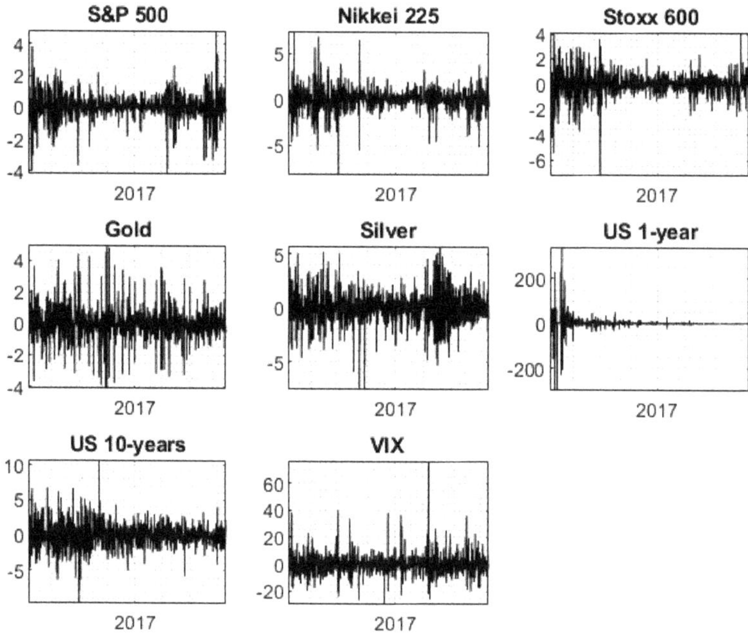

Figure 3. Daily log returns of the eight cryptopredictors from 8 August 2015 to 28 February 2019.

4. Methodology

Studies have provided strong evidence of time-varying volatility in macroeconomic variables, however VARs with constant volatility are used in this paper. By using constant volatility, the performance of point forecasting should not be affected that much by conditional heteroscedasticity, which is the case for heteroscedastic models such as GARCH and stochastic volatility. Heteroscedasticity is a major concern in the regression analysis, as well as in the analysis of variance, as it can invalidate statistical tests. These tests assume that the errors, obtained by modelling, are uniform and uncorrelated. For example, the ordinary least squares (OLS) estimator is still unbiased in the case of heteroscedasticity, thus is inefficient because the actual variance and covariance are underestimated.

In this paper, three types of specifications are analysed: the standard VAR model, VAR with stochastic volatility and VAR with GARCH. The reason for multiple specifications of the model is to really see if the forecasting performance of a more complex model is better than a simple model. The Bayesian approach gives some advantages, as the parameter uncertainty can be mitigated. The probabilistic statements can be computed without assumption. Another advantage is that the estimation of complex nonlinear models with many parameters is feasible. For the stochastic volatility, two different models are investigated: one where the normal distribution is used and the other where the student-t distribution is used. These procedures by using these models are not the same, thus could end up with different results. This way, there can also be a conclusion about which distribution would give more accurate forecasts between all the models.

As stated in Catania et al. (2019), the number of lags of the VAR models is selected equal to three based on the BIC. The lag of interest of the cryptopredictors is the first lag. Thus, eight models are discussed and used in this paper: Bayesian VAR(3), Bayesian VARX(3), Bayesian VAR(3)-SV, Bayesian VARX(3)-SV, Bayesian VAR(3)-GARCH, Bayesian VARX(3)-GARCH, Bayesian VAR(3)-SVt and Bayesian VARX(3)-SVt. These models are constant parameter vector autoregressive and among the most common models applied in financial and macroeconomic forecasting (see Koop and Korobilis (2010); Lutkepohl (2007)). Regarding time-varying parameters, we left this issue as future research. To compare the models with each other, the Bayesian VAR(3) is chosen to be the benchmark. In the next subsections, the models used for the in-sample analysis and the forecasting exercise are explained briefly.

4.1. Bayesian VAR

First, the focus is on the benchmark model; the Bayesian VAR(3) model is described as follows:

$$y_t = \beta_1 y_{t-1} + \beta_2 y_{t-2} + \beta_3 y_{t-3} + \epsilon_t, \quad \epsilon_t \sim N(0, \Sigma_{\epsilon_t}), \text{ for } t = 1, \cdots, T,$$

with T the number of total days of the data. Since this model is for every cryptocurrency, the equation above can be rewritten in stacked form:

$$Y_t = Z_t \beta + \epsilon_t, \quad \beta = vec(\beta_1, \beta_2, \beta_3),$$
$$Z_t = (I_N \otimes X_t),$$

where $X_t = [y_{t-1}, y_{t-2}, y_{t-3}]'$, for every cryptocurrency.

Bayesian VARX

To introduce possible dependence to other variables, it is possible to extend the Bayesian VAR model, by including other variables of interest. The so-called VARX model can be described as:

$$y_t = \beta_1 y_{t-1} + \beta_2 y_{t-2} + \beta_3 y_{t-3} + \sum_{j=1}^{8} \gamma_j W_{j,t} + \epsilon_{i,t}, \quad \epsilon_t \sim N(0, \Sigma_{\epsilon_t}), \text{ for } t = 1, \cdots, T,$$

with T the number of total days of the data and where γ_j and $W_{j,t}$ are the parameter and cryptopredictor, respectively. Since this model is for every cryptocurrency, the equation above can be rewritten in stacked form:

$$Y_t = Z_t \beta + \epsilon_t, \quad \beta = vec(\beta_1, \beta_2, \beta_3, \gamma_1, \cdots, \gamma_8),$$
$$Z_t = (I_N \otimes X_t),$$

with T the number of total days of the data and where $X_t = [y_{t-1}, y_{t-2}, y_{t-3}, W_{1t}, \cdots, W_{8t}]'$, for every cryptocurrency.

4.2. Bayesian VAR-SV

In the following section, the models with time-varying volatility are described in detail by differentiating between SV and GARCH. First, the Bayesian VAR(3) with stochastic volatility is similar to the previous model, however there is a difference in the innovations term. This allows the model to take different approaches over time, for example in times of high uncertainty there could be a higher variance in the innovations. For this reason, one should use stochastic volatility, since the model adapts to the movement and volatility of the time series.

The Bayesian VAR-SV(3) model is described in the following way:

$$y_t = \beta_1 y_{t-1} + \beta_2 y_{t-2} + \beta_3 y_{t-3} + \epsilon_t,$$
$$\epsilon_t = A^{-1}\Lambda_t^{0.5}\varepsilon_t, \varepsilon_t \sim N(0, I_k), \Lambda_t \equiv \mathrm{diag}(\lambda_{1t}, \cdots, \lambda_{kt}),$$
$$\log(\lambda_t) = \log(\lambda_{t-1}) + \nu_t,$$
$$\nu_t = (\nu_{1t}, \nu_{2t}, \cdots, \nu_{kt})' \sim N(0, \Phi), \text{ for } t = 1, \cdots, T$$

with T the number of total days of the data and where A is a lower triangular matrix with non-zero coefficients below the diagonal, which are ones. Λ_t is a diagonal matrix which contains the time-varying variances of shocks. This model implies that the reduced form variance-covariance matrix of innovations to the VAR is $var(\epsilon_t) \equiv \Sigma_t = A^{-1}\Lambda_t(A^{-1})'$ (Clark and Ravazzolo (2015)).

4.3. Bayesian VAR-GARCH

The Bayesian VAR(3) with GARCH(1,1) innovations is almost the same as the VAR-SV model, however there is a difference in the innovations term. This allows the model to take different approaches over time, for example in times of high uncertainty there could be a higher variance in the errors. It also has a memory over time so it can compare the observations with the past to get a better estimate of the predictions. For this reason, one should use GARCH over SV, because of the memory over time.

The Bayesian VAR(3) with GARCH(1,1) innovations is described in the following way:

$$y_t = \beta_1 y_{t-1} + \beta_2 y_{t-2} + \beta_3 y_{t-3} + \epsilon_t,$$
$$\epsilon_t = H_t^{0.5}\eta_t, \eta_t \sim N(0, I_k), H_t = D_t R_t D_t, D_t = \mathrm{diag}(h_{1t}^{0.5}, \cdots, h_{kt}^{0.5}),$$
$$h_t = \omega + B\epsilon_{t-1}^{(2)} + Gh_{t-1}, \text{ for } t = 1, \cdots, T,$$

with T the number of total days of the data. R is the conditional correlation matrix. h_t follows a GARCH(1,1) model where $h_t = [h_{1t}, h_{2t}, \cdots, h_{kt}]'$ and $\epsilon_t^{(2)} = [\epsilon_{1t}^2, \epsilon_{2t}^2, \cdots, \epsilon_{kt}^2]'$ are conditional variances and squared errors, respectively. ω and B and G are matrices of coefficients (Carnero and Eratalay (2014)).

4.4. Bayesian VAR-SVt

The following model description is similar to the VAR-SV, but now with a student-t distribution. This model, referred to as VAR-SVt, is described as:

$$y_t = \beta_1 y_{t-1} + \beta_2 y_{t-2} + \beta_3 y_{t-3} + \epsilon_t,$$
$$\epsilon_t = A^{-1}\Lambda_t^{0.5}\varepsilon_t, \varepsilon_t \sim t(0, I_k, \eta), \Lambda_t \equiv \mathrm{diag}(\lambda_{1t}, \cdots, \lambda_{kt}),$$
$$\log(\lambda_t) = \log(\lambda_{t-1}) + \nu_t,$$
$$\nu_t = (\nu_{1t}, \nu_{2t}, \cdots, \nu_{kt})' \sim t(0, \Phi, \eta), \text{ for } t = 1, \cdots, T$$

with T the number of total days of the data and η the degrees of freedom. A is a lower triangular matrix with non-zero coefficients below the diagonal which are ones, Λ_t is a diagonal matrix, which contains the time-varying variances of shocks. This model implies that the reduced form variance–covariance matrix of innovations to the VAR is $var(\epsilon_t) \equiv \Sigma_t = A^{-1}\Lambda_t(A^{-1})'$ (Clark and Ravazzolo (2015)).

4.5. Forecasting

To forecast the cryptocurrencies, the methodology used is called a rolling window. The estimation part is from 8 August 2015 to 8 August 2017, i.e. a two-year estimation window. Using the results from this estimation, the point forecast one-day ahead is calculated. The next forecast is done by estimating a day later than before, thus from 8 September 2015 to 8 September 2017 . This procedure continues until the end of the data is reached (28 February 2019), i.e. 567 days, thus the number of one-day ahead forecasts is 567. As a prior for the SV and GARCH models, the Minnesota prior is used as a start. This approach is standard and can be extended to other priors; for this paper, the standard approach is sufficient enough to investigate the cryptocurrencies. For every one-day forecast, a total of 6000 simulations are drawn and the first 1000 simulations are burned. This burning of the first simulation is due to the fact that the first simulations can be correlated and/or inaccurate. Over time, the simulations are independent of each other and can be used for measures.

4.6. Measures

To compare the performances of the forecasts, we use five different types of measures. The first three are measures of point forecasts, while the last two are measures of density forecasts. The difference between measures using point forecasts and measures using density forecasts is that measures using point forecasts use the mean of the simulations, while measures using density forecasts use all simulations. Measures using density forecasts give a great view of the full simulation and are not be averaged out as the measures using point forecasts. However, measures using point forecasts still give a good interpretation of the performance and are more efficient in time.

The first measure is the so-called 95% credible interval, which is an interval obtained by simulations. The 2.5% and 97.5% quantiles of the simulations are the lower and upper bounds, respectively. The idea behind this credible interval is that in 95% of the cases the forecast will be in this interval. Another measure is the sign predictability, in this paper referred as the "success rate", which is the percentage of the forecasts which are in the right direction, as the actual observations. When the actual observation goes down and the forecast as well, then it counts as a "success". It is also a "success" when the actual observation goes up and the forecast as well. In the two other cases, it counts as a "fail"; in this way, the "success rate" is built. We do not perform sign predictability tests for the reason indicated by Christoffersen and Diebold (2006). Tests that rely on the sign give no information about volatility dynamics, which is potentially valuable for detecting sign predictability.

The third measure is called the Root Mean Squared Error (RMSE). The RMSE is preferred over the Mean Squared Error (MSE) since it is on the same scale as the data. Some authors (e.g., Armstrong (2001)) recommend the use of the RMSE since it is more sensitive to outliers than commonly used Mean Absolute Error (MAE). The RMSE is computed for each cryptocurrency series, i = Bitcoin, Ethereum, Ripple and Litecoin:

$$RMSE_i = \sqrt{\frac{\sum_{t=R}^{T-1}(\hat{y}_{i,t+1} - y_{i,t+1})^2}{T-R}}$$

where R is the length of the rolling window, T is the number of observations, $\hat{y}_{i,t+1}$ is the ith cryptocurrency forecast at time t, and $y_{i,t+1}$ is the actual observation at time t.

The fourth type of measure is for evaluating the density forecasts; this measure is called the Log Predictive Score (LS). In the same way as for the RMSE, it is computed for each series:

$$LS_i = \sum_{t=R}^{T-1} \ln f(y_{i,t+1})$$

where $f(y_{i,t+1})$ is the predictive density for $y_{i,t+1}$, given the information up to time t. The fifth measure is the Continuous Rank Probability Score (CRPS). This is a continuous extension of the RPS and can be defined by considering an integral of the Brier scores over all possible thresholds x. Denoting the predicted cumulative density function by $F(x) = p(X \leq x)$ and the observed value of X by y_i, the continuous ranked probability score can be written for each series as:

$$CRPS_i = E\left(\int_{-\infty}^{\infty}[F(x) - H(x - y_i)]^2 dx\right),$$

where $H(x - y_i)$ is the Heaviside function that takes the value 0 when the observed value is smaller than the threshold, and 1 otherwise (Jolliffe and Stephenson 2003, Forecast Verification).

For the RMSE, LS and CRPS, we apply the *t*-test by Diebold and Mariano (1995) for each model versus the benchmark. This test gives a *p*-value which indicates a certain significance level. If in a table a value has one asterisk, then the model performs better, by a significance level of 5%, than the benchmark model. If in a table a value has two asterisks, then the model performs better, by a significance level of 1%, than the benchmark model. The first row of the tables contain the results of the RMSE, LS and CRPS of the benchmark, which is the BVAR model. Ratios of each models RMSE and CRPS to the benchmark are done such that entries less than 1 indicate that the given model yields forecasts more accurate than those from the benchmark. The differences of each models LS to the benchmark are performed such that a positive number indicates a model beats the baseline.

The other procedure we use is the model confidence set procedure of Hansen et al. (2011) using a *R* package called *MCS*, detailed by Bernardi and Catania (2016). The model confidence set procedure compares all the predictions jointly and deletes a model if it is significantly worse, finally ending up with the best possible models of the models that were put in. The models which have a grey background in tables are chosen to be not significantly worse than the other models.

5. Results

As stated in Section 4.6, we use different measures for point and density forecasting. Initially, the focus is on point forecasting. The first results of the forecasts are given in Table 2; these are the percentages of actual observations outside of the 95% credible interval obtained by simulation. To compare the BVAR model with the BVAR-GARCH model, the forecasts of the BVAR-GARCH model is only for Ripple not more often in the 95% credible interval. This would imply that the forecasts are less volatile using the BVAR-GARCH model compared to the BVAR model, and for Ripple this would be the opposite. This is in line with the expectations since the kurtosis of Ripple (see Table 1) is significantly higher than the other cryptocurrencies. The BVAR-SV and BVARX-SV models have the highest percentages of all the cryptocurrencies except for Bitcoin. This would suggest that using Stochastic Volatility will not give a good prediction overall using credible intervals. The results between the BVAR model and the BVARX model are close to each other, thus there is not a clear distinction between these two models. However, the BVARX-GARCH model is the model that stands out the most, which gives the most forecasts in the 95% credible interval, the only exceptions are the BVAR-GARCH model for Ethereum and the BVARX-SV model for Bitcoin.

Overall, the use of the cryptopredictor variables would be helpful to simulate forecasts due to the fact that in almost every case using the cryptopredictor variables would give a lower percentage of actual observations outside of the 95% credible interval. Using a student-t distribution in the SV model is only for Bitcoin more often out of the interval, which is expected as Bitcoin is the least volatile of the cryptocurrencies. Including the cryptopredictor variables into the SV-t model, this percentage is only smaller for Ripple, however not by a lot.

Table 2. Percentage of actual observations outside of the 95% credible interval retrieved by simulation.

Cryptocurrency	Bitcoin	Ethereum	Ripple	Litecoin
BVAR	8.9947	5.1146	4.7619	6.5256
BVAR-SV	5.8201	21.517	14.991	16.755
BVAR-GARCH	5.9965	3.7037	5.4674	4.4092
BVARX	9.1711	4.5855	4.9383	6.7019
BVARX-SV	3.5273	13.404	8.9947	8.9947
BVARX-GARCH	5.6437	4.0564	4.0564	3.351
BVAR-SVt	7.7601	6.5256	9.7002	10.582
BVARX-SVt	8.1129	6.3492	9.1711	10.582

For every cryptocurrency, the credible intervals are also plotted (see Figures A1–A4 in Appendix A). In these figures, the credible interval of the BVAR models are pretty steady for all cryptocurrencies, hence these models are not capturing the volatile movements of the data that well. When one uses a more expanded version, e.g., the BVAR-SV or BVAR-GARCH model, the credible levels captures the movements better; when there are shocks, the credible levels adapt to its movement. However, the BVARX-SV models stands out the most; there is much noise in the credible levels, thus using the predictors would not be helpful to give a more narrow credible interval to predict one day ahead.

Table 3 shows the results for the second point forecasting measure previously described. This predictability is not statistically tested but gives an insight into the accuracy of the movement of the forecasts. The returns are used to see if the direction of predictions is correct. The BVAR-SV model is compared to the BVAR model and BVAR-GARCH model in all cases more in the right direction. Another observation is that only for Ethereum and Ripple including the cryptopredictor variables predict the direction more precisely. The reason for this behaviour would be that Ripple is more dependent on market movement than the other cryptocurrencies. However, the percentages are under 50% or close to 50%, which would imply that these models (BVAR and BVAR-GARCH) cannot predict the movement very precise. That statement only applies for now on the prediction of the cryptocurrency going up or down.

An important observation of this table is that the stochastic volatility models have the best scores overall and are in some cases about 60–67%, which is much more precise than for example 35.45% of the BVAR-GARCH for Bitcoin. This is especially the case for the SV model with a student-t distribution, thus using a SV model with student-t distribution is the best way, among these models, to forecast the direction of the cryptocurrencies.

Table 3. Percentage of forecasts in the right direction (up or down).

Cryptocurrency	Bitcoin	Ethereum	Ripple	Litecoin
BVAR	51.675	43.563	48.325	44.621
BVAR-SV	51.852	55.556	55.556	55.732
BVAR-GARCH	35.45	37.39	38.801	38.448
BVARX	47.795	45.15	49.735	43.034
BVARX-SV	51.852	56.085	56.614	50.794
BVARX-GARCH	35.097	41.446	41.975	36.861
BVAR-SVt	61.905	62.963	61.905	67.901
BVARX-SVt	62.434	62.963	58.025	67.725

Moving to the last point forecast measure, Table 4 contains the results of the ratio of the RMSE. For these results, the RMSE of the benchmark model (BVAR) and the ratios of the other models are reported. As expected in the descriptive statistics, Ripple is the cryptocurrency with the highest RMSE due to the high kurtosis.

For Ripple and Litecoin, the SV models are significantly better than the benchmark model. The GARCH model is in all cases not significantly better than the benchmark; the cause could be that cryptocurrencies do not follow such dynamics. We could state that including the cryptopredictor variables does not affect the RMSE of the models enough to increase the performance of the forecasts. For Bitcoin, there is no model significantly better performing than the VAR, this could be caused by the aforementioned stability of Bitcoin compared to the other cryptocurrencies.

Table 4. Ratio of RMSE against benchmark.

Cryptocurrency	Bitcoin	Ethereum	Ripple	Litecoin
BVAR	4.6091	5.6996	7.6627	6.7055
BVAR-SV vs. BVAR	0.99466	0.99466	0.98465 **	0.97735 **
BVAR-GARCH vs. BVAR	1.0072	1.0106	1.0189	1.0163
BVARX vs. BVAR	1.0111	1.0113	1.0057	1.0098
BVARX-SV vs. BVAR	0.99585	0.99598	0.98555 **	0.98187 *
BVARX-GARCH vs. BVAR	1.013	1.02	0.99486	1.0065
BVAR-SVt vs. BVAR	0.99593	0.98915 **	0.98254 **	0.98709 **
BVARX-SVt vs. BVAR	0.99744	0.98927 *	0.98349 **	0.98774 **

Notes: (1) The "X" indicates models with the cryptopredictor variables included, the "t" indicates that the student-t distribution is used. (2) For BVAR, the benchmark model, the table reports the RMSE, for other models it reports the ratio between the RMSE of the current model and the benchmark. Entries less than 1 indicate that forecasts from current model are more accurate than forecasts from the benchmark model. (3) ** and * indicate RMSE ratios are significantly different from 1 at 5% and 10%, according to the Diebold–Mariano test. (4) Gray cells indicate models that belong to the Superior Set of Models delivered by the Model Confidence Set procedure at confidence level 10%.

The grey areas indicate the model confidence set; this also confirms our conclusion that using the SV model is in almost every case (except for Litecoin and VARX-SV) in this set. If one wants to forecast these cryptocurrencies with one of these models, then the preferred option, by looking at the RMSE, is using stochastic volatility.

Tables 5 and 6 contain the results of the density measures CRPS and PL. The results of the CRPS measure are not that different from the RMSE. One difference is that by the CRPS, GARCH outperforms the VAR for Bitcoin and for Ripple if the cryptopredictor variables are included. Hence, the density of Bitcoin and Ripple follow the dynamics of a GARCH model more than the benchmark. However, the SV model also outperforms the GARCH model since the values of the SV model are in many cases lower. In the model, confidence set is now also the GARCH for Bitcoin included.

Table 5. Ratio of CRPS against benchmark.

Cryptocurrency	Bitcoin	Ethereum	Ripple	Litecoin
BVAR	2.4707	3.1043	3.9479	3.453
BVAR-SV vs. BVAR	0.95108 **	0.99346	0.90827 **	0.9735 *
BVAR-GARCH vs. BVAR	0.96574 **	1.0443	0.99732	1.0226
BVARX vs. BVAR	1.0125	1.012	1.007	1.0131
BVARX-SV vs. BVAR	1.066	1.0298	0.93993 **	0.99681
BVARX-GARCH vs. BVAR	0.97812 *	1.042	0.97615 *	1.0216
BVAR-SVt vs. BVAR	0.95964 **	0.98594	0.88674 **	0.96403 **
BVARX-SVt vs. BVAR	0.96002 **	0.98764	0.88773 **	0.96525 **

Notes: (1) The "X" indicates models with the cryptopredictor variables included, the "t" indicates that the student-t distribution is used. (2) For BVAR, the benchmark model, the table reports the CRPS, for other models it reports the ratio between the CRPS of the current model and the benchmark. Entries less than 1 indicate that forecasts from current model are more accurate than forecasts from the benchmark model. (3) ** and * indicate CRPS ratios are significantly different from 1 at 5% and 10%, according to the Diebold–Mariano test. (4) Gray cells indicate models that belong to the Superior Set of Models delivered by the Model Confidence Set procedure at confidence level 10%.

The conclusion drawn from the first measure of density forecast (CRPS) is that for Ethereum the case is now the same as the case for Bitcoin by using the RMSE; there is no model significantly better than the benchmark. The reason could be that the density of the forecasts of Ethereum are not following the movement captured by the used models, such that the predictability of Ethereum is low caused by its uncertainty being higher than those of the other cryptocurrencies.

Regarding the density forecast for CRPS, the main conclusion is that including stochastic volatility in the model formulation lead to better results with respect to the benchmark (VAR model) and to GARCH specification. In particular, the inclusion of student-t specification of the errors in the SV models leads to better results and to great improvements for every cryptocurrency. If one includes the cryptopredictors in the analysis, there are not so great improvements except when the errors are student-t specified for stochastic volatility.

Table 6. Differences of PL against benchmark.

Cryptocurrency	Bitcoin	Ethereum	Ripple	Litecoin
BVAR	−3.2676	−3.1777	−3.7552	−3.8476
BVAR-SV vs. BVAR	0.28254	−1.6413 **	−0.030439	−0.17147
BVAR-GARCH vs. BVAR	−0.081207	−0.76657 *	0.27199	0.27338
BVARX vs. BVAR	−0.023045	−0.0085887 *	−0.025829	−0.027074
BVARX-SV vs. BVAR	0.28375	−0.85084 **	0.25762	0.39481
BVARX-GARCH vs. BVAR	0.239	−0.27849	0.3654	0.40684
BVAR-SVt vs. BVAR	0.38974	0.067936	0.59546	0.63765
BVARX-SVt vs. BVAR	0.43121	0.064834	0.55927	0.4663

Notes: (1) The "X" indicates models with the cryptopredictor variables included, the "t" indicates that the student-t distribution is used. (2) For BVAR, the benchmark model, the table reports the PL, for other models it reports the difference between the PL of the current model and the benchmark. Entries greater than 0 indicate that forecasts from current model are more accurate than forecasts from the benchmark model. (3) ** and * indicate PL differences are significantly different from 0 at 5% and 10%, according to the Diebold–Mariano test. (4) Gray cells indicate models that belong to the Superior Set of Models delivered by the Model Confidence Set procedure at confidence level 10%.

The predictive likelihood (PL, or log predictive score (LS)) has some different results compared to the previous measures. At first, the predictive likelihood is very close to each other if one compares the cryptocurrencies, which indicates that the models perform the same for the cryptocurrencies. Only for Ethereum there are models significantly better performing than the VAR. The SV models are in that case the most significant and the GARCH and VAR including the cryptopredictor variables are less significant.

Overall, the model confidence set is as before containing the SV models. However, this time the SV-t models are not in this set, only for Litecoin including the cryptopredictor variables. Litecoin has however almost a full set, only the SV-t model is not in it, thus Litecoin is not following a single model, but can be explained by multiple models. The GARCH models are now in the model confidence set as well, which illustrates that the log score of the forecasts are describable as GARCH movements.

Regarding the density forecast for PL, the main conclusion is that including stochastic volatility in the model formulation leads for Ethereum to better results with respect to the benchmark (VAR model) and to GARCH specification. Contrarily, the CRPS inclusion of the student-t specification of the errors in the SV model lead to no significant better results. If one includes cryptopredictors in the analysis, there are only for Ethereum improvements if there is no student-t specification.

Robustness Check

In this section, we perform the forecasting exercises by including different univariate models. We report the results for different possible benchmark models. We consider the following two univariate models: an autoregressive model with one lag (AR(1)) and an autoregressive model with the first three lags (AR(3)) based on the BIC criterion.

Table 7 reports the point and density forecasting for the AR(1) and AR(3) versus the benchmark model considered in Section 5. All models are run by using the usual Bayesian priors for 5000 iterations. Furthermore, we perform the root mean square error (RMSE) and the CRPS for the four main cryptocurrencies. As stated in Table 7, the results for the point and density forecasting are qualitatively similar to multivariate benchmark case, VAR(3).

Table 7. Point (RMSE) and Density forecasting (CRPS) for Bayesian AR(1), AR(3) and VAR(3).

Models	Bitcoin	Ethereum	Ripple	Litecoin
RMSE				
BAR(1)	4.6033	5.6470	7.5795	6.5794
BAR(3)	4.6069	5.6517	7.5984	6.6076
BVAR(3)	4.6091	5.6996	7.6627	6.7055
CRPS				
BAR(1)	2.4717	3.0790	3.8395	3.4161
BAR(3)	2.4730	3.0809	3.8816	3.4245
BVAR(3)	2.4707	3.1043	3.9479	3.453

6. Conclusions

Recently, cryptocurrencies have attracted attention from researchers and financial institutions due to their importance. In this paper, a comparison of the performance of several models has been investigated to predict four of the most capitalised cryptocurrencies: Bitcoin, Ethereum, Ripple and Litecoin. A set of cryptopredictors is applied and eight model combinations are proposed for combining these predictors. The results show statistically significant improvements in point forecasting for all the cryptocurrencies when using a combination of stochastic volatility and a student-t distribution. In density forecasting for all cryptocurrencies, the stochastic volatility model gives the best predictability. One recommendation for future research is to allow different weights across time and time-varying parameters to improve the point and density forecasting. Moreover, other cryptopredictors based on the dynamics of the cryptomarket might be interesting for modelling.

Author Contributions: The work was equally divided between the two coauthors. The origin and development of the paper was a joint initiative. R.B. focused on collection of data and econometric analysis; L.R. worked on writing results and the working paper.

Funding: This research was supported by the European Union Horizon 2020 research and innovation programme under the Marie Sklodowska-Curie grant agreement No 796902.

Acknowledgments: We thank the editor, two anonymous referees and Lennart Hoogerheide for helpful comments and suggestions to improve this work. Luca Rossini acknowledges financial support from the European Union Horizon 2020 research and innovation programme under the Marie Sklodowska-Curie grant agreement No 796902.

Conflicts of Interest: The authors declare no conflict of interest.

Appendix A. Results

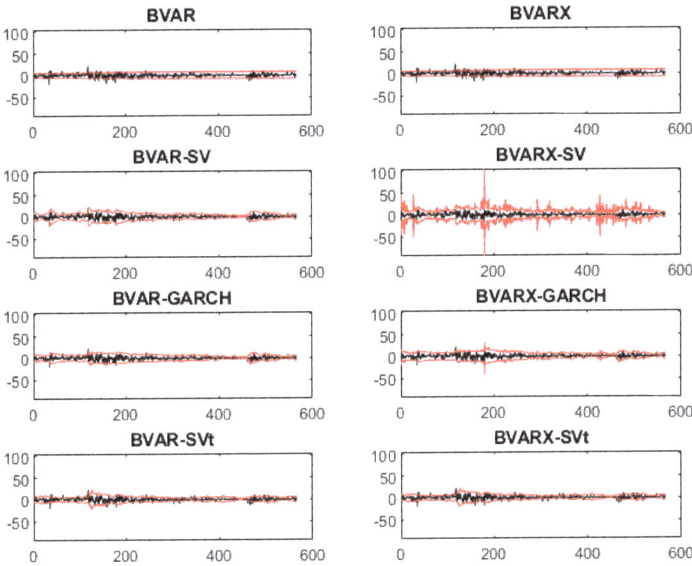

Figure A1. Credible interval for Bitcoin.

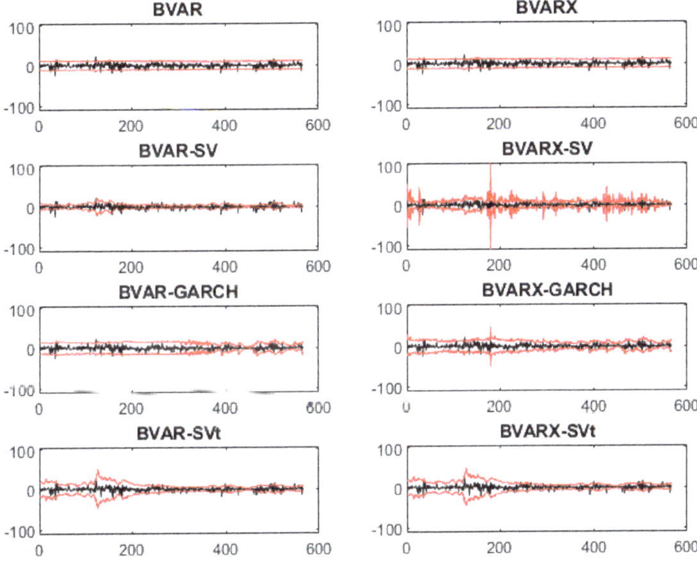

Figure A2. Credible interval for Ethereum.

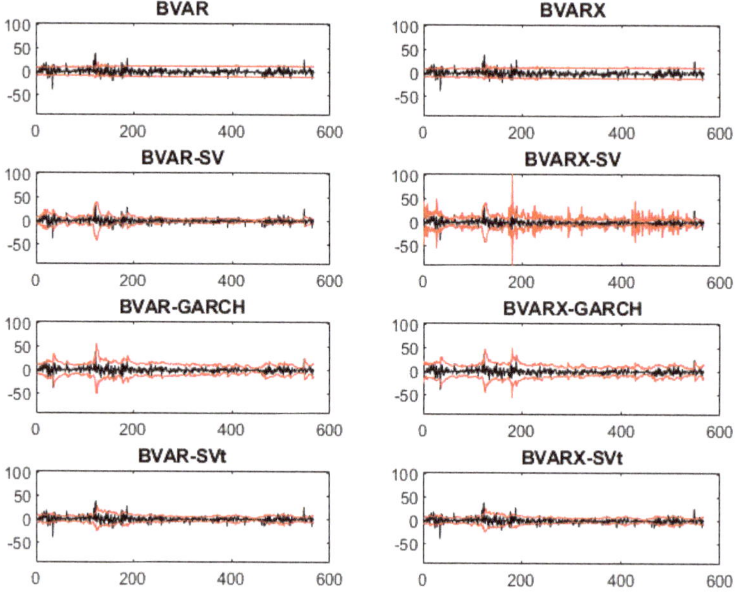

Figure A3. Credible interval for Litecoin.

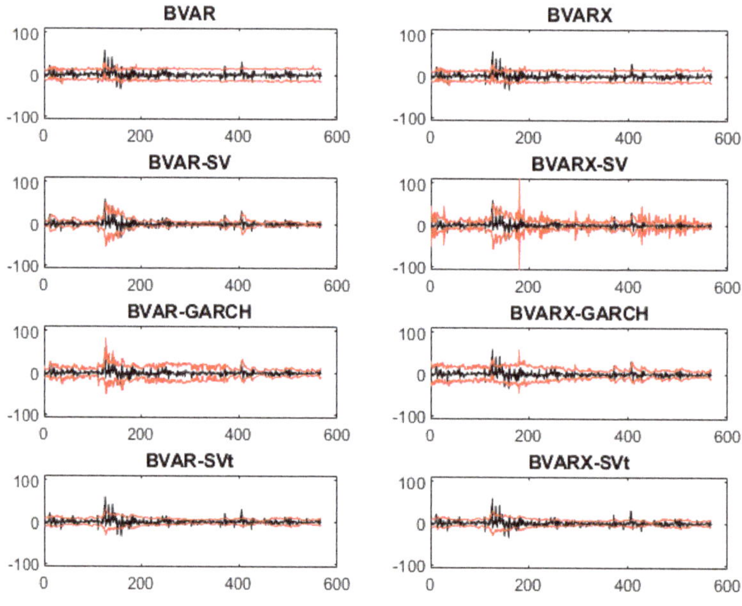

Figure A4. Credible interval for Ripple.

References

Armstrong, J. Scott. 2001. Evaluating Forecasting Methods. In *Principles of Forecasting: A Handbook for Researchers and Practitioners*. Norwell: Kluwer Academic Publishers.

Bernardi, Mauro, and Leopoldo Catania. 2016. Portfolio optimisation under flexible dynamic dependence modelling. *Journal of Empirical Finance* 48: 1–18. [CrossRef]

Bianchi, Daniele. 2018. *Cryptocurrencies as an Asset Class? An Empirical Assessment*. Warwick: WBS Finance Group Research Paper.

Bloomberg. 2017a. Japan's BITpoint to Add Bitcoin Payments to Retail Outlets. Available online: https://www.bloomberg.com/news/articles/2017-05-29/japans-bitpoint-to-add-bitcoin-payments-to-100-000s-of-outlets (accessed on 9 September 2019).

Bloomberg. 2017b. Some Central Banks Are Exploring the Use of Cryptocurrencies. Available online: https://www.bloomberg.com/news/articles/201706-28/rise-of-digital-coins-has-central-banks-considering-eversions (accessed on 9 September 2019).

Bloomberg. 2018. *Big Investors May Be Dragging Bitcoin Toward Market Correlation*. New York: Bloomberg.

Capgemini and BNP Paribas. 2017. World Payments Report 2017. Payments Volume. Available online: https://www.worldpaymentsreport.com/#non-cashpayments-content (accessed on 9 September 2019).

Carnero, M. Angeles, and M. Hakan Eratalay. 2014. Estimating VAR-MGARCH models in multiple steps. *Studies in Nonlinear Dynamics and Econometrics* 18: 339–65. [CrossRef]

Catania, Leopoldo, Stefano Grassi, and Francesco Ravazzolo. 2018. Predicting the volatility of cryptocurrency time-series. In *Mathematical and Statistical Methods for Actuarial Sciences and Finance*. Cham: Springer.

Catania, Leopoldo, Stefano Grassi, and Francesco Ravazzolo. 2019. Forecasting cryptocurrencies under model and parameter instability. *International Joural of Forecasting* 35: 485–501. [CrossRef]

Cheah, Eng-Tuck, and John Fry. 2015. Speculative bubbles in Bitcoin markets? An empirical investigation into the fundamental value of Bitcoin. *Economics Letters* 130: 32–36. [CrossRef]

Christoffersen, Peter F., and Francis X. Diebold. 2006. Financial asset returns, direction-of-change forecasting, and volatility dynamics. *Management Science* 52: 1273–87. [CrossRef]

Chu, Jeffrey, Saralees Nadarajah, and Stephen Chan. 2015. Statistical analysis of the exchange rate of bitcoin. *PLoS ONE* 10: e0133678. [CrossRef] [PubMed]

Clark, Todd E., and Francesco Ravazzolo. 2015. Macroeconomic Forecasting Performance under Alternative Specifications of Time-Varying Volatility. *Journal of Applied Econometrics* 30: 551–75. [CrossRef]

Cointelegraph. 2017. South Korea Officially Legalizes Bitcoin, Huge Market for Traders. Available online: https://cointelegraph.com/news/south-korea-officiallylegalizes-bitcoin-huge-market-for-traders (accessed on 9 September 2019).

D'Agostino, Antonello, Luca Gambetti, and Domenico Giannone. 2013. Macroeconomic forecasting and structural change. *Journal of Applied Econometrics* 28: 82–101. [CrossRef]

Diebold, Francis X., and Robert S. Mariano. 1995. Comparing predictive accuracy. *Journal of Business and Economic Stastistics* 13: 253–63.

Dyhrberg, Anne Haubo. 2016. Hedging capabilities of bitcoin. Is it the virtual Gold? *Finance Research Letters* 16: 139–44. [CrossRef]

Ethereum. 2014. Ethereum Wiki. Available online: https://github.com/ethereum/wiki/wiki/White-Paper/ (accessed on 9 September 2019).

Fernández-Villaverde, Jesús, and Daniel Sanches. 2016. *Can Currency Competition Work?* NBER Working Papers 22157. New York: National Bureau of Economic Research.

Forbes. 2017. Emerging Applications for Blockchain. Available online: https://www.forbes.com/sites/forbestechcouncil/2017/07/18/emerging-applicationsfor-blockchain (accessed on 9 September 2019).

Griffin, John M., and Amin Shams. 2018. *Is Bitcoin Really Un-Tethered?* Technical Report, SSRN Working Paper. Rochester: SSRN.

Hansen, Peter R., Asger Lunde, and James M. Nason. 2011. The model confidence set. *Econometrica* 79: 453–97. [CrossRef]

Hencic, Andrew, and Christian Gouriéroux. 2015. Noncausal Autoregressive Model in Application to Bitcoin/USD Exchange Rates. In *Econometrics of Risk*. Edited by Van-Nam Huynh, Vladik Kreinovich, Songsak Sriboonchitta and Komsan Suriya. Studies in Computational Intelligence. Springer, Cham, vol. 583.

Hotz-Behofsits, Christian, Florian Huber, and Thomas Otto Zörner. 2018. Predicting cryptocurrencies using sparse non–gaussian state space models. *Journal of Forecast* 36: 627–40. [CrossRef]

Johannes, Michael, Arthur Korteweg, and Nicholas Polson. 2014. Sequential learning, predictive regressions, and optimal portfolio returns. *Journal of Finance* 69: 611–44. [CrossRef]

Jolliffe, Ian T., and David B. Stephenson, eds. 2003. *Forecast Verification*. A Practitioner's Guide in Atmospheric Science. Hoboken: John Wiley and Sons Ltd., 240p.

Koop, Gary, and Dimitris Korobilis. 2010. Bayesian Multivariate Time Series Methods for Empirical Macroeconomics. *Foundations and Trends in Econometrics* 3: 267–358. [CrossRef]

Koop, Gary, and Dimitris Korobilis. 2013. Large time-varying parameter VARs. *Journal of Econometrics* 177: 185–98. [CrossRef]

Litecoin. 2014. Litecoin Wiki. Available online: https://litecoin.info/Litecoin/ (accessed on 9 September 2019).

Lütkepohl, Helmut. 2007. *New Introduction to Multiple Time Series Analysis*. Berlin: Springer Publishing Company, Incorporated.

Muglia, Camilla, Luca Santabarbara, and Stefano Grassi. 2019. Is Bitcoin a Relevant Predictor of Standard & Poor's 500? *Journal of Risk and Financial Management* 12: 93.

Nakamoto, Satoshi. 2008. Bitcoin: A Peer-to-Peer Electronic Cash System. Available online: http://citeseerx.ist. psu.edu/viewdoc/summary?doi=10.1.1.221.9986 (accessed on 9 September 2019).

Ripple. 2012. Welcome to Ripple. Available online: https://ripple.com/ (accessed on 9 September 2019).

Sapuric, Svetlana, and Angelika Kokkinaki. 2014. Bitcoin is volatile! Isn't that right? Paper presented at Business Information Systems Workshops, Larnaca, Cyprus, May 22–23, pp. 255–65.

Sims, Christopher A. 1980. Macroeconomics and Reality. *Econometrica* 48: 1–48. [CrossRef]

Sims, Christopher A., and Tao Zha. 2006. Were there regime switches in US monetary policy? *American Economic Review* 96: 54–81. [CrossRef]

Stavroyiannis, Stavros, Vassilios Babalos, Stelios Bekiros, Salim Lahmiri, and Gazi Salah Uddin. 2019. The high frequency multifractal properties of Bitcoin. *Physica A: Statistical Mechanics and its Applications 1873–2119* 520: 62–71. [CrossRef]

Yermack, David. 2015. *Is Bitcoin a real currency? An Economic appraisal*. New York: NYU—Stern School of Business.

Journal of
Risk and Financial Management

Article

Is Bitcoin a Relevant Predictor of Standard & Poor's 500?

Camilla Muglia, Luca Santabarbara and Stefano Grassi *

Department of Economics and Finance, University of Rome 'Tor Vergata', Via Columbia 2, 00133 Rome, Italy;
camilla.muglia@gmail.com (C.M.); luca-santa@hotmail.it (L.S.)
* Correspondence: stefano.grassi@uniroma2.it

Received: 14 May 2019; Accepted: 17 May 2019; Published: 31 May 2019

Abstract: The paper investigates whether Bitcoin is a good predictor of the Standard & Poor's 500 Index. To answer this question we compare alternative models using a point and density forecast relying on Dynamic Model Averaging (DMA) and Dynamic Model Selection (DMS). According to our results, Bitcoin does not show any direct impact on the predictability of Standard & Poor's 500 for the considered sample.

Keywords: cryptocurrency; Bitcoin; forecasting; point forecast; density forecast; dynamic model averaging; dynamic model selection; forgetting factors

---

1. Introduction

The idea of cryptocurrency and the related technology, Blockchain, was suggested in 2009 by an anonymous user known as Satoshi Nakamoto. He posted a paper to a cryptographic mailing list introducing a new electronic cash system with very low transaction costs able to avoid the presence of a central bank: the Bitcoin, see Nakamoto (2009). In the last ten years, cryptocurrencies have become more and more popular among researchers and investors, with around 2000 cryptocurrencies available at the time of writing. In recent months, the Bitcoin has experienced a dramatic price increase and consequently, the global interest in cryptocurrencies has spiked substantially. Despite the price increase, there are other numerous reasons for this intensified interest, just to mention a few: Japan and South Korea have recognised Bitcoin as a legal method of payment (Bloomberg 2017a; Cointelegraph 2017); some central banks are exploring the use of the cryptocurrencies (Bloomberg 2017b); a large number of companies and banks created the Enterprise Ethereum Alliance[1] to make use of the cryptocurrencies and the related technology called blockchain (Forbes 2017). Finally, the Chicago Mercantile Exchange (CME) started the Bitcoin futures on 18 December 2017, see Group (2017), Nasdaq and the Tokyo Financial Exchange will follow, see Bloomberg (2017b).

Although Bitcoin is a relatively new currency, there have already been some studies on this topic: Hencic and Gourieroux (2015) applied a non-causal autoregressive model to detect the presence of bubbles in the Bitcoin/USD exchange rate. The study of Cheah and Fry (2015) focused on the same issue. Fernández-Villaverde and Sanches (2016) analysed the existence of price equilibria among privately issued fiat currencies and Yermack (2015) wondered whether the cryptocurrency can be considered a real currency. Sapuric and Kokkinaki (2014) measured the volatility of the Bitcoin exchange rate against six major currencies. Chu et al. (2015) provided a statistical analysis of the log–returns of the exchange rate of Bitcoin versus the USD. Catania and Grassi (2018) analysed the main characteristics of cryptocurrency volatility.

---

[1] Source: https://entethalliance.org/members/.

Moreover Bianchi (2018) tried to investigate some of the key features of cryptocurrency returns and volatilities, such as their relationship with traditional asset classes, as well as the main driving factors behind the market activity. He found that returns on cryptocurrencies are moderately correlated with commodities and a few more assets.

Other studies have analyzed cryptocurrency manipulation and predictability. For instance, Hotz-Behofsits et al. (2018) applied a time-varying parameter VAR with t-distributed measurement errors and stochastic volatility. Griffin and Shams (2018) investigated whether Tether (another cryptocurrency backed by USD) is directly manipulating the price of Bitcoin, increasing its predictability. Catania et al. (2019) studied cryptocurrencies' predictability using several alternative univariate and multivariate models. They found statistically significant improvements in point forecasting when using combinations of univariate models and in density forecasting when relying on a selection of multivariate models.

Many institutions tried to investigate the relationship between Bitcoin and the stock market. In some articles, it was speculated that the Bitcoin can improve stock market's predictability, in this case, Bitcoin could be used as a leading indicator. In an article by Bloomberg (2018), Morgan Stanley's analysts stated that "big investors may be dragging Bitcoin toward Market correlation": the increasing risk of this cryptocurrency may have had an attraction for investors who were seeking for high gains. Stavroyiannis and Babalos (2019) examine the dynamic properties of Bitcoin and the Standard & Poor's 500 (S&P500) index. They study whether Bitcoin can be classified as a possible hedge, diversifier, or safe-haven with respect to the US markets. They found that it does not hold any of the hedge, diversifier, or safe-haven properties and it exhibits intrinsic attributes not related to US markets.

To the best of our knowledge, there are still no studies to confirm that Bitcoin is a good stock market predictor. This paper tries to fill this gap, analyzing whether Bitcoin could be used as a leading indicator for the S&P500.

To answer this question, we allow for parameter and model uncertainty, avoiding Markov Chain Monte Carlo (MCMC) estimation at the same time. This is accomplished using the forgetting factors methodology (also known as discount factors) which have been recently proposed by Raftery et al. (2010) and found to be useful in economic and financial applications, see Dangl and Halling (2012) and Koop and Korobilis (2012) (KK). Another advantage of this methodology is to provide, in close form, both the marginal and predictive likelihood (PL), which are useful in model selection.

The rest of the paper proceeds as follows: Section 2 presents the general model and the estimation strategy; Section 3 presents the Dataset; Section 4 discusses the empirical results; finally, Section 5 reports some conclusions.

2. Models and Estimation Strategy

Let $\mathbf{y}_t \equiv (y_1, \ldots, y_t)'$ denote the time series of interest and $\mathbf{x}_t \equiv (x_1, \ldots, x_t)'$ the series of exogenous variables, then the model can be written as:

$$
\begin{aligned}
y_t &= \mathbf{z}_t \gamma_t + \varepsilon_t, & \varepsilon_t &\sim \mathrm{N}(0, \mathrm{H}_t), \\
\gamma_t &= \gamma_{t-1} + \eta_t, & \beta_t &\sim \mathrm{N}(0, \mathrm{Q}_t),
\end{aligned}
\tag{1}
$$

where $\mathbf{y}_t$ is a scalar representing the observed time series at time t, $\mathbf{z}_t = \{y_{t-1}, \ldots, y_{t-p}, x_{t-1}, \ldots, x_{t-q}\}$ is a $1 \times m$ vector ($m = p + q$) stacking all the lags of the series of interest and of the exogenous variable; $\gamma_t = \{\gamma_{1,t}, \ldots, \gamma_{j,t}\}$ is an $m \times 1$ vector containing the time varying states γs, which are assumed to follow a random-walk dynamic. Finally, the errors, ε_t and β_t, are assumed to be mutually independent at all leads and lags. The H_t contains the time-varying volatilities of the series. The state space model (SSM) of Equation (1) has been used in several recent papers, see among others, Primiceri (2005) and Koop and Korobilis (2012).

In order to estimate the quantities of interest, maximum likelihood or Bayesian estimation based on MCMC can be used. However, these two estimation approaches end up being computationally complex and, most of the time, infeasible. To reduce the computational burden, KK proposed two main adjustments to the usual MCMC.

The first is to replace the variance-covariance matrix Q_t with an approximation. Latent states—γ_t—can then be obtained with a closed-form expression avoiding maximum likelihood or MCMC, see Supplementary Materials. The second adjustment is to replace the measurement error variance matrix H_t with an Exponential Weighted Moving Average (EWMA) type filter.

As discussed in Supplementary Materials, this methodology requires the specification of the hyperparameters λ, α and κ and the specification of the initial condition of the states γ_0 and Σ_0. Refer to KK for an extensive discussion of the problem.

3. Dataset Description

Table 1 reports the dataset used for the analysis, with the transformation and the data source. The sample goes from 11 August 2015 to 19 July 2018 and consists of 740 daily observations. The crypto–market is open 24 h a day, seven days a week; hence, for computing returns we use the closing price at midnight (UTC). As discussed in Catania et al. (2019), the data are available from https://coinmarketcap.com/ with daily frequency; unfortunately, hourly data that could allow for a more precise analysis are not freely available. To investigate non-stationary issues, three Unit-Root tests have been performed: Augmented Dickey-Fuller (ADF) Test, Philips-Perron (PP) Test and Kwiatkowsky, Phillips, Schmidt and Shin (KPSS) Test. All of them confirm the stationarity of each transformed series, results are available from the authors upon request.

Table 1. Data overview and transformation. The table reports the series divided by type, Financial predictors, Commodity predictors and Crypto predictors. The series are available for the period 11 August 2015 to 19 July 2018. For each variable the table reports the abbreviation code, the full name, the data source and the transformation applied.

Code	Full Name	Transformation	Data Source
Analyzed serie			
S&P500	Standard & Poor's 500	Log-First-Difference	Thomson Reuters Eikon
Financial predictors			
EF300	FTSEuroFirst300	Log-First-Difference	Thomson Reuters Eikon
NASDAQ	Nasdaq 100 Index	Log-First-Difference	Thomson Reuters Eikon
VIX	CBOE Market Volatility Index	Log-First-Difference	Thomson Reuters Eikon
1mUS	1-month US Treasury Constant Maturity Rate	First-Difference	Federal Reserve System
10yUS	10-years US Treasury Constant Maturity Rate	First-Difference	Federal Reserve System
Commodity predictors			
OIL	ICE Brent Crude Eletronic Energy Future	Log-First-Difference	Thomson Reuters Eikon
GOLD	SPDR Gold Shares	Log-First-Difference	Thomson Reuters Eikon
Crypto predictors			
BTC	Bitcoin	Log-First-Difference	Coinmarketcap
BHL	Bitcoin High minus Bitcoin Low	Log	Coinmarketcap

Figure 1 reports Bitcoin closing price (BTC) which shows a steep rise in 2017 reaching the value of almost 20,000 US dollars in December 2017. This ascending trend was severely interrupted at the beginning of 2018, when price quickly dropped down to $6000. At the time of writing, BTC's price is fluctuating between 5000 and 6000 dollars.

The series reported in Table 1 are divided in: financial predictors, such as VIX; commodity predictors, such as GOLD and crypto predictors such as BTC. Among the financial predictors, the VIX, see Figure S1 in Supplementary Materials (Panel (c)), is the most volatile, as expected. It displays a very steep peak between January and February 2018, the same period in which BTC's price started to fall.

Table S1 in Supplementary Materials reports the correlation matrix of the predictors. As the table shows the BTC appears to be highly positively correlated with all the financial indexes: S&P500, EF300 and NASDAQ.

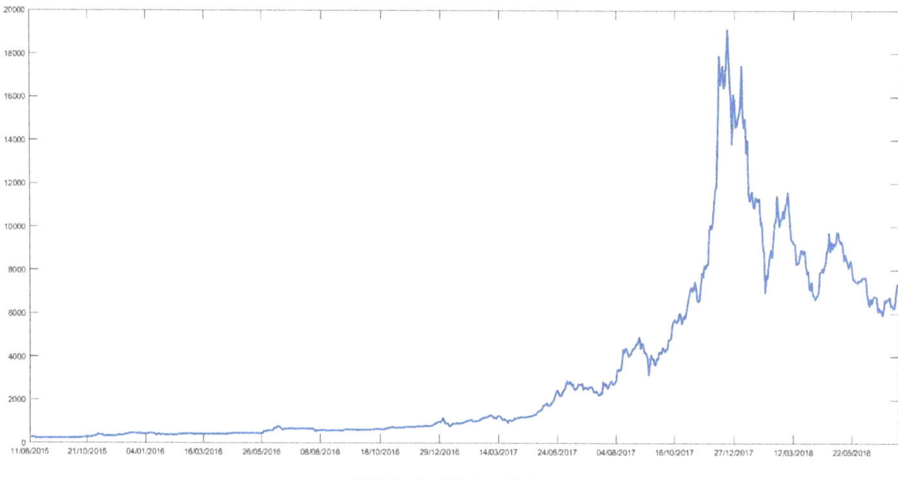

BTC Daily Closing Price

Figure 1. The figure reports the Bitcoin (BTC) closing price from August 2015 to July 2018. The plot clearly shows the steep rise in the price 2017 and the sharp drop in 2018.

4. Analysis

The out-of-sample period begins on 1st September 2016 and the forecast horizon ranges from $h = 1$ to $h = 7$ days ahead. The analysis compares the performances of two models: the first—M_1—includes all the predictors: financial, commodity and crypto predictors, see Table 1. The second, M_2, excludes crypto predictors. The benchmark model, denoted with M_0, is an ARMA(1,1)-GARCH(1,1) model. M_1 and M_2 can suffer from massive model uncertainty due to the number of possible predictor's combination at each time point t. For example, M_1 has $2^9 = 512$ models at each point in time. To mitigate this fact, we use the DMA and DMS as described in Koop and Korobilis (2012) and reported in Supplementary Materials. As already mentioned, the methodology requires fixing three hyperparameters: the forgetting factor λ for the parameter variation; the decay factor κ for the EWMA; and, finally, the discount weight α that weights each model based on forecast performances.

The results reported in this section are based on $\kappa = 0.94$. This value suits daily data, see Riskmetrics (1996) and Prado and West (2010). The other parameters are set to $\alpha = 0.99$ and $\lambda = 0.99$, coherently with Raftery et al. (2010). In Section 4.2 a robustness analysis for the forgetting factors α and λ is carried out. Moreover, we also tried to optimize at each time point λ_t using a standard data-driven approach minimizing the expected prediction error. Unfortunately, the optimized λ_t with crypto time series seems to be very unstable; we leave this issue as a topic of further research.

The analysis begins with the investigation of the posterior inclusion probabilities of each predictor: the higher the probability the higher the predictor's influence over the dependent variable. Figure 2 depicts the posterior probabilities of BTC (Panel (a)), and of BHL (Panel (b)). Time-varying posterior probabilities of inclusion for the other exogenous variables are reported in Supplementary Materials.

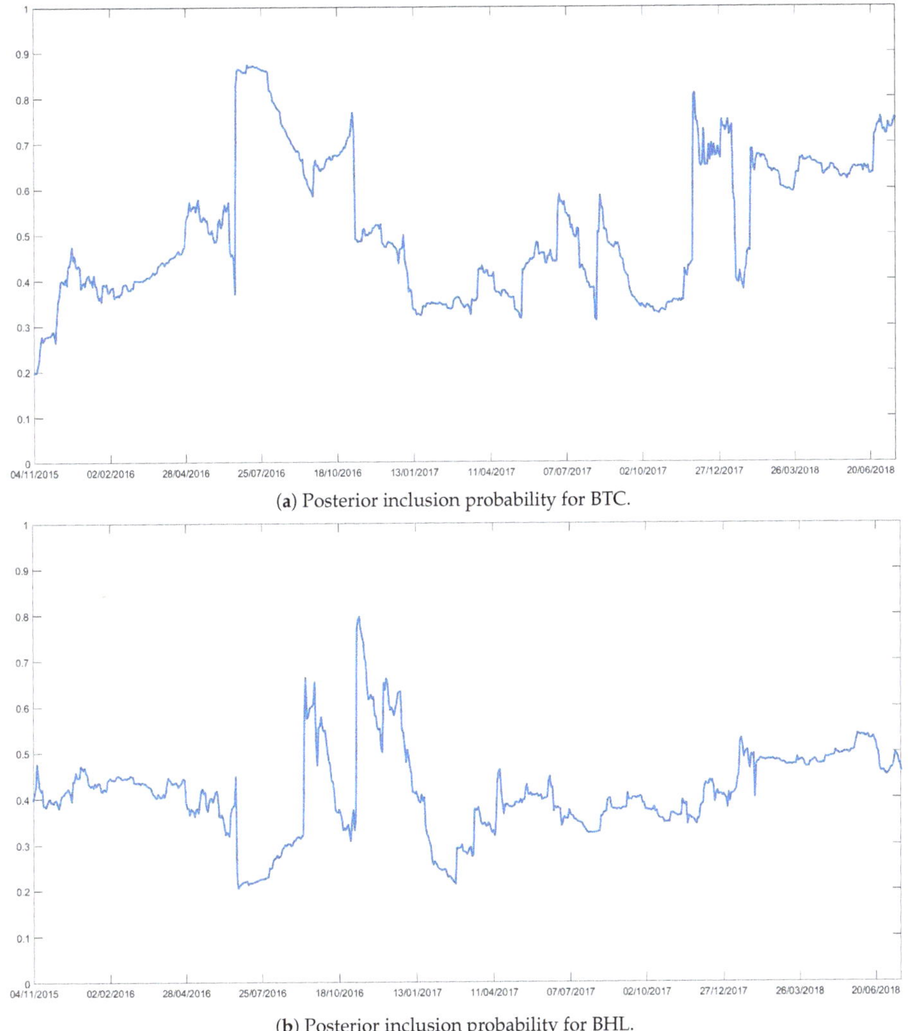

(**a**) Posterior inclusion probability for BTC.

(**b**) Posterior inclusion probability for BHL.

Figure 2. Posterior inclusion probabilities. Panel (**a**) shows posterior inclusion probability for BTC. Panel (**b**) shows posterior inclusion probability for BHL.

The figures show that the importance of each predictor switches rapidly over time, with a high inclusion probability of BTC in some specific periods. One important change is in 2016 when the inclusion probability suddenly jumped from 0.5 to 0.9 increasing the correlation with the S&P500 and potentially its role as a leading indicator.

After a calm period during 2017, the BTC gained importance once again at the end of the same year with a steep rise in price. During this period, a lot of articles pointed out a correlation between BTC and financial markets. Bloomberg (2018) stated that "big investors may be dragging Bitcoin toward market correlation" and see BTC as an asset which guarantees the highest potential risk/return combination in the market. This may have attracted the interest of big investors able to move huge amounts of funds and consequently correlate BTC to the USA stock market. Another article by Cointelegraph (2018) asserted that BTC might be correlated with VIX, but there is no evidence that it may influence the

S&P500 index. An extensive analysis of the latter issue is carried out in the next sections using point and density forecast.

4.1. Forecast Metrics

To assess the leading property of BTC we use point and density forecast. For the point forecasts, we use the mean absolute forecast error (MAFE) for each forecast horizon, $h = 1, \ldots, 7$:

$$\text{MAFE}_h = \frac{1}{T - R} \sum_{t=R}^{T-h} \left| \hat{y}_{i,t+h|t} - y_{i,t+h} \right|, \tag{2}$$

where T is the number of observations, R is the length of the rolling window, $\hat{y}_{t+h|t}$ is the S&P500 forecast made at time t for horizon h and y_{t+h} is the realization.

To evaluate the density forecasts, we use predictive log score (LS) that is commonly viewed as the broadest measure of density accuracy, see Geweke and Amisano (2010). As for the MAFE, we compute the LS for each horizon:

$$s_h(y_i) = \sum_{t=R}^{T-h} \ln \left(f(y_{t+h}|I_t) \right), \tag{3}$$

where $f(y_{t+h}|I_t)$ is the predictive density for y_{t+h} constructed using information up to time t.

We report the MAFEs and the LSs as a ratio of each model's with respect to the baseline. Entries smaller than 1 indicate that a given model yields forecasts that are more accurate than those from the baseline and differences in score relative to the baseline, such as a negative number, indicates a model that beats the baseline. In order to statistically assess the differences between alternative models, we apply the Diebold and Mariano (1995) test for equality of the average loss (with loss defined as squared error and negative log score) of each model versus the ARMA(1,1)-GARCH(1,1) benchmark and we also employ the Model Confidence Set procedure of Hansen et al. (2011) using the R package MCS detailed in Bernardi and Catania (2016) to jointly compare all predictions. Differences are tested separately for each forecast horizon.

4.2. Point Forecast

Point forecast is evaluated through MAFE for both DMA and DMS as well as for their special case, Bayesian Model Averaging (BMA). For each forecast horizon, the errors are calculated using the following combination of forgetting and discount factors: $\lambda = \alpha = 0.99$, $\lambda = \alpha = 0.95$, $\lambda = 1$ and $\alpha = 0.99$, $\lambda = 0.99$ and $\alpha = 1$, and finally $\lambda = \alpha = 1$. In all the cases, the decay factor is fixed to $\kappa = 0.94$.

Table 2 compares point forecast for M_1 and M_2 as a ratio M_0 (top) and against M_0 (bottom). From the upper table, it emerges that the errors are increasing in accordance with the forecast horizon. Moreover, when h increases, the ratio increases, meaning that the benchmark model displays better results than DMA and DMS. Table S8 in Supplementary Materials B shows that increasing the forecasting horizon to $h = 10$ does not improve the forecasting performance of M_1 and M_2. However, Section 4.3, which analyses density forecasts results, reveals different outcomes.

Another peculiarity is that forecasts improve when α and λ tend to 1. When $\alpha = \lambda = 0.95$ we get the worst forecast performance for DMA and DMS, while the best results are obtained with BMA. This may be due to the nature of the series: the presence of outliers and high peaks in BTC series may distort the point forecast.

To see if BTC improves predictability over the S&P 500 a DM test is performed with a level of significance equal to $\alpha = 95\%$. Results are reported in Supplementary Materials Table S2. There is no evidence of an improvement in prediction when the BTC is added to the set of predictors. Further results for different forecast horizons are reported in Supplementary Materials.

Using point forecast it seems that BTC does not improve predictability over the S&P 500 index.

Table 2. Point forecast: M_1 vs. M_0 top table and M_2 vs. M_0 bottom table. Results are reported as the ratio between the model considered over the benchmark. From both the tables it emerges that the simplest model, the ARMA(1,1)-GARCH(1,1), forecasts better than both DMA and DMS.

M_1 vs. M_0

		DMA	DMS	DMA	DMS	DMA	DMS	DMA	DMS	BMA
		$\lambda = 0.99$	$\lambda = 0.99$	$\lambda = 0.95$	$\lambda = 0.95$	$\lambda = 0.99$	$\lambda = 0.99$	$\lambda = 1$	$\lambda = 1$	$\lambda = 1$
		$\alpha = 0.99$	$\alpha = 0.99$	$\alpha = 0.95$	$\alpha = 0.95$	$\alpha = 1$	$\alpha = 1$	$\alpha = 0.99$	$\alpha = 0.99$	$\alpha = 1$
$\kappa = 0.94$										
$h = 1$	MAFE	1.006	1.000	1.063	1.089	1.013	1.011	1.014	1.013	1.026
$h = 2$	MAFE	1.388	1.392	1.474	1.467	1.393	1.402	1.403	1.403	1.408
$h = 3$	MAFE	1.651	1.668	1.760	1.798	1.651	1.659	1.667	1.655	1.658
$h = 4$	MAFE	1.903	1.904	2.104	2.133	1.913	1.916	1.920	1.917	1.934
$h = 5$	MAFE	2.121	2.125	2.368	2.401	2.118	2.118	2.151	2.150	2.188
$h = 6$	MAFE	2.285	2.280	2.499	2.528	2.287	2.287	2.369	2.358	2.366
$h = 7$	MAFE	2.481	2.466	2.699	2.702	2.483	2.482	2.619	2.621	2.611

M_2 vs. M_0

		DMA	DMS	DMA	DMS	DMA	DMS	DMA	DMS	BMA
		$\lambda = 0.99$	$\lambda = 0.99$	$\lambda = 0.95$	$\lambda = 0.95$	$\lambda = 0.99$	$\lambda = 0.99$	$\lambda = 1$	$\lambda = 1$	$\lambda = 1$
		$\alpha = 0.99$	$\alpha = 0.99$	$\alpha = 0.95$	$\alpha = 0.95$	$\alpha = 1$	$\alpha = 1$	$\alpha = 0.99$	$\alpha = 0.99$	$\alpha = 1$
$\kappa = 0.94$										
$h = 1$	MAFE	1.002	1.000	1.059	1.065	1.013	1.011	1.017	1.015	1.039
$h = 2$	MAFE	1.386	1.387	1.462	1.460	1.391	1.390	1.403	1.402	1.403
$h = 3$	MAFE	1.652	1.663	1.752	1.782	1.655	1.661	1.669	1.657	1.670
$h = 4$	MAFE	1.904	1.910	2.112	2.128	1.908	1.910	1.917	1.914	1.923
$h = 5$	MAFE	2.123	2.131	2.367	2.399	2.110	2.109	2.159	2.159	2.154
$h = 6$	MAFE	2.288	2.289	2.506	2.527	2.291	2.295	2.385	2.374	2.386
$h = 7$	MAFE	2.482	2.473	2.692	2.687	2.483	2.483	2.618	2.613	2.614

4.3. Density Forecast

Density forecast is more informative than point forecast, as it is a measure of the prediction uncertainty. The PL, which is the basis of density forecast, comes as a by-product of the adopted estimation strategy. Table 3 reports the LS: the evidence is striking and the results are almost opposite to those in Section 4.2. Both M_1 and M_2 provide statistically superior forecasts with respect to M_0.

Table 3. Log Score (LS), computed over the forecast horizon. Results are reported relative to the benchmark specification (ARMA(1,1)-GARCH(1,1)) for which the absolute score is reported. Values in **bold** indicate rejection of the null hypothesis of Equal Predictive Ability between each model and the benchmark according to the Diebold-Mariano test at the 5% confidence level. Grey cells indicate those models that belong to the Superior Set of Models delivered by the Model Confidence Set procedure at confidence level 10%. As the table shows, the difference between M_1 and M_2 is very poor.

Days Ahead	M_0	$M_1 - M_0$	$M_2 - M_0$
$h = 1$	-1659.997	$\mathbf{-1023.949}$	-1024.600
$h = 2$	-1651.352	-1767.424	$\mathbf{-1763.904}$
$h = 3$	-1647.144	-2188.181	$\mathbf{-2187.612}$
$h = 4$	-1643.063	$\mathbf{-2496.529}$	-2498.355
$h = 5$	-1639.526	$\mathbf{-2733.322}$	-2740.850
$h = 6$	-1636.366	-2930.505	$\mathbf{-2927.831}$
$h = 7$	-1631.968	-3097.841	$\mathbf{-3093.876}$

The first column reports the PL for the benchmark model (M_0), and the other columns report the differences of M_1 and M_2 with respect to the benchmark. Among the three models, M_0 shows the worst results in contrast with the results of Section 4.2. The best forecast result is obtained for M_1 when $h = 1$; however, the difference between M_1 and M_2 is almost irrelevant. Following the same strategy previously adopted the DM test is carried out, with a significance level of 95%.

The DM statistics, equal to -2.236, suggest that the null hypothesis of equal forecasting ability is rejected. As discussed in Harvey et al. (1997), the DM test could be over-sized when the forecast horizon is greater than one, so in those cases, we used the modified test given by:

$$S_1^* = \left[\frac{P + 1 - 2h + P^{-1}h(h-1)}{P}\right]^{1/2} S_1,$$

where S_1 is the original statistics, h is the forecast horizon, P is the forecast evaluation period. The modified version of DM test maintains the same null hypothesis of equal forecasting ability. Whereas, the alternative is that model M_2 is more accurate than model M_1.

H_1 is accepted in this case since the test shows a very high p-value (0.987). In other words, model M_2 is performing better than M_1 in terms of forecasting. Finally, the MCS indicates that DMS and DMA has similar performance across horizons and they are both superior to the benchmark.

Therefore, the density forecast shows a different outcome to that of the point forecast. While the benchmark model performs better than DMA and DMS in terms of MAFEs, the opposite is true when the density forecast is considered. DMA and DMS give much better predictions for the S&P 500 when the PL is considered.

The main goal of the paper is to understand whether BTC can be assumed to be a good predictor for the S&P 500. Point forecast does not give any contribution to answering this question. A more precise result is reached when the density forecast is used. Even though the PL are close to each other, it has been found that the model that excludes the BTC related series outperforms the one that includes them at lag one. For the other lags, the results are mixed and almost all the models are included in the MCS without a clear superior model. This indicates that BTC does not seem to improve the predictability of the S&P 500 index.

Table S9 in Supplementary Materials reports the results for $\alpha = \lambda = 0.99$ and $\kappa = 0.94$ when the Dow Jones (DJ) index is substituted to S&P500. It emerges that, using DJ, the BTC improves the result of both point and density forecast for shorter horizon (one or two days ahead). These results are promising and carrying out an extensive analysis for different markets is a topic for further research.

5. Conclusions

This work investigates whether BTC can be used as a leading indicator for the S&P500 index. We use the methodologies recently introduced by Raftery et al. (2010), which allow the predictor's weight to change dynamically over time. The study is based on two distinct models: the first—M_1—includes all the predictors; the second—M_2—excludes the crypto-predictors. The benchmark model—M_0—is estimated using an ARMA(1,1)-GARCH(1,1).

The forecasting analysis is based on both point and density forecast. Results coming from the point forecast are not very satisfactory: the M_0 outperforms both M_1 and M_2. Density forecast provides a totally different outcome: M_1 and M_2 strongly outperform M_0. Unfortunately, in this case, the DM and the MCS do not give clear evidence about which of the two models is the best. Accordingly, from our results we can conclude that BTC does not show any predictive power over the S&P500 index. In the coming years, cryptocurrencies will surely receive more and more consideration and there is the possibility that our result may be disavowed.

Supplementary Materials: The supplementary materials are available online at http://www.mdpi.com/1911-8074/12/2/93/s1.

Author Contributions: Conceptualization, C.M., L.S. and S.G.; methodology, S.G.; software, C.M., L.S. and S.G.; validation, S.G.; formal analysis, C.M., L.S. and S.G.; investigation, C.M. and L.S.; data curation, C.M. and L.S.; writing—original draft preparation, C.M. and L.S.; writing—review and editing, S.G.; supervision, S.G.; project administration, S.G.

Funding: This research received no external funding.

Acknowledgments: We thank Francesco Ravazzolo for helpful comments.

Conflicts of Interest: The authors declare no conflict of interest.

References

Bernardi, Mauro, and Leopoldo Catania. 2016. Portfolio Optimisation under Flexible Dynamic Dependence Modelling. *Journal of Empirical Finance* 48: 1–18. [CrossRef]

Bianchi, Daniele. 2018. *Cryptocurrencies as an Asset Class? An Empirical Assessment*. Technical Report, SSRN Working Paper. Rochester: SSRN.

Bloomberg. 2017a. Japan's BITPoint to Add Bitcoin Payments to Retail Outlets. Available online: https://www.bloomberg.com/news/articles/2017-05-29/japan-s-bitpoint-to-add-bitcoin-payments-to-100-000s-of-outlets (accessed on 29 May 2017).

Bloomberg. 2017b. Some Central Banks Are Exploring the Use of Cryptocurrencies. Available online: https://www.bloomberg.com/news/articles/2017-06-28/rise-of-digital-coins-has-central-banks-considering-e-versions (accessed on 28 June 2017).

Bloomberg. 2018. Big Investors May Be Dragging Bitcoin Toward Market Correlation. Available online: https://www.bloomberg.com/news/articles/2018-02-07/big-investors-may-be-dragging-bitcoin-toward-market-correlation (accessed on 7 February 2018).

Catania, Leopoldo, and Stefano Grassi. 2018. *Modelling Crypto-Currencies Financial Time Series*. Technical Report, CEIS Working Paper. Glasgow: CEIS.

Catania, Leopoldo, Stefano Grassi, and Francesco Ravazzolo. 2019. Forecasting Cryptocurrencies under Model and Parameter Instability. *International Journal of Forecasting* 35: 485–501. [CrossRef]

Cheah, Eng-Tuck, and John Fry. 2015. Speculative bubbles in Bitcoin markets? An empirical investigation into the fundamental value of Bitcoin. *Economics Letters* 130: 32–37. [CrossRef]

Chu, Jeffrey, Saralee Nadarajah, and Stephen Chan. 2015. Statistical Analysis of the Exchange Rate of Bitcoin. *PLoS ONE* 10: e0133678. [CrossRef] [PubMed]

CME Group. 2017. CME Group Announces Launch of Bitcoin Futures. Available online: http://www.cmegroup.com/media-room/press-releases/2017/10/31/cme_group_announceslaunchofbitcoinfutures.html (accessed on 31 October 2017).

Cointelegraph. 2017. South Korea Officially Legalizes Bitcoin, Huge Market for Traders. Available online: https://cointelegraph.com/news/south-korea-officially-legalizes-bitcoin-huge-market-for-traders (accessed on 21 July 2017).

Cointelegraph. 2018. So Is There a Correlation Between Bitcoin and Stock Market? Yes, but No. Available online: https://cointelegraph.com/news/so-is-there-a-correlation-between-bitcoin-and-stock-market-yes-but-no (accessed on 13 February 2018).

Dangl, Thomas, and Mark Halling. 2012. Predictive Regressions with Time-Varying Coefficients. *Journal of Financial Econometrics* 106: 157–81. [CrossRef]

Diebold, Francis, and Roberto Mariano. 1995. Comparing Predictive Accuracy. *Journal of Business and Economic Stastistics* 13: 253–63.

Fernández-Villaverde, Jesus, and Daniel Sanches. 2016. *Can Currency Competition Work?* NBER Working Papers 22157. New York: National Bureau of Economic Research.

Forbes. 2017. Emerging Applications for Blockchain. Available online: https://www.forbes.com/sites/forbestechcouncil/2017/07/18/emerging-applications-for-blockchain (accessed on 15 March 2012).

Geweke, John, and Gianni Amisano. 2010. Comparing and Evaluating Bayesian Predictive Distributions of Asset Returns. *International Journal of Forecasting* 26: 216–30. [CrossRef]

Griffin, Jonh, and Amin Shams. 2018. *Is Bitcoin Really Un-Tethered?* Technical Report, SSRN Working Paper. Rochester: SSRN.

Hansen, Peter, Asger Lunde, and James Nason. 2011. The Model Confidence Set. *Econometrica* 79: 453–97. [CrossRef]

Harvey, David, Leybourne, Stephen, and Paul Newbold. 1997. Testing the equality of prediction mean squared errors. *International Journal of Forecasting* 13: 281–91. [CrossRef]

Hencic, Andrew, and Christian Gourieroux. 2015. Noncausal Autoregressive Model in Application to Bitcoin/USD Exchange Rate. In *Econometrics of Risk. Studies in Computational Intelligence*. Edited by Van-Nam Huynh, Vladik Kreinovich, Songsak Sriboonchitta and Komsan Suriya. Cham: Springer, vol. 583.

Hotz-Behofsits, Christian, Florian Huber, and Thomas Zorner. 2018. Predicting Crypto-currencies Using Sparse Non-Gaussian State Space Models. *Journal of Statistical Software* 37: 627–40. [CrossRef]

Koop, Gary, and Dimitris Korobilis. 2012. Forecasting Inflation Using Dynamic Model Averaging. *International Economic Review* 53: 867–86. [CrossRef]

Nakamoto, Satoshi. 2009. Bitcoin: A Peer-to-Peer Electronic Cash System. Available online: https://Bitcoin.org/Bitcoin.pdf (accessed on 31 October 2008).

Prado, Raquel, and Mike West. 2010. *Time Series: Modeling, Computation, and Inference.* Boca Raton: CRC Press.

Primiceri, Giorgio 2005. Time Varying Structural Vector Autoregressions and Monetary Policy. *Review of Economic Studies* 72: 821–52. [CrossRef]

Raftery, Adrian. E., Miroslav Kárnỳ, and Pavel Ettler. 2010. Online Prediction under Model Uncertainty via Dynamic Model Averaging: Application to a Cold Rolling Mill. *Technometrics* 52: 52–66. [CrossRef] [PubMed]

Riskmetrics. 1996. *Riskmetrics—Technical Document*, 4th ed. Technical Report. New York: J.P. Morgan/Reuters.

Sapuric, Svetlana, and Angelika Kokkinaki. 2014. Bitcoin is Volatile! Isn't That Right? Paper presented at the Business information Systems Workshops, Larnaca, Cyprus, May 22–23.

Stavroyiannis, Stavros, and Vassilios Babalos. 2019. *Dynamic Properties of the Bitcoin and the US Market.* Technical Report. Rochester: SSRN.

Yermack, David 2015. Is Bitcoin a Real Currency? An Economic Appraisal. In *Handbook of Digital Currency—Bitcoin, Innovation, Financial Instruments, and Big Data.* Cambridge: Academic Press, pp. 31–43.

Journal of
Risk and Financial Management

Article

Optimism in Financial Markets: Stock Market Returns and Investor Sentiments

Chiara Limongi Concetto [1,2] **and Francesco Ravazzolo** [1,3,*]

[1] Faculty of Economics and Management, Free University of Bozen-Bolzano, 39100 Bolzano, Italy; Chiara.Limongi@economics.unibz.it
[2] Sparkasse—Cassa di Risparmio, 39100 Bolzano, Italy
[3] Centre for Applied Macro and Commodity Prices, BI Norwegian Business School, 0484 Oslo, Norway
* Correspondence: francesco.ravazzolo@unibz.it

Received: 8 April 2019; Accepted: 7 May 2019; Published: 13 May 2019

Abstract: This paper investigates how investor sentiment affects stock market returns and evaluates the predictability power of sentiment indices on U.S. and EU stock market returns. As regards the American example, evidence shows that investor sentiment indices have an economic and statistical predictability power on stock market returns. Concerning the European market instead, investigation provides weak results. Moreover, comparing the two markets, where investor sentiment of U.S. market tries to predict the European stock market returns, and vice versa, the analyses indicate a spillover effect from the U.S. to Europe.

Keywords: Bayesian econometrics; portfolio choice; sentiments; stock market predictability

JEL Classification: C11; C22; G11; G12

---

1. Introduction

Optimism, also known as market sentiment, reveals the movements in the financial markets dictated by the psychological perception of determined operations or trades. This could create situations of mispricing, leading investors to lower returns than they expected. These movements in sentiment can conduct price distant from economic fundamentals and pose new research questions. For example, is optimism, and consequently pessimism, a factor of influence in financial markets? Accordingly, investor sentiment, which captures these fluctuations, is increasingly a topic of research relevance.

Several studies have been conducted in order to examine the presence and the effects of sentiment in financial markets. Before of an investment, investors behave differently. According to their propensity to the risk and the future expectations, they are divided into rational and irrational traders. Many individuals, defined irrational, in making decisions underreact or overreact to fundamentals and returns. Therefore, evaluation and decision-making are biased with the result of mispricing, i.e., moving from its fundamental value. Definitions as overconfidence, conservatism, and representativeness can explain the concept, but there is no academic consensus on a theory or a right formula to quantify it. We dedicate the next section to a literature review and discussion on what has been found on the relationship between investor sentiments and stock market returns.

The aim of this paper is to extend the research on investor sentiments and stock market returns in three directions. First, the majority of studies investigates this relationship with American stock markets, because of their financial significance and the higher likelihood to access the data. One of the few exception is (Fernandes et al. 2013) that provide an examination of the Portuguese market. This paper would like to contribute to the literature by analysing and comparing a strong and stable market like the U.S. to a smaller one, but with economic significance, like Europe.

Second, we apply Bayesian inference allowing us to set priors such as that the posterior distribution of the parameters of the predictive return regression can better learn from the data. This is particular useful when the sample size is small and priors help to reduce parameter uncertainty as in our European case.

Third, we evaluate the out-of-sample predictability power of investor sentiment acting on this association and interpret the economic effects of the findings. Using various indices, which measure sentiment both in an implicit and explicit way, the U.S. and the European market are studied over the periods 1990–2014 and 2001–2017, respectively. Extending previous evidence, we add sentiment indices as a further regressor to those typically considered in stock market predictability; see, for example, the list in (Welch and Goyal 2008). The forecasts in both examples start from the year 2008 because of its economical relevance due to the financial crisis. Further analyses compare the two markets to each other, searching for a spillover effect. In this case, investor sentiment of U.S. market tries to predict the European stock market returns, and vice versa.

As regards the American example, we find that sentiment indices have a negative impact on the stock market returns and provide accurate predictions of next month stock returns. Excluding it from the set of regressors decreases substantially the economic and statistical predictability power. With respect to the European market, evidence show weak findings. Only the Consumer Confidence Index provides in-sample evidence of predictability, but none gives out-of-sample more accurate predictions that the random walk in mean benchmark. Finally, the results show the presence of a spillover effect between the two markets. From an economic standpoint, Europe, which has been affected by globalisation and quick communication, is more prone to follow the influence of the American sentiment, because of the stronger U.S. economy.

The structure of the paper is as follows: Section 2 provides the literature review, deepening what is investor sentiment and diversifying between its measurements. Section 3 deals with the methodology, the empirical applications, and the relative results. Section 4 sums up the conclusion and suggests issues for future works.

2. Literature Review

This chapter provides a brief definition of investor sentiment, supported by theories, extended to behavioural reasons and effects; and a review of the empirical analyses on its relationship with stock markets.

2.1. Investor Sentiment

First of all, it is pivotal to define what investor sentiment is and why it has become more important in recent times. Investor sentiment is also known as *market sentiment* since it reveals the movements in the financial markets dictated by the psychological perception of determined operations or trades. Investors are subject to the sentiment of the market, i.e., to the belief about future expectations and investment risks that are not consistent with the statistical data or real facts. When the business performance is driven by emotions, a distortion of the price from its fundamental value occurs, entailing the risk in itself to be misunderstood from the investors and worsen the situation. Therefore, sentiment represents generally the attitude of economic agents, from consumers to investors, towards the market.

Barberis, Shleifer, and Vishny (Barberis et al. 1998) introduce an investor sentiment, focusing on overreaction and underreaction. They explain that information could be misleading. Indeed, optimistic announcements drive the investors to an exaggerated optimism about future news and, therefore, to overreaction, which leads stock prices to increase. Unfortunately, the following "news announcements are likely to contradict his optimism, leading to lower returns" (Barberis et al. 1998). This idea simply resumes the evidence that optimistic investors tend to overreact and, in the end, receive less of what they expected. Furthermore, another mechanism arises: conservatism, which "states that individuals are slow to change their beliefs in the face of new evidence" (Barberis et al. 1998). Then, investors, divided into optimistic and pessimistic traders, behave differently according to the weight they designate to a particular announcement, and are unlikely to change their mind, even though a strong proof is supplied. This wrong assessment leads to persistent mispricing and a deterioration of the final wealth.

Baker and Wurgler (Baker and Wurgler 2006) argue that the issue of mispricing derives from an "uninformed" sentimental demand shock. According to behavioural finance, there is a strong debate on market efficiency, since the allocation of capital could be prone to encounter several risks (for example, fundamental and noise trader risk) during the investment and implies costs due to mispricing (Barberis and Thaler 2003).

2.2. Empirical Investigation

Various authors have contributed to influence the scientific field with a great number of papers regarding the investor sentiment and its effects. Hereafter, we provide a brief summary of the ones we consider the most worthy and appropriate previous studies on this topic.

Fisher and Statman (Fisher and Statman 2000) investigate three different groups of investors: individuals, newsletter writers, and Wall Street strategists. While the first two are almost perfectly correlated, there is no correlation of them with the last group. The study reveals that the future S&P500 returns have a negative and statistically significant relationship with individual investors and strategists of Wall Street.

Additionally, Brown and Cliff (Brown and Cliff 2005) prove that sentiment is negatively related to future returns. Then, if the investor sentiment is high (low), it will imply lower (higher) stock returns in the future. Smaller companies tend to be less affected by sentiment, while large firms even in long horizon are more influenced, with a consequently higher level of predictability power.

Baker and Wurgler (Baker and Wurgler 2006) explore the effect of the investor sentiment on cross section of stock returns. The results suggest that the sentiment is inversely proportional to stock returns—small, young, extreme growth, unprofitable, distressed, high volatility, and non-dividend-paying stocks. Another salient conclusion is that firm characteristics, that theoretically should not exercise any unconditional predictive power, show instead conditional patterns (for example, the U shape) as the sentiment is conditioned. This outcome can be explained as a compensation for the systematic risks, where some countermeasures, as the orthogonalisation of the investor sentiment index to macroeconomic circumstances, demonstrate inconsistency with this interpretation.

Baker and Wurgler (Baker and Wurgler 2007) examine in depth, theoretically and empirically, the investor sentiment, looking for an optimal way to measure it and to discern and quantify the consequences of it. They confirm that sentiment influences the cost of capital, with effects on the allocation of investments.

Lemmon and Portniaguina (Lemmon and Portniaguina 2006) investigate the time-series relationship between investor sentiment and stock returns using consumer confidence as a measure of investor optimism. Lemmon and Portniaguina (Lemmon and Portniaguina 2006) distinguish from a rational and an irrational part, the letter proxy by regression residuals. They find that a negative relationship between the sentiment and the stock market returns exists, even if a mispricing seems to be eventually corrected by noise traders.

From an international point of view, Schmeling (Schmeling 2009) researches if consumer confidence could have an impact on the expected stock returns in 18 industrialised countries. As before, Schmeling (Schmeling 2009) shows that sentiment has a negative relationship with forecasts of aggregate stock market returns. In addition, he provides a cultural explanation of why some countries have higher sentiment; indeed, most of them are more prone to overreact and to have a herding behaviour.

On the other hand, Verma and Soydemir (Verma and Soydemir 2006) point out that rational and irrational factors are both constituent parts of the investor sentiment, individual, as well as institutional. Furthermore, they brought to light a significant phenomenon: the contagion effect. The exploration consists of searching for an influence of one country's sentiment upon the assets of other markets. Their research evidences that the U.S. investor sentiment affects Mexico and Brazil, at an institutional stage, and U.K. at both the institutional and individual level.

Verma, Baklaci, and Soydemir (Verma et al. 2008) consider the impact of arbitrageurs and noise traders' sentiment on both the Dow Jones Industrial Average and the S&P500 returns. They find that irrational investor sentiment has a stronger effect on stock returns than rational one, justifying it with the speed of processing information about economic fundamentals.

Chung, Hung, and Yeh (Chung et al. 2012) also inspect investor sentiment in the business cycles and report that the predictability of the sentiment is meaningful only during the expansion, while in periods of recession there is no significance. Therefore, the investor sentiment results to be regime-dependent.

Huang et al. (Huang et al. 2014) propose a new investor sentiment, denoted as *aligned*, which outperforms the others, in terms of fitting, reducing incredibly the noise component, and predictability, with good results even in the out-of-sample forecasting method. Widely basing on the previous predictor of Baker and Wurgler (Baker and Wurgler 2006), they compare the results between the Baker and Wurgler (BW) sentiment and the aligned sentiment partially least square (SPLS).

Finally, Fernandes, Gonçalves, and Vieira (Fernandes et al. 2013) provide an examination of the "small" Portuguese stock market. Starting from the same hypothesis of the majority of the essays cited before, they investigate whether there exists predictability not only of aggregate stock returns, but also at industrial indices levels for Portugal, over the period 1997–2009. Using the residuals of the Economic Sentiment Indicator (ESI) for Europe and applying the principal component analysis technique to obtain macroeconomic factors, they document that sentiment shows a negative relation to returns. In addition, they inspect for the presence of a contagious effect of the U.S. investor sentiment on the local market.

3. Methodology

3.1. Indices and Models

Many different indicators have been proposed as investor sentiment index. Additionally, there are several different measurement mechanisms to build it. They can be divided mostly into two macro-categories: direct and indirect measures. Direct measures are all the indices, where the data are obtained through surveys conducted to consumers, investors or other agents, who explicitly give a response and their sentiment towards some specific questions and issues. The indirect measure is, instead, a financial or pure mathematical index used as a proxy to define the new sentiment indicator.

In the surveys, investors usually divide into bull, neutral, or bear. Alternatively, they are asked to express an opinion through numbers indicating high or low expectations. Some examples are the American Association of Individual Investors (AAII), which officially conducts and publishes surveys on investors; the Conference Board Consumer Confidence Index, which elaborates the surveys on individuals' expectations about issues in macroeconomics; and others that can deal with businesses or industrial sectors.

The literature provides many example of indirect measurements that can be assumed as sentiment indices. The more applied are: the IPOs, the number and average of first-day returns on Initial Public Offerings; NYSE turnover, measuring trading volume; CEFD, closed-end fund discount, since it seems to be inversely correlated to sentiment; dividend premium, which is the difference between average market-to-book ratios of payers and non-payers. All these proxies are considered as subject to sentiment, even though with probably different timing. Consequently, Baker and Wurgler, and Huang et al. (Baker and Wurgler 2006; Huang et al. 2014) combine more of these proxies to create one unique index.

Huang et al. (Huang et al. 2014) and before Baker and Wurgler (Baker and Wurgler 2006, 2007) study how the investor sentiment works and which factors are its constituents. Both indices are constructed from the same set of variables. Both the BW investor sentiment, created by Baker and Wurgler (Baker and Wurgler 2006, 2007), and the aligned one (here-hence denominated as SPLS), created by (Huang et al. 2014), are obtained from the following six individual sentiment proxies:

- Close-end fund discount rate (CEFD);
- Share turnover (TURN);
- Number of IPOs (NIPO);
- First-day returns of IPOs (RIPO);
- Dividend premium (PDND); and
- Equity share in new issues (EQTI).

In constructing the sentiment index, Huang et al. (Huang et al. 2014) and Baker and Wurgler (Baker and Wurgler 2006) use equal structure and the same choice of proxies (see above). The reference equation to create investor sentiment is written as follows:

$$\text{Sent}_t = \text{CEFD}_t\,\beta_1 + \text{TURN}_t\,\beta_2 + \text{NIPO}_t\,\beta_3 + \text{RIPO}_t\,\beta_4 + \text{PDND}_t\,\beta_5 + \text{EQTI}_t\,\beta_6 \tag{1}$$

Baker and Wurgler (Baker and Wurgler 2006) apply a first principal component, Huang et al. (Huang et al. 2014) prefer the partial least squares. According to (Huang et al. 2014), PC fails to produce significant forecasts because it can accumulate approximation errors coming from parts of the variations of the proxies. Hence, every one of the aforementioned proxy is moved on average with six months smoothing, standardised, and elaborated upon other regressions on industrial production, durable, and nondurable consumption, service consumption, employment, and a series of dummy variables in order to reduce the business cycle variation. In addition, the residuals coming from these regressions are used as proxy to be combined to build a new investor sentiment index. This procedure is the orthogonalisation to macro variables in order to compensate for systematic risk and to prevent high correlations, if the raw data are conditioned from macroeconomic factors.

Then, Huang et al. (Huang et al. 2014) apply a linear regression model where they regress sentiment indices at time t to predict returns at t + 1. We extend the regression in two directions. First, we include in the linear regression a set of control variables. Indeed, investor sentiment indices could proxy other information and we control for it. The resulting model is:

$$R_{t+1} = \alpha + \beta\,\text{Sent}_{t,k} + \delta X_t + \varepsilon_{t+1}, \varepsilon_{t+1} \sim \text{i.i.d.}\left(0, \sigma^2\right), k = 1, \ldots, K \tag{2}$$

where Rt+1 is the excess market return at time t + 1, Sentt,k is the investor sentiment at time t, and k is one of the K alternative investor sentiment indices, Xt is a set of predictors described in the next section. Second, we apply Bayesian inference. Barberis (Barberis 2000), Kandel and Stambaugh (Kandel and Stambaugh 1996), and Hodrick (Hodrick 1992) are among the first papers to advocate the use of Bayesian inference for investigating stock market predictability. Bayesian inference allows to set priors such as that the posterior distribution of the parameters of the predictive return regression can better learn from the data. This is particular useful when the sample size is small and priors help to reduce parameter uncertainty. Moreover, priors can be set to improve long-term asset allocation and to remove biases. Recently, Pettenuzzo, Timmermann, and Valkanov (Pettenuzzo et al. 2014) documented that economic constraints based on prior beliefs systematically reduce uncertainty about model parameters, reduce the risk of selecting a poor forecasting model, and improve both statistical and economic measures of out-of-sample forecast performance. We apply a normal-inverted gamma prior for our linear regression. We set prior mean values equal to OLS estimates and large prior variance values to keep the likelihood dominant on the prior. Degrees of freedom are set equal to 10% of the sample size. Our priors result in a closed form solution for parameter posteriors and predictive distributions. Precisely, the parameters β will follow a Student's *t* posterior distribution and the predictive density will also be *t*-Student distributed. See (Koop 2003) for exact values.[1] The estimation is run recursively.

---

[1]   We also investigate uniform flat priors. For the US example the results are almost identical; for the EU exercise we find large parameter uncertainties and lower forecast accuracy.

Up to the last observation posterior distributions and predictive densities are computed to predict the following value. In the next period, when new data are available, the process is repeated to obtain further predictions.

3.2. Data

The data span from January 1990–December 2014 (300 months) for the U.S. example, whereas the European example range from June 2001 through April 2017 (191 months). The European sample is unfortunately quite limited since the data are not available before the selected start point for all the components of the variables considered. As for the U.S. example, the length of the sample ends in 2014, because the data for the (Baker and Wurgler 2006, 2007) investor sentiment and the aligned investor sentiment calculated by (Huang et al. 2014) are available only until that year.

The dataset for the analysis in the U.S. market consists of the following variables:

- *Stock excess market returns of U.S. market*, SEMRUS: calculated from price of S&P500, including dividends and in excess of the risk free rate (3-month US treasury bill);
- *Continuous compounding of S&P500*, COMPOUND: calculated without dividends, in excess of risk free rate (10-year US treasury bill);
- *Investor sentiment index*, BW: calculated by (Baker and Wurgler 2006), through the PC method;
- *Orthogonalised investor sentiment index*, BWORT: calculated by (Baker and Wurgler 2006), the orthogonalisation is applied in order to reduce the systematic risk;
- *Aligned investor sentiment index*, SPLS: calculated by (Huang et al. 2014), through the PLS method;
- *Orthogonalised aligned investor sentiment index*, SPLSORT: calculated by (Huang et al. 2014), the orthogonalisation is applied for the same reasons as before;
- *Conference Board Consumer Confidence Index of US*, CB_CONS: calculated through surveys on expectations about business conditions, employment and income, from consumers over a six-month horizon;
- *CBOE's Volatility of S&P500*, VIX: annualised standard deviation, also known as uncertainty index, it is calculated from near expectations (one-month horizon) about stock market volatility.

Therefore, our sample includes four indirect measures and two direct measures of sentiment. The indirect measures of sentiment are downloaded from the Guofu Zhou website.

On the other hand, the dataset for the European consists of the following variables:

- *Stock excess market returns of EU market*, SEMREU: calculated from price of Euro Stoxx 50, including dividends and in excess of the risk free rate (3-month Euribor);
- *Continuous compounding of Euro Stoxx 50*, COMPOUND: calculated without dividends, in excess of risk free rate (10-year German government bond);
- *Economic Sentiment Indicator of European countries*, ESI_EU: published monthly by the European Commission, it consists of five sectoral confidence indicators (based on results from business surveys), which are: industry (40%), services (30%), consumers (20%), construction (5%) and retail trade (5%);
- *Economic Sentiment Indicator of Eurozone*, ESI_EUZONE: composite calculated only for the Eurozone countries;
- *Consumer Confidence Indicator of Europe*, CONSCONF: calculated from surveys on the financial situation of households, the general economic situation, unemployment expectations and savings, over one year horizon;
- *Industrial Confidence Indicator of Europe*, INDUCONF: calculated from surveys on production expectations, order books and stocks of finished products;
- *Economic Sentiment Indicator of Germany*, ZEW_DEU: calculated from surveys on expectations about macroeconomic development, financial and industrial profit situation over the following six months;

- *Ifo Business Climate Index*, IFO: dealing with the assessments of business situation and future expectations, it is calculated from surveys on different sectors from enterprises, such as manufacturing, construction, wholesaling and retailing, over a six-month horizon.

Therefore, the European example includes only direct measures of sentiment.

Our list of control for the U.S. stock market includes the 15 economic variables which are popular stock return predictors and are directly linked to economic fundamentals and risk aversion. We use the updated data From (Welch and Goyal 2008). Most of the predictors fall into four broad categories, namely: (i) valuation ratios capturing some measure of 'fundamentals' to market value such as the dividend yield, the earnings–price ratio, the 10-year earnings–price ratio or the book-to-market ratio; (ii) measures of bond yields capturing level effects (the three-month T-bill rate and the yield on long-term government bonds), slope effects (the term spread) and default risk effects (the default yield spread, defined as the yield spread between BAA and AAA rated corporate bonds, and the default return spread, defined as the difference between the yield on long-term corporate and government bonds); (iii) estimates of equity risk, such as the long-term return and stock variance (a volatility estimate based on daily squared returns); (iv) three corporate finance variables, namely the dividend payout ratio (the log of the dividend–earnings ratio), net equity expansion (the ratio of 12-month net issues by NYSE-listed stocks over the year-end market capitalization) and the percentage of equity issuance (the ratio of equity issuing activity as a fraction of total issuing activity). Finally, we consider a macroeconomic variable, inflation, defined as the rate of change in the consumer price index, and the net payout measure, which is computed as the ratio between dividends and net equity repurchases (repurchases minus issuances) over the last 12 months and the current stock price. As in (Welch and Goyal 2008), lag inflation is lagged an extra month to account for the delay in CPI releases.

For the European exercise, we could not collect all the 15 predictors and have eight variables: the dividend yield, the earnings–price ratio, the book-to-market ratio, the short-term interest rate, the long-term yield, the term spread, the default risk, the default return spread (where 10-years German bund rates are used as the government rate), stock variance (European VIX, VSTOXX), and inflation.

3.3. Empirical Results

3.3.1. The U.S. Market

The dependent variable is the excess market return, continuously compounded log return on the S&P 500 index (including dividends), minus the risk-free rate. The risk free rate is represented by the three-month U.S. Treasury bill.

Figure 1 shows four of the sentiment indices used for the U.S. market. Both the BW index and the SPLS have a similar pattern, since they are constructed starting from the same six variables, even though using different methods (PC and PLS, respectively). For this reason, the sentiment indices cannot be applied all together, but regress in separate equations.

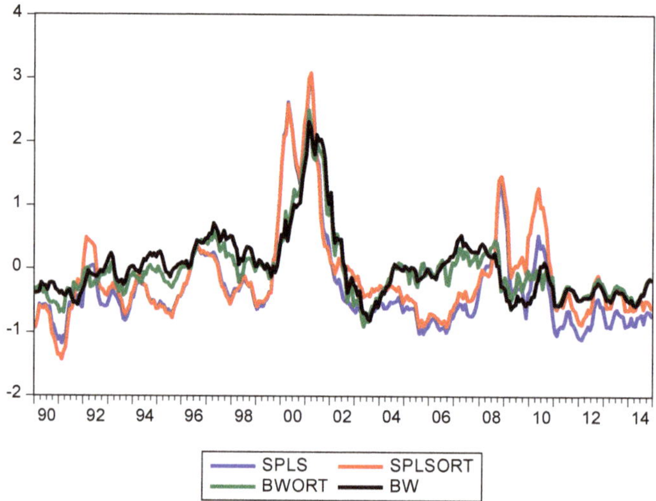

Figure 1. Plot of the sentiment indices group for the entire range of 1990–2014.

Figure 2 reports two sentiment indices, SPLS, and BWORT, and stock market returns. The figure documents that the latter variable is much more volatile than the sentiment, with great positive and negative peaks in short periods. As discussed in (Baker and Wurgler 2006, 2007), first, orthogonalisation applied to sentiment indices reduces the systematic risk. Second, the sentiment changes are more difficult to be detected, and its volatility expressed only in periods of high speculation.

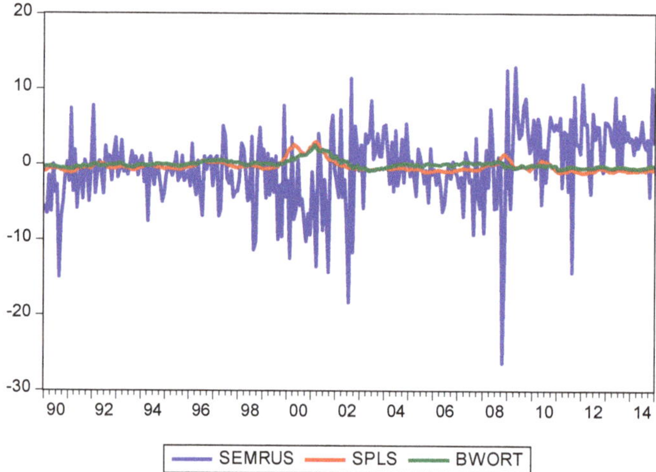

Figure 2. Plot of the sentiment indices, SPLS and BWORT, and the stock market returns, SEMRUS, for the entire range of 1990–2014.

Table 1 reports the results of the U.S. regression. The first four variables refer to indirect sentiment indices; the last two to (direct) consumer or market indices. All coefficients have negative posterior means, almost all the posterior mass has negative mass as the Bayesian *t*-statistics confirms and the posterior distribution assigns probability to positive numbers lower than 1%. The coefficient and the forecasts evaluation are consistent with the literature, proving that there exists a negative relationship between stock market returns and investor sentiment, supported by (Baker and Wurgler 2006, 2007;

Huang et al. 2014). Economically, one-percentage change in the independent variable is associated with an average decrease of −2.20 (for the BW) in the excess market return.

Table 1. Set of regressions run on the U.S. market.

Variable	Post Mean ß	Bayesian *t*-Stat	Positive Post. Distr.	MSPE Ratio
SPLS	−1.079	−1.965	0.050	0.933 **
BW	−2.200	−3.149	0.002	0.926 **
SPLSORT	−1.041	−2.068	0.040	0.940 **
BWORT	−2.350	−3.318	0.001	0.939 **
CB_CONS	−0.046	−1.685	0.093	0.938 **
VIX	−0.259	−5.150	0.000	0.954 **

Note: This table reports the posterior mean of the sentiment indices used in the various regressions with US data; the Bayesian *t*-statistics, computed as the ratio of the posterior mean and the posterior standard deviation of the parameter; the probability of the positive posterior distribution. The last column gives the out-of-sample mean square error (MSPE) relative to the MSPE of the random walk benchmark. A MSPE ratio lower than 1 means that the alternative model based on the sentiment index outperforms the random walk benchmark. We measure statistical significance relative to the benchmark model using the (Diebold and Mariano 1995) *t*-tests for equality of the average loss. Asterisks indicate significance at * 10% and ** 5% levels. All results are based on the whole forecast evaluation period January 2008–December 2014.

As next step, we produce one-month forecasts from January 2008 to December 2014 using an expanding window approach. We compute mean square prediction errors (MSPE) by comparing each (point) forecast to the realization. We also compute forecasts using the standard benchmark model used for studying return predictability, the random walk in mean. We report MSPE ratios by dividing the MSPE of each of our models based on one of the sentiment indices by the MSPE of the benchmark. A MSPE ratio lower than 1 means that the alternative model based on the sentiment index outperforms the random walk benchmark. A MSPE ratio larger than 1 means that the benchmark is more accurate. We also test the difference of the MSPE based on the alternative model and the one based on the benchmark model using the (Diebold and Mariano 1995) test; see (West 1996) for theoretical foundations.

Among the sentiment indices, we find that BW provides the most accurate predictions of stock market returns with a reduction on MSPE relative to the benchmark of almost 7.5%. The difference is statistically significant. This result contrasts with (Huang et al. 2014), who found the SPLS being more accurate in the out-of-sample analysis. The SPLS is still statistically superior to the benchmark, but adding the control variables in (Welch and Goyal 2008) reduces marginally its economic gains. When testing the difference in MSPE of the models based on BW and SPLS indices, the null of equal predictability is not rejected.

When comparing to the other indices, we find that all models statistically outperform the benchmark model and the VIX variable gives the lower gains. Interesting, an index like the CB_CONS, which is made up of opinions and should be more inclined to errors, seems to be more appropriate (economically, but not statistically) to represent the investor sentiment, providing a larger predictability power than a financial variable as the VIX. We notice that the VIX and the stock variance in (Welch and Goyal 2008) dataset are highly correlated and this can create some imprecision on estimation. Finally we run two further set of regression models. The first one is a model based only on the (Welch and Goyal 2008) regressors and exclude the sentiment indices. The model gives a 3% reduction on MSPE relative to the benchmark, confirming the predictability power of the sentiment indices which all results on lower ratios. The second set of models removes control variables and apply the six sentiment indices individually in each regression. MSPE gains reduces, but BW and CB_CONS still provide a statistical significant reduction up to 5%, providing further evidence of their predictability power.

3.3.2. The European Market

In this section, we deal with the analysis and interpretation of the EU example. The excess stock market returns of the Euro Stoxx 50 is predicted through different European sentiment indices and a set of control variables.

Figure 3 plots the sentiment group on the entire sample, formed by the two Economic Sentiment Indicators, one for all Europe and one for the Eurozone, and the Consumer and Industrial Confidence Index. For making visible the trend of the series, the mean value is subtracted to the variables ESI_EU and ESI_EUZONE, levelling them to the other two indices. The two sentiment indices cannot be used all together because of multicollinearity issue since INDUCONF and CONSCONF are two of the five component sectors of the ESI.

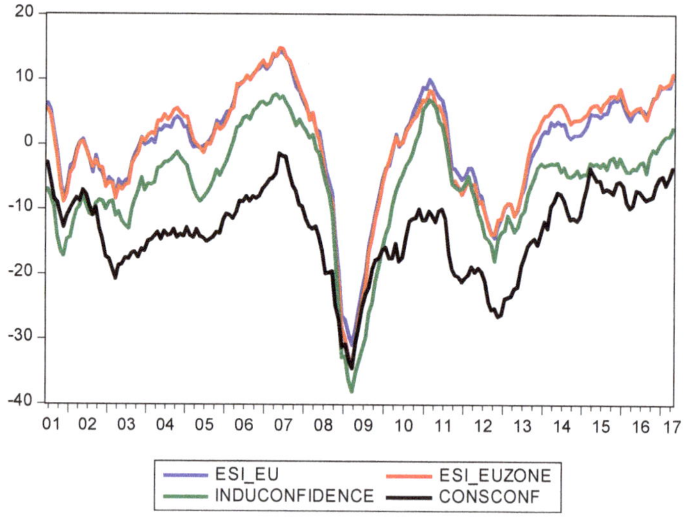

Figure 3. Plot of the sentiment indices group for the entire range 2001–2017.

Figure 4 show the volatile pattern of Euro Stoxx 50 compared to Consumer and Industrial Indices. At the end of the 2008 the negative peak in sentiment indices due to the financial crises is evident. On the contrary, on the same period, in particular the following months, stock returns recorded an increasing evolution with positive peaks.

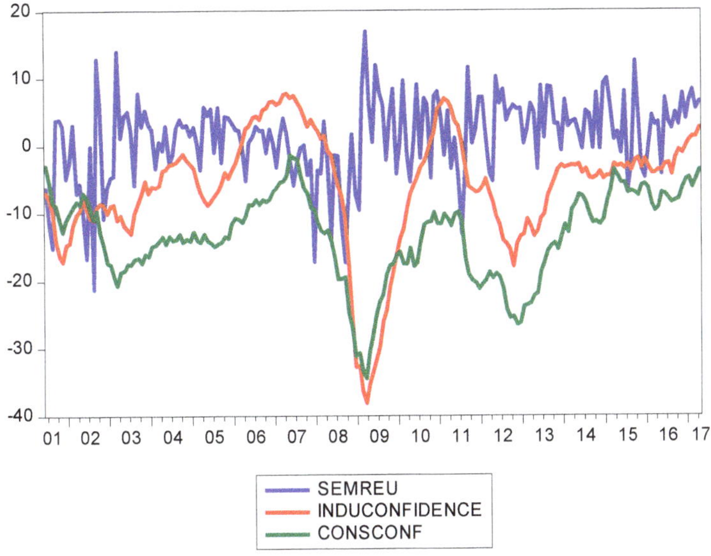

Figure 4. Plot of the economic indices, CONSCONF and INDUCONF, and the stock market returns, SEMREU, for the entire range 2001–2017.

Table 2 shows regression results. In this example, the Economic Sentiment Indicator and two specific components of it substitute the BW and SPLS indices. The economic indicators we choose are German industrial confidence index, ZEW_DEU and IFO indicators. The choice of these two German indices comes from different reasons. First, Germany is considered as a leading country in Europe, with a stronger economic and political stability. Second, Germany is an industrial and financial centre, with contacts to many European regions. Finally, the surveys reflect optimistic and pessimistic share for the future expected economic development not only in Germany, but also in France, Italy, and other relevant countries.

Table 2. Set of regressions on the EU market.

Variable	Post Mean ß	Bayesian *t*-Stat	Positive Post. Distr.	MSPE Ratio
ESI_EU	−0.040	−0.410	0.663	1.000
ESI_EUZONE	−0.040	−0.332	0.740	0.999
CONSCONF	−0.490	−2.690	0.006	1.000
INDUCONF	0.012	0.143	0.894	1.002
ZEW_DEU	0.013	0.723	0.463	1.036
IFO	0.052	0.503	0.584	1.030

Note: This table reports the posterior mean of the sentiment indices used in the various regressions with European data; the Bayesian *t*-statistics, computed as the ratio of the posterior mean and the posterior standard deviation of the parameter; the probability of the positive posterior distribution. The last column gives the out-of-sample mean square error (MSPE) relative to the MSPE of the random walk benchmark. A MSPE ratio lower than 1 means that the alternative model based on the sentiment index outperforms the random walk benchmark. We measure statistical significance relative to the benchmark model using the (Diebold and Mariano 1995) *t*-tests for equality of the average loss. Asterisks indicate significance at * 10% and ** 5% levels. All results are based on the whole forecast evaluation period January 2008–April 2017.

Except for the Consumer Confidence Index, posterior probabilities of other variables assign large probabilities to positive numbers. Therefore, apart from CONSCONF, there is no strong evidence on the role of sentiment indices to drive the EU stock market. From the economic point of view, this can be justified by the fact that Europe has not a strong financial impact comparable to the volumes of the U.S., which has been historically the leader of the worldwide markets. Fernandes, Gonçalves, and

Vieira (Fernandes et al. 2013) concluded that the Portuguese market has tendency to be affected by the sentiment, because of the high level of collectivism in the country. The herding is counterbalanced by the presence of institutional investors, which are considered as rational. This statement could lead to think that it is likely to notice a majority of rational investors in the EU market, because of institutional level, than noise traders. The forecasting exercise over the sample 2008–2017 confirms evidence and all models perform similarly in terms of MSPE. None models statically outperform the random walk benchmark.

3.3.3. Spillover Effect

Our forecasting sample deals with the period during and after the financial crisis, which had a global effect. Therefore, we investigate the possibility that the markets are not independent, where booms and recessions spread around different geographic regions.

Table 3 shows the results of predicting the European stock returns with U.S. sentiment indices. In these regressions, we exclude the set of control variables and just focus on the spillover effects. The output demonstrates a spillover effect for almost all the U.S. sentiment indices to European markets. Only the VIX does not support this evidence. The survey indicator CB_CONS is the only with a positive coefficient. BW produces the lowest MSPE, but it is not statistically significant relative to the benchmark model. One explanation for the result is that European investors misinterpret U.S. sentiment fluctuations, also due to the large capitalization of the U.S. market, confusing them with fundamental news and reacting to them in their European portfolio.

Table 3. Set of estimations run using the U.S. sentiment in order to predict the EU stock returns.

Variable	Post Mean ß	Bayesian *t*-Stat	Positive Post. Distr.	MSPE Ratio
SPLS	−3.880	−3.061	0.003	1.095
BW	−3.195	−3.055	0.003	0.990
SPLSORT	−4.964	−3.588	0.001	1.064
BWORT	−3.283	−2.902	0.005	1.018
CB_CONS	0.097	2.224	0.029	1.037
VIX	−0.161	−1.566	0.121	1.037

Note: This table reports the posterior mean of the sentiment indices used in the various regressions; the Bayesian *t*-statistics, computed as the ratio of the posterior mean and the posterior standard deviation of the parameter; the probability of the positive posterior distribution. The last column gives the out-of-sample mean square error (MSPE) relative to the MSPE of the random walk benchmark. A MSPE ratio lower than 1 means that the alternative model based on the sentiment index outperforms the random walk benchmark. We measure statistical significance relative to the benchmark model using the (Diebold and Mariano 1995) *t*-tests for equality of the average loss. Asterisks indicate significance at * 10% and ** 5% levels. All results are based on the whole forecast evaluation period January 2008–April 2017.

Table 4 reports the estimations of the U.S. stock returns through the European sentiment indices. As shown, all the variables have almost all the posterior mass in the negative support. Economically, it seems that the Economic Sentiment Indicator, elaborated by the European Commission, has a stronger link with American investors, enabling predictions on stock returns, than with the EU market. The model based on it outperforms the random walk benchmark at a 5% significance level. We notice that gains are, however, smaller than using U.S. sentiment indices. Zew and Ifo indices were not inserted in this table because of the unavailability of data for the entire range.

Table 4. Set of estimations run using the EU sentiment indices in order to predict the U.S. market.

Variable	Post Mean ß	Bayesian *t*-Stat	Positive Post. Distr.	MSPE Ratio
ESI_EU	−0.120	−3.997	0.000	1.021
ESI_EUZONE	−0.127	−4.387	0.000	0.997
CONSCONF	−0.191	−4.862	0.000	0.976 *
INDUCONF	−0.117	−3.550	0.001	1.060

Note: This table reports the posterior mean of the sentiment indices used in the various regressions; the Bayesian *t*-statistics, computed as the ratio of the posterior mean and the posterior standard deviation of the parameter; the probability of the positive posterior distribution. The last column gives the out-of-sample mean square error (MSPE) relative to the MSPE of the random walk benchmark. A MSPE ratio lower than 1 means that the alternative model based on the sentiment index outperforms the random walk benchmark. We measure statistical significance relative to the benchmark model using the (Diebold and Mariano 1995) *t*-tests for equality of the average loss. Asterisks indicate significance at * 10% and ** 5% level. All results are based on the whole forecast evaluation period January 2008 to December 2014.

To sum up, Tables 3 and 4 document a link between financial markets and the two markets are not independent, but interdependent.

4. Conclusions

This paper applies the sentiment index in regression models to predict US and European stock market returns. Many measurements are experimented, from direct sentiment indices, like surveys, to indirect measures of investor sentiment, such as the ones calculated by (Huang et al. 2014; Baker and Wurgler 2006, 2007). Differently than the previous literature, we control for a set of variables often used in return predictability and apply Bayesian inference to reduce parameter uncertainty due to the short sample, in particular for the European example.

As regards the American example, the results showed that globally sentiment has a negative impact on the stock market returns and BW resulted to have the highest predictive power. With respect to the European market, evidence shows weak findings and no relationship is found. Finally, the results show the presence of spillover effect between the two markets. Therefore, it can be concluded that U.S. and EU are two interdependent markets. In the end, this idea can justify the weak outputs on the European markets. From an economic standpoint, affected from globalisation and quick communication, Europe could be more prone to follow the influence of the American sentiment, because of the stronger economy.

Unfortunately, due to unavailability of data, the analysis is conducted on a limited range. The short period is a limitation on estimating the best model, since there could be omitted factors influencing the estimation. The use of Bayesian priors limits somewhat such effects. However, in future works it could be interesting to explore the difference between the rational and irrational factors of the sentiment, deepening the irrational analysis (i.e., the residual part).

Author Contributions: The work was equally divided between the two coauthors. The origin and development of the paper was a joint initiative. C.L.C. focused on collection of data and econometric analysis; F.R. worked on writing results and the working paper.

Funding: This work was supported by the Open Access Publishing Fund of the Free University of Bozen-Bolzano.

Acknowledgments: We thank the editor, two anonymous referees and Stefano Grassi for helpful comments and suggestions to improve this work. Chiara Limongi Concetto thanks the Italian Banking, Insurance, and Finance Federation to award the RIFET (Rome Investment Forum Empowers Talents) 2017 award.

Conflicts of Interest: The authors declare no conflict of interest.

References

Baker, Malcom, and Jeffrey Wurgler. 2006. Investor sentiment and the cross-section of stock returns. *The Journal of Finance* 61: 1645–80. [CrossRef]

Baker, Malcom, and Jeffrey Wurgler. 2007. Investor sentiment in the stock market. *Journal of Economic Perspectives* 21: 129–51. [CrossRef]

Barberis, Nicholas. 2000. Investing for the long run when returns are predictable. *Journal of Finance* 55: 225–64. [CrossRef]

Barberis, Nicholas, and Richard Thaler. 2003. A Survey of behavioral finance. In *Handbook of the Economics of Finance, (1051–1121).* Edited by George M. Constantinides, Milton Harris and René Stulz. Amsterdam: Elsevier Science B.V.

Barberis, Nicholas, Andrei Shleifer, and Robert Vishny. 1998. A model of investor sentiment. *Journal of Financial Economics* 49: 307–43. [CrossRef]

Brown, Gregory, and Michael Cliff. 2005. Investor sentiment and asset valuation. *Journal of Business* 78: 405–40. [CrossRef]

Chung, San-Lin, Chi-Hsou Hung, and Chung-Ying Yeh. 2012. When does investor sentiment predict stock returns? *Journal of Empirical Finance* 19: 217–40. [CrossRef]

Diebold, Francis Xavier, and Robert Mariano. 1995. Comparing predictive accuracy. *Journal of Business and Economic Statistics* 13: 253–63.

Fernandes, Carla Manuela de Assunção, Paulo Miguel Marquez Gonçalves, and Elisabete Fatima Simões Vieira. 2013. Does sentiment matter for stock market returns? Evidence from a small European market. *Journal of Behavioral Finance* 14: 253–67. [CrossRef]

Fisher, Kenneth, and Meir Statman. 2000. Investor sentiment and stock returns. *Financial Analysts Journal* 56: 16–23. [CrossRef]

Hodrick, Robert. 1992. Dividend yields and expected stock returns: Alternative procedures for inference and measurement. *Review of Financial Studies* 5: 357–86. [CrossRef]

Huang, Dashan, Fuwei Jiang, Jun Tu, and Guofu Zhou. 2014. Investor sentiment aligned: A powerful predictor of stock returns. *Review of Financial Studies* 28: 791–37. [CrossRef]

Kandel, Shmuel, and Robert Stambaugh. 1996. On the predictability of stock returns: An asset allocation perspective. *Journal of Finance* 51: 385–424. [CrossRef]

Koop, Gary. 2003. *Bayesian Econometrics*. Hoboken: Wiley.

Lemmon, Michael, and Evgenia Portniaguina. 2006. Consumer confidence and asset prices: some empirical evidence. *Review of Financial Studies* 19: 1499–529. [CrossRef]

Pettenuzzo, Davide, Allan Timmermann, and Rosen Valkanov. 2014. Forecasting stock returns under economic constraints. *Journal of Financial Economics* 114: 517–53. [CrossRef]

Schmeling, Michael. 2009. Investor sentiment and stock returns: Some international evidence. *Journal of Empirical Finance* 16: 394–408. [CrossRef]

Verma, Rahul, and Gökçe Soydemir. 2006. The Impact of U.S. individual and institutional investor sentiment on foreign stock markets. *Journal of Behavioral Finance* 7: 128–44. [CrossRef]

Verma, Rahul, Hasan Baklaci, and Gökçe Soydemir. 2008. The impact of rational and irrational sentiments of individual and institutional investors on DJIA and S&P500 index returns. *Applied Financial Economics* 18: 1303–17.

Welch, Ivo, and Amit Goyal. 2008. A comprehensive look at the empirical performance of equity premium prediction. *Review of Financial Studies* 21: 1455–508. [CrossRef]

West, Kenneth. 1996. Asymptotic inference about predictive ability. *Econometrica* 64: 1067–84. [CrossRef]

MDPI

St. Alban-Anlage 66

4052 Basel

Switzerland

Tel. +41 61 683 77 34

Fax +41 61 302 89 18

www.mdpi.com

Journal of Risk and Financial Management Editorial Office

E-mail: jrfm@mdpi.com

www.mdpi.com/journal/jrfm